THE POETRY OF WAR

Poets from Homer to Bruce Springsteen have given voice to the intensity, horror, and beauty of war. The greatest war poets praise the victor while mourning the victim; they honor the dead while raising deep questions about the meaning of honor. Poets have given memorable expression to the personal motives that send men forth to fight: idealism, shame, comradeship, revenge. They have also helped shape the larger ideas that nations and cultures invoke as incentives for warfare: patriotism, religion, empire, chivalry, freedom. *The Poetry of War* shows how poets have shaped and questioned our basic ideas about warfare. Reading great poetry, Winn argues, can help us make informed political judgments about current wars. From the poems he discusses, readers will learn how soldiers in past wars felt about their experiences, and why poets in many periods and cultures have embraced war as a grand and challenging subject.

JAMES ANDERSON WINN is Professor of Engl ton University. He is the author of, among o of *Words: Reflections on the Hu 3) and the award-winning (1987).

THE POETRY OF WAR

JAMES ANDERSON WINN

CAMBRIDGE
UNIVERSITY PRESS

CAMBRIDGE UNIVERSITY PRESS
Cambridge, New York, Melbourne, Madrid, Cape Town, Singapore, São Paulo

Cambridge University Press
The Edinburgh Building, Cambridge CB2 8RU, UK

Published in the United States of America by Cambridge University Press, New York

www.cambridge.org
Information on this title: www.cambridge.org/9780521710220

First published 2008

Printed in the United Kingdom at the University Press, Cambridge

A catalogue record for this publication is available from the British Library

ISBN 978-0-521-88403-7 hardback
ISBN 978-0-521-71022-0 paperback

In memory of Maynard Mack

Contents

Illustrations

Acknowledgments

I have incurred many debts in the years devoted to this book. Since 1998, it has been my privilege to chair the Department of English at Boston University. Colleagues there who have read my drafts and supported my dreams include Renata Adler, Julia Brown, Aaron Fogel, Bob Levine, Jack Matthews, Lee Monk, Robert Pinsky, Christopher Ricks, Chuck Rzepka, Andy Stauffer, and Rosanna Warren. I could neither have written this book nor discharged my administrative duties without the daily support of Bill Carroll, Jim Siemon, Christopher Martin, and the indispensable Harriet Lane. Colleagues and friends from other institutions have been no less important; for substantial help, let me single out Paula Backscheider of Auburn, Linda Gregerson and Steven Mullaney of Michigan, Paul Hammond of Leeds, David Morris of Virginia, Cedric Reverand II of Wyoming, and Robert Sullivan of Notre Dame. Two younger colleagues, both of whom were students in my first graduate seminar at the University of Michigan, have also given me much support; they are Anna Battigelli of Plattsburgh State and Eric Jager of UCLA.

Because I have written this book for general readers, I have been especially grateful to friends from other walks of life who have read some or all of it. They include Jack Bogle, Steven Clifford, Mary Connelly, John Lansing, Elizabeth Levy, the Honorable Kenneth McKenzie, Thomas Mitchell, Arthur Paxton, John Rosenthal, and Larry Spraggs.

Megan Buckley and Janet Rosen of the Sheree Bykofsky Agency in New York believed in this book and worked hard on its behalf. Two readers engaged by Cambridge University Press produced substantial reports that helped me improve the final version; I salute them for their attention to detail and their critical engagement with the book's largest claims.

Though by far the most important, the personal debts are the most difficult to describe in the few words I have here. Mara Jayne Miller intervened decisively at many points in the book's development; I am grateful for her unfailing candor. My father, Albert C. Winn, himself the author of a fine study of war in the Bible, was a shrewd and helpful reader, as he has been throughout my life. My children, Ellen Polly Winn and Philip Legaré Winn, have given me constant and unflagging support. Lucy Chapman has made me freshly aware of harmony, joy, and miracle – three crucial alternatives to war.

Some who I hoped would appreciate this book did not live to see it in print. My Michigan colleague and tennis partner, Dan Fader, a pioneer in writing seriously about literature for a broad readership, died before I had a chance to ask his help and counsel. My mother, Grace Walker Winn, a passionate lifelong worker for peace, died when the project was in its early stages. And my academic father, Maynard Mack, who was my toughest reader for all my other work, died before I had a draft I dared to send him. In appreciation of his high critical standards, his insistence on the moral capacities of literature, and his unabashed love of great poetry, I have humbly dedicated this effort to his memory.

Boston, February 2007

Introduction: Terrible beauty

War rages in our world, as it has for all of human history. Each morning news stories from Iraq, Afghanistan, Lebanon, Palestine, Chechnya, and Darfur report the violent deaths of combatants and civilians. Even Americans, long accustomed to the notion that such events could only happen overseas, are still reeling from the attack on the World Trade Center, which has forced us to confront our fear of death and our grief at the deaths of others. Recent history raises with new urgency the question of how to respond – politically, morally, and artistically – to the intensity and horror of war.

Soldiers in combat employ a stripped-down language of curses, screams, and commands – a language far removed from the reflective and formal idiom of poets. Yet in order to come to grips with the full range of their thoughts and feelings about war, soldiers, mourners, victims, and prophets have often turned to poetry. Even before poems were written down, soldiers trusted poets to make their deeds immortal, and poets embraced warfare as a grand and challenging subject.

Despite these ancient connections, war and poetry are fundamentally different activities. War dismembers bodies, scattering limb from limb. Poetry re-members those bodies and the people who lived in them, making whole in verse what was destroyed on the battlefield. The technology of warfare tears people, armies, and cities apart; it divides in order to conquer. The technology of poetry binds together all the ways that words can move us; it combines in order to enrich. In the history of warfare, the great technological changes have been innovations designed to make existing weapons and skills useless: the stirrup, the cannon, the tank, the guided missile. In the history of poetry, even the most original poems depend on past practice, building older forms and ideas into their texture. War obliterates the past; poetry feeds upon the past.

Professional soldiers, however, are often backward-looking, conservative, tribal. Their "values and skills," as the military historian John Keegan has argued, "are those of a world apart, a very ancient world, which exists in parallel with the everyday world but does not belong to it. Both worlds change over time, and the warrior world adapts in step to the civilian. It follows it, however, at a distance."[1] This formula also applies to poets, whose values and skills are those of an ancient world, and whose modes of expression have often followed those of the prosaic world at a distance. A shared sense of preserving older skills and values has sometimes drawn warriors and poets together, despite the stark differences between their crafts. The Japanese Samurai, an extreme example, managed to suppress guns and gunpowder for 250 years. They knew about the new technology, but they feared it would make their skill with swords obsolete, so they rigorously controlled the making of guns and retained a power based on the art of swordsmanship. It should not surprise us that the other art on which the Samurai prided themselves was the making of poems.[2]

Critics eager to dismiss poetry have typically used the imagery of gender to separate the brutal, sweeping violence of warfare from the subtle, delicate energy of poetry, treating violence as manly, poetry as feminine. Resisting that crude formula, poets have often found beauty in violence. Homer, describing the blood flowing down a hero's wounded thigh, thinks of a woman using red dye to color a piece of ivory, an ornate work of art.[3] Bertran de Born, a medieval troubadour, links the pleasure he feels when hearing the birds sing in springtime with the pleasure he feels when seeing dead knights in ditches, with splintered lances stuck through their sides.[4] Some brave poets have even acknowledged the dark connection between violence and the erotic. They have seen the links between sexual desire and military aggression, but they have also described the sacrifices made in war as acts of love that lead to the birth of beauty.

In his great poem on the Easter Rising of 1916, William Butler Yeats develops this idea in haunting and memorable terms. Although their attempted revolution failed, Yeats credits the Irish patriots who briefly occupied the Dublin Post Office with changing the emotional landscape of Ireland. From their "excess of love" came a hope for freedom that the poet could picture as beauty:

> We know their dream; enough
> To know they dreamed and are dead;
> And what if excess of love
> Bewildered them till they died?
> I write it out in a verse–
> MacDonagh and MacBride
> And Connolly and Pearse
> Now and in time to be,
> Wherever green is worn,
> Are changed, changed utterly:
> A terrible beauty is born.[5]

As the patriots showed their love for Ireland by mounting a doomed revolt that led to their deaths, Yeats shows his love for them by fitting their names into his meter and rhyme-scheme, using the power of verse to keep their memory alive.

Two years later, Robert Graves addressed an affectionate poem to his fellow-soldier and fellow-poet Siegfried Sassoon, who had served with him in the same regiment throughout the First World War. Expressing amazement at their survival, Graves admits that he and Sassoon found beauty in death, and argues that they drew life and breath from the numerous dead:

> Show me the two so closely bound
> As we, by the wet bond of blood,
> By friendship blossoming from mud,
> By Death: we faced him, and we found
> Beauty in Death,
> In dead men, breath.[6]

By calling the force that binds the two men "the wet bond of blood," Graves bravely acknowledges the softer aspects of his feelings for Sassoon. A friendship blossoming from mud suggests the conventional motif of the flower that springs from a grave, but it also allows the two males a metaphorical fertility. Together, they have given birth to a blossoming friendship. All of this rich imagery, however, is a prelude to the revelation of the true bonding force: Death. By staring Death in the face, Graves claims, the two men found beauty. From the dead men all around them, they drew breath.

Figure 1. Robert Graves in Oxford (1920).

We need poems like these to counter the mindless simplifications of war propaganda. Too often, soldiers learn to think in terms of *us* versus *them*, treating the enemy as if he were not even human. Such ugly terms as *Hun, Jap,* or *Gook* bear witness to our need to define the other side as utterly unlike us. Merely patriotic poets have sometimes been complicit in this process of flattening, misusing their art to versify slogans and cheers. Poets true to their calling, however, use the full range of poetry's powers to express the full range of our contradictory responses to war, including our ability to find beauty amid the horror.

Like the ocean, great fires, and destructive storms, war is attractive to poets as an instance of the *sublime,* an experience bringing together awe, terror, power, and reverence on a grand scale. When Yeats writes of the "terrible beauty" of the Easter Rising, he may be thinking of the way the English put down the revolution by indiscriminately shelling the center of Dublin, starting fires that burned much of the city. In acknowledging the beauty inherent in fire and destruction, Yeats participates in a long tradition stretching back to Homer. Poets celebrating eighteenth-century revolutions were especially fond of the military sublime. In *The Columbiad*, a book-length poem on the American Revolution, Joel Barlow describes the Battle of Saratoga as if it were the Last Judgment, invoking the sublime in all its glory:

> Now roll like winged storms the solid lines,
> The clarion thunders and the battle joins;
> Thick flames in vollied flashes load the air.
> And echoing mountains give the noise of war;
> Sulphureous clouds rise reddening round the height,
> And veil the skies and wrap the sounding fight.[7]

Like many eighteenth-century poets, Barlow believed that ancient languages were better suited to epic grandeur than modern ones. But he also believed that modern war, because of its scale and horror, was a better subject for poetry than ancient war. He makes both points in the preface to *The Columbiad*:

The shock of modern armies is, beyond comparison, more magnificent, more sonorous and more discoloring to the face of nature, than the ancient could have been; it is consequently susceptible of more pomp and variety of description. Our heaven and earth are not only shaken and tormented with greater noise, but filled and suffocated with fire and smoke. If Homer, with his Grecian tongue and all its dialects, had had the battle of Blenheim* to describe, the world would have possessed a picture and a piece of music which it will never possess.[8]

Barlow's enthusiasm for war as an occasion for the sublime music of epic poetry is political as well as aesthetic. In an earlier passage, he predicts that "righteous Freedom" and "protected Industry" will cure the rage of war.[9] Convinced that "good wars" could advance the inevitable progress of mankind toward freedom, democracy, and

---

* The major battle of the War of the Spanish Succession, in which forces under the Duke of Marlborough defeated the French on 13 August 1704.

brotherhood, Enlightenment poets often connected the magnificence of warfare to the supposed nobility of its aims. Their words helped create the idea of a "war to end all wars." Modern commentators, aware of the terrible failure of that hope, have been less likely to associate the beauty of combat with political progress. According to the critic Walter Benjamin, writing on the eve of World War II, our capacity to experience warfare as beauty has nothing to do with virtue or freedom. It comes from the dulling of our senses by technology and the twisted logic of Fascism:

Fascism ... expects war to supply the artistic gratification of a sense perception that has been changed by technology. ... Mankind, which in Homer's time was an object of contemplation for the Olympian gods, now is one for itself. Its self-alienation has reached such a degree that it can experience its own destruction as an aesthetic pleasure of the first order. This is the situation of politics which Fascism is rendering aesthetic.[10]

In our own times, witnesses to war have tried to separate the beauty of combat from *any* political or moral meaning, arguing that it has "the aesthetic purity of absolute moral indifference – a powerful, implacable beauty." Those words come from Tim O'Brien's *The Things They Carried*, a profoundly lyrical treatment of the war in Vietnam. Many who served in that war were deeply skeptical about its aims, but O'Brien, one of the most eloquent of those skeptics, has the courage to write about the war in language we may recognize as sublime:

For all its horror, you can't help but gape at the awful majesty of combat. You stare out at tracer rounds unwinding through the dark like brilliant red ribbons. You crouch in ambush as a cool, impassive moon rises over the nighttime paddies. You admire the fluid symmetries of troops on the move, the great sheets of metal-fire streaming down from a gunship, the illumination rounds, the white phosphorus, the purply orange glow of napalm, the rocket's red glare. It's not pretty, exactly. It's astonishing. It fills the eye. It commands you. You hate it, yes, but your eyes do not. Like a killer forest fire, like cancer under a microscope, any battle or bombing raid or artillery barrage has the aesthetic purity of absolute moral indifference – a powerful, implacable beauty – and a true war story will tell the truth about this, though the truth is ugly.[11]

By quoting a phrase from "The Star Spangled Banner," O'Brien signals his awareness of his poetic forebears. When he speaks of "the rocket's red glare" in the same breath with napalm and white phosphorus, he invokes the tradition of the military sublime and undercuts it at the same time. Like Francis Scott Key, he sees the incendiary beauty of bombardment. Unlike Key or Barlow, he cannot connect that terrible beauty to the ideas of liberty and progress.

Despite the skepticism about the political and moral meaning of war expressed so memorably by O'Brien, a doubt he shares with many modern poets, politicians continue to draw on older poetic traditions when seeking support for military ventures. Sometimes they are entirely unaware that the chivalric, patriotic, or magnificent language they are using comes from poets; sometimes they willfully flatten or misrepresent the traditions on which they draw. I have written this book to complicate that picture, to show that poetry can offer thoughtful readers precious insights into war – moral, political, and aesthetic ways of understanding war that are valuable precisely because they are not simple, flat, or formulaic.

Poetry is an art of memory, and in poems on war, memory is both a purpose and a subject. When poets assure the dead that their heroic acts will not be forgotten, living readers are more likely to believe those claims if the poems are memorable. Before the alphabet, poetry served to strengthen memory and preserve essential knowledge by giving stories and beliefs a rhythmic and musical shape.[12] In the modern world, we preserve knowledge in print and on hard drives, but we still commit some essential truths to memory, using the rhythm and music of poetry to help us hold them in our hearts. In Yeats's refrain, for example, the repetition of the word *changed* has incantatory power, and the strong triple rhythms of the second line make it impossible to forget:

> All changed, **changed** utterly,
> A terrible beauty is born.

Because its formal techniques for engaging our memory have ancient origins, poetry connects us to old ways of hearing and feeling. Like their forebears, modern poets must choose words that make sense, and even if they have abandoned traditional meters, they must fit those words to some meaningful rhythm, some shapely form. A reader attentive to both syntax and form will hear several kinds of meaning at once in poetic language.

At a different level, poetry helps cultures remember their pasts, and because every poet is inevitably dependent on earlier poets, we may hear in each new poem enriching echoes of poems from the past. Many poems about war attempt to honor heroism and sacrifice by evoking the weapons, customs, and poetic diction of earlier eras, deliberately distancing us from the ugly details of the current conflict. Sometimes this process yields only sentimental nostalgia, but in other cases, the summoning of past heroes and their language casts a fresh light on the present.

The formal ordering of verse and the echoing of previous poems are ways for poets to enclose or contain the horror, to assert control over the uncontrollable. By using traditional patterns of meter and older conventions of language to describe scenes of present chaos and violence, poets offer a more thoughtful account of war than television or print journalists, who must focus on the immediate moment and the hard facts. Poetic form and poetic allusion, which require contemplation and consideration, encourage readers to look at war from more than one perspective, and thus to think more deeply about its meaning.

Poets have given memorable expression to the personal motives that send men forth to fight: glory, honor, shame, comradeship, revenge. They have also helped to shape the larger, more corporate ideas that nations and cultures invoke as incentives for warfare: patriotism, religion, empire, chivalry, freedom. Some poets devote their talents to celebrating courage. Others focus on regretting loss. The greatest war poets do both at once: they praise the victor while mourning the victim; they honor the dead while raising deep questions about the meaning of honor. Even when the poet's main purpose is to praise the heroic efforts of one side, the fruitful ambiguity inherent in poetic form allows doubts, fears, and sympathy for the enemy to infiltrate the lines of verse.

Practicing the skills required to make words both meaningful and musical, to find images from the past that illuminate the present, helps poets develop the moral subtlety required to honor courage and sacrifice while regretting cruelty and loss. Because they are used to keeping both syntax and meter in play, poets are able to sustain other kinds of tension between conflicting forces. Some of the modes of emphasis made possible by poetic form lend themselves to irony, allowing poets to signal doubts about their own assertions. In *John Brown's Body*, Stephen Vincent Benét's long narrative poem on the American Civil War, the poet uses irony to explore the fundamental tension between poetry and war. Late in the war, a teenaged sentry remembers ancient poems while guarding the tent of Robert E. Lee:

> The aide-de-camp knew certain lines of Greek
> And other such unnecessary things
> As birds and music, that are good for peace
> But are not deemed so serviceable for war.[13]

According to this account, poetry is unnecessary for war, which requires more pragmatic kinds of knowledge. Like birds and music, poetry is only good for peace. But by writing a book-length poem on the Civil War, Benét reveals his belief that poetry is by no means unnecessary in wartime. By using the word *deemed*, he lets us know that he is reporting popular opinion, not his own. Ironies of this kind allow poets to express conflicting ideas simultaneously, which is often necessary when speaking of war.

These lines appeared in the English textbook used in my junior high school, and my first response to reading them was to imagine being the poetic sentry. From early childhood, I had heard my parents recite verse of all kinds, and like most eighth-graders in Alabama, I treasured stories about the conflict that Southerners insisted on calling "the War Between the States." One of my great-grandfathers, they told me, ran away from home as a boy to join the Confederate army. Another served as an infantry captain and carried fragments of Yankee bullets in his body. My great-great-grandfather's fastest ship ran the blockade of Charleston harbor seven times, and my mother still had a silver fork from the captain's table. A century after the fighting, the names of battlefields – Antietam, Spottsylvania, Chancellorsville – were still sacred, potent sounds. The oral history I grew up hearing was vague about large-scale strategy and downright hazy about the war's end, but it was rich in heroic anecdote. Repeated with reverence and emotion, the words of heroes were poetry to my ears. There was General Barnard Bee at Bull Run, a battle he would not survive, giving a new name to a great Confederate strategist:

> There stands Jackson like a Stone Wall;
> Rally behind the Virginians.[14]

And Jackson's own haunting death speech:

> Let us cross over the river, and rest
> Under the shade of the trees.[15]

Though spoken as prose, both these quotations fall readily into meter. For a boy with a poetic imagination, words like these made it possible to believe that eloquence was a mark of heroism. Brave men, I thought, must speak poetically – especially in times of crisis. Yet Benét's lines, which impressed me so much that I learned them by heart, challenged that notion and questioned the value of poetry in wartime – and through his irony, as I was just beginning to see, the poet cast further doubt on both the romanticizing of war and the pragmatic dismissal of poetry.

When they subject patriotism, courage, and youthful idealism to withering irony, poets are usually seeking a way to keep despair at the loss of youth and its bright hopes from swamping their poems in teary sentiment. Benét was the son of a career military officer, and the grandson of two men who fought on opposite sides in the Civil War. But when America entered World War I, the poet was still in his teens and unable to see without spectacles. Although he memorized the eye chart, it took only three days for the Army to detect his handicap. His service, out of uniform, took place in a code room in Washington, not a trench in Flanders.[16] The aide-de-camp – sensitive, poetic, and shadowed by death – is a fantasy version of the poet's own youthful self, which may help to explain why the older narrator treats him ironically:

> He was a youth with an inquisitive mind
> And doubtless had a failing for romance,
> But then he was not twenty, and such faults
> May sometimes be excused in younger men
> Even when such creatures die, as they have done
> At one time or another, for some cause
> Which we are careful to point out to them
> Much later, was no cause worth dying for,
> But cannot reach them with our arguments
> Because they are uneconomic dust.[17]

Meter is an essential part of the narrator's voice. The cool, impassive tone in which he expresses his disdain for younger men depends upon his fitting such detached, worldly phrases as "uneconomic dust" into blank verse, a form used by Shakespeare, Milton, and Wordsworth. By speaking in meter, the narrator avoids confronting the pain of war directly, and gains a more distant and critical perspective on romantic attitudes toward war. But irony is always a play of double meanings, and in this case, grief threatens to break through the mask of detachment. The fact that the sentry is not yet twenty, which the narrator offers as a reason for excusing his romantic faults, is also a reason for sympathy and sorrow. During the last years of the Civil War, many on both sides were in their teens. "Such creatures" often died, as did the equally youthful soldiers drafted in Germany and England in the final years of the Great War. Although the narrator affects a worldly, aged cynicism, Benét was not yet thirty when he wrote these lines, and still quite susceptible to the romantic notions his narrator dismisses as a failing. The poet is as present in the romanticism of the youthful sentry as he is in the skepticism of the older narrator. In this poem as in many others, irony is not only a way for the poet to keep his own emotions at bay; it is also a way of encouraging the reader to consider several conflicting interpretations of war at the same time.

Although death in war is often sharp and sudden, poems on war stretch time in both directions. Benét's strong feelings about World War I – sorrow at the appalling loss of life, anger at having been denied service, and survivor guilt as he considered the many fine poets among the dead – were surely powerful motives for his decision to write a long poem on the Civil War. And the unnecessary poem his Confederate soldier carries in his memory is not a lyrical reverie about birds and music but a stirring epic about "spear-handling kings"[18] – the *Iliad*, first in a long line of powerful poems on war. The best such poems use memory to link the heroism of the moment to past tradition; they use prophecy to move beyond the violent moment to some consideration of its lasting meaning. From this wider perspective, it is possible to celebrate bravery while lamenting war's costs, to sing both victor and victim. The war poets I most admire enlist the forces of memory, meter, and irony to help us confront, in all its contradictory power, the terrible beauty of war.

CHAPTER I

Honor and memory

In May of 1962, General Douglas MacArthur addressed the corps of cadets at West Point. At the end of his career, and at the beginning of the war in Vietnam, he took as his subject three "hallowed words": "Duty ... honor ... country."[1] *Honor* is the oldest, most basic concept in this triad. It existed before there were countries, and before those countries imposed duties on their citizens. Ancient Greek warriors did not have a strong sense of nation, but they had an acute sense of personal honor. So did medieval knights, who were the original free lancers. The *Oxford English Dictionary* defines honor as "high respect, esteem, or reverence, accorded to exalted worth or rank."[2] Different periods and cultures have represented such respect, esteem, and reverence with different symbols – including material goods, aristocratic titles, and rituals of deference – but MacArthur, speaking in a nation without an aristocracy, evoked the idea of honor by using poetic language. He told the young men that they were "the Nation's ... gladiators in the arena of battle," alluding to ancient Rome but suppressing the fact that Roman gladiators were slaves. He spoke of "a code of conduct and chivalry," invoking the myth of virtuous knighthood but ignoring the brutality of real medieval knights. And he described his fellow soldiers, men loyal to this "great moral code," as "those who guard this beloved land of culture and ancient descent," inventing a noble and lengthy ancestry for a country whose real history is democratic and short.

As these deliberately vague and supposedly poetic gestures reveal, MacArthur hoped to intensify the idea of honor by appealing to an imagined tradition. After announcing that Duty, Honor, and

Country were his themes, he said that he possessed "neither that eloquence of diction, that poetry of imagination, nor that brilliance of metaphor to tell you all that they mean" – a false show of humility that betrays his keen interest in poetry. In this speech as in others, MacArthur drew frequently upon poetic devices. By claiming that "the American man-at-arms" had "drained deep the chalice of courage," he deployed the Christian and chivalric imagery of the Holy Grail, first developed in medieval poems. By describing the soldier as writing "his own history … in red on his enemy's breast," he combined the bayonet and the pen, transforming the soldier into a writer. And by self-consciously employing alliteration to recall his comrades in the First World War, "bending under soggy packs on many a weary march, from dripping dusk to drizzling dawn," he even tried to *sound* poetic.

MacArthur's need to speak of war in this kind of language shows how deeply the poetry of World War I, in which he was a decorated combatant, had penetrated his imagination. Paul Fussell, the most sensitive analyst of that poetry, has shown how the poets of the Great War began by employing an "essentially feudal language" in which horses were *steeds*, friends were *comrades*, and the dead were *the fallen*.[3] By invoking the "man-at-arms" and the "chalice of courage," MacArthur echoed that feudal idiom, and the connection runs deeper than imagery. Like the poets of 1914, MacArthur was eager to apply the language of exalted rank to the ordinary soldier: "I do not know the dignity of their birth," he said, remembering the American dead, "but I do know the glory of their death."

The notion that death might give glory, dignity, and even nobility to men who could not have claimed such honors in civilian life was a common poetic theme in the early days of the Great War, memorably developed by the British poet Rupert Brooke. Before the war, Brooke was as famous for his good looks as for his poems. Yeats called him "the handsomest man in England"; Virginia Woolf swam naked with him in a country stream.[4] The five sonnets Brooke published during the first year of the war were widely read and quoted, even from pulpits.[5] They gained added significance when he died in 1915.

In "The Soldier," the speaker imagines his English dust as *richer* than the surrounding earth of a foreign grave:

Figure 2. Rupert Brooke in Ottawa (1913).

If I should die, think only this of me:
That there's some corner of a foreign field
That is forever England. There shall be
In that rich earth a richer dust concealed;
A dust whom England bore, shaped, made aware, . . .[6]

The richness of the soldier's imagined dust comes in part from its being human remains, as opposed to the miscellaneous organic matter of the surrounding soil, but Brooke does not make that point. Instead, he emphasizes the fact that the dust is *English*, and therefore richer than anything else in the *foreign* field – a patriotic claiming of privilege for all things English. Benét's wry phrase about "uneconomic dust" is probably a skeptical American response to this very poem and its nationalistic claims, and may reflect his recognition of the other kind of privilege that lurks behind the cover of Brooke's patriotism: the idea of class. If we apply the sequence of verbs ("bore, shaped, made aware") to Brooke himself, we may imagine an Englishman born into an upper-class family and shaped by an elite education at Rugby and Cambridge, with an acute awareness that he could express as poetry. For the enlisted men the poet commanded as an officer, the experience of being born, shaped, and made aware by an England imagined as a mother was surely different. And if Brooke sincerely believed that any English soldier, no matter how humble his origins, could enrich the soil of Flanders with his dust, the dust he particularly imagined was that of a privileged, sensitive poet.

Like MacArthur magically transforming America into a "land of culture and ancient descent," Brooke magically awards his own social standing and poetic awareness to the generic and nameless soldier of his poem. Although he did not foreground this process, his eulogists did. Winston Churchill, writing a few days after Brooke's death, treated him as a model for others, emphasizing his education and his physical beauty:

The thoughts to which he gave expression in the very few incomparable war sonnets which he has left behind will be shared by many thousands of young men moving resolutely and blithely forward into this, the hardest, cruelest, and the least-rewarded of all the wars that men have fought. They are a whole history and revelation of Rupert Brooke himself. Joyous, fearless, versatile, deeply instructed, with classic symmetry of mind and body, he was all that one would wish England's noblest sons to be in days when no sacrifice but the most precious is acceptable, and the most precious is that which is most freely proffered.[7]

In emphasizing the value of sacrifice, Churchill draws on ideas Brooke had expressed poetically in "The Dead," where he extends the idea of wealth to casualties of all ranks and classes. The dead, though once poor, are now rich; they have made precious gifts to the rest of us:

> Blow out, you bugles, over the rich Dead!
> There's none of these so lonely and poor of old,
> But, dying, has made us rarer gifts than gold.[8]

The wages of common soldiers may be paltry, but their deaths are the coin in which Honour, imagined as a king, pays handsome wages to the living:

> Honour has come back, as a king, to earth,
> And paid his subjects with a royal wage;
> And Nobleness walks in our ways again;
> And we have come into our heritage.

In a grand, generous gesture, Brooke associates the deaths of enlisted men with "Nobleness" and the national heritage, but he is honest enough to describe them as "lonely and poor" before their deaths.

The ironies to which I am pointing are inherent in the concept of honor in many periods. Only through bloodshed can the lonely, poor soldier become a full participant in the noble heritage of the nation, as Shakespeare's Prince Henry claims in a speech that describes the comradeship of soldiers as a blood-tie linking kings and commoners:

> For he to day that sheds his blood with me
> Shall be my brother: be he ne'er so vile,
> This day shall gentle his condition.[9]

The most striking word here is *gentle*, transformed by the context from an adjective to a verb and given strong emphasis by its metrical placement. As Shakespeare's poetry transforms the normal function of that word, so warfare is supposed to transform the vile condition of the ordinary soldier, making him a gentleman.

Though Shakespeare's play was often quoted at the time (and later), the Great War put such traditional claims under severe pressure. By 1916, over a million combatants were dead, and if monuments continued to describe the dead as "glorious," their deaths were often muddy and anonymous, leaving no identifiable remains. The remaining poets – still mostly officers – began to reject the stock vocabulary of chivalric terms and abstract nouns that had seemed so apt a few years earlier. In a sonnet called "The Poet as Hero,"

Figure 3. Siegfried Sassoon (1916).

Siegfried Sassoon explained why he was now "scornful, harsh, and discontented, / Mocking and loathing War":

> You are aware that once I sought the Grail,
> Riding in armour bright, serene and strong;
> And it was told that through my infant wail
> There rose immortal semblances of song.
> But now I've said good-bye to Galahad,
> And am no more the knight of dreams and show:
> For lust and senseless hatred make me glad,
> And my killed friends are with me where I go.
> Wound for red wound I burn to smite their wrongs;
> And there is absolution in my songs.[10]

For Sassoon, chivalric myth is no longer an adequate motive for combat, and reaching into the dream world of fairy tales is no longer an adequate purpose for poetry. Brutalized by combat and disillusioned with knightly honor, he now takes pleasure in lust and senseless hatred. Poetry, which once served to glorify combat, is now a way of seeking absolution. But Sassoon cannot easily escape from poetic language. "I burn to smite their wrongs," he says, expressing his hope to avenge his dead comrades. Despite himself, he remembers Renaissance love poetry, in which burning often represents desire, and the King James Version of the Old Testament, in which Samson and Gideon *smite* their foes.

Some eight months after writing this poem, Sassoon wrote an eloquent public letter refusing to continue his service. Thanks to the timely intervention of Robert Graves, he was not court-martialed, but sent to a hospital in Scotland to recover from "shell shock." Among his fellow patients was another bitter poet, Wilfred Owen, who later returned to the front and died just days before the Armistice. In a preface he drafted for a planned collection of war poems, Owen told his readers not to expect invocations of glory, honor, or other grand abstractions.

This book is not about heroes. English Poetry is not yet fit to speak of them. Nor is it about deeds, or lands, nor anything about glory, honour, might, majesty, dominion, or power, except War. Above all I am not concerned with Poetry. My subject is War, and the pity of War. The Poetry is in the pity. Yet these elegies are to this generation in no sense consolatory. They may be to the next. All a poet can do today is warn. That is why the true Poets must be truthful.[11]

Owen refuses to write about glory and honor, and rejects the liturgical traditions linking those abstractions with the might, majesty, dominion, and power of God. His subject, he says, is war, and the pity of war. When he says he is not concerned with Poetry, he obviously does not mean that he is abandoning verse, which he continued to write until the end. He is rejecting what Poetry with a capital P had come to mean – a stock vocabulary of knightly images and lofty abstractions. In the new poetry exemplified by Owen's later poems, a realistic account of war replaces the false fantasies of knighthood; pity replaces glory and honor. Yet Owen's rejection of the language of glory and honor, his

Figure 4. Wilfred Owen.

determination to treat the dead with a pity felt directly and personally, may owe something to his own experience of class condescension. Sassoon, whom he admired extravagantly, sneered at his "Grammar School accent."[12]

The attack on traditional poetry mounted by Owen and others disillusioned by the Great War may be among the reasons why later wars have produced fewer poems, but it was not a complete success. Less than fifty years later, in a nation supposedly free from the cruelties of class snobbery, General MacArthur brought back the imagery of the Grail and spoke reverently of glory and honor and the other abstractions that Sassoon and Owen had rejected as false. In a passage he must have thought especially poetic, he invoked "the witching melody of faint bugles blowing reveille, of far drums beating the long roll." Here he remembered not only Brooke's bugles, but those of a nineteenth-century American poet, Richard Hovey, who had written a strikingly similar passage in the 1890s, when MacArthur was a teenager, describing

> The bugles of the dead
> Blowing from spectral ranks an answering cry!
> The ghostly roll of immaterial drums,
> Beating reveille in the camps of dream.[13]

As these examples suggest, poetry has often helped to dress warfare in the borrowed robes of honor and nostalgia. In every period, poets have invoked the weapons, vocabulary, myths, and cultural values of previous eras in order to make their own times seem grander, more heroic, more noble. Politicians and military leaders, in turn, have not hesitated to use such poetry for their own purposes. Poetry's complicity in making the notion of honor attractive matters deeply because honor, especially when embraced by nations, can trigger violence on a large scale. The classicist Donald Kagan, a thoughtful analyst of the origins of war, claims a continuous history for honor as a motive for warfare:

Thucydides found that people go to war out of "honor, fear, and interest." . . . That fear and interest move states to war will not surprise the modern reader, but that concern for honor should do so may seem strange. If we take honor to mean fame, glory, renown, or splendor, it may appear applicable only to an earlier time. If, however, we understand its significance as deference, esteem, just due, regard, respect, or prestige we will find it an important motive of nations in the modern world as well. . . . The reader may be surprised by how small a role . . . considerations of practical utility and material gain, and even ambition for power itself, play in bringing on wars and how often some aspect of honor is decisive.[14]

Kagan makes good these claims by demonstrating that the way decision-makers at the beginning of World War II or the Cuban missile crisis thought about their honor had elements in common with the way ancient Greeks and Romans thought about theirs. In reminding us of these continuities, he denies us the easy comfort of imagining that modern leaders have become less concerned with honor than leaders in earlier cultures. The meaning of honor has changed many times in the years separating us from the ancients. Shifting cultural attitudes toward religion, class, and sex have helped shape conceptions of honor specific to particular times and places. But in many of those times and places, the seductive music of poetry has been a powerful force persuading fighters that their ugly work has something to do with a glorious, fabled past.

I first became aware of General MacArthur's speech on "Duty, Honor, Country" while serving in an Army band in 1969. On a blistering summer day, we put on our woolen dress uniforms and went to play at an annual ceremony of commemoration in Norfolk, Virginia, where the general's remains lie in a marble memorial. Words from his speech are carved into the walls, where tourists gawk at them. As we rode the bus to Norfolk, standing up to preserve the creases in our trousers, one of our sergeants, a career bandsman, implored us to heed the patriotic message of MacArthur's speech, repeating "Duty, Honor, Country" over and over again, as if chanting a liturgy. To me, it seemed especially ironic that this particular sergeant was a Puerto Rican, borrowing MacArthur's words to express his devotion to a country in which he was often treated as a second-class citizen.

On that day, it was very easy to be cynical – both about MacArthur's speech and about the sergeant's unblinking acceptance of its message. If the only writers enlisting the power of poetry in the service of honor were would-be poets like MacArthur or thin sentimental poets like Richard Hovey, cynicism might be an adequate response. But the same forces are also at work in some of the finest lyrics in English, those written by the Cavalier poets of the seventeenth century. Although I did not remember it on that hot day in Norfolk, I know I was moved when I first read the best-known Cavalier poem on honor: "To Lucasta, Going to the Wars," by Richard Lovelace, published in 1649. It was in my high-school textbook on English literature, and it still appears in textbooks today. If asked for one poetic phrase about honor, many readers of English poetry might recall the concluding lines:

> I could not love thee (dear) so much,
> Lov'd I not Honour more.[15]

These words have entered our cultural memory as a timeless and general example of the soldier's farewell to his lady, but the poem they conclude is an exercise in denial. Like the other Cavaliers, Lovelace refused to acknowledge the sweeping changes that took place during his life. Although you would never know it from the poem, he lived in a time when revolutions toppled monarchs, religious strife tore countries apart, and war became efficient and faceless. In the Thirty Years' War (1618–1648), Gustavus Adolphus of Sweden devised formations that assured nearly continuous gunfire, with the result that some 300,000 Germans died in combat. Malnutrition, disease, and marauding troops caused millions of civilian casualties; modern scholars estimate the losses at 15–20 percent of the population. In the English Civil Wars (1641–1649), soldiers faced increasingly effective artillery and musket fire. Civilians did not die in numbers comparable to those on the Continent, but suffering was widespread. Like the American Civil War two centuries later, this conflict divided families and turned friends into enemies. Sieges frequently ended with the execution of troops who had surrendered, and Parliamentary soldiers wantonly destroyed precious artifacts that they considered symbols of the old regime: stained glass windows, cathedral organs, country houses. The wars overturned settled hierarchies in state, Church, and society, and ended with the public beheading of Charles I, a monarch once thought sacred.

To many living in them, these times seemed modern, even revolutionary. In the words of one popular song, the world was "turned upside down."[16] Yet poets, both on the Continent and in Britain, clung to the conventions of epic and chivalric literature and avoided depicting the mechanized slaughter of the present. If poems were our only evidence, we might imagine that seventeenth-century wars still featured single combat by heroic nobles.

The English Cavalier poets, doomed celebrants of the losing side in the Civil Wars, used poetry to ignore or suppress the new ideas and weapons that defined their times. Their deliberately traditional language makes their poems seem closer to the troubadour songs of the twelfth century than to the radical ballads of the 1640s. Yet the chivalric formulas of these poets, already outdated in their own period, had a long afterlife, influencing the way later writers, including the World War I poets and General MacArthur, described and imagined themselves. Their language about honor, based on classical and chivalric sources and cast in memorable lyric form, retains some power today. The persistence of Cavalier poems in our cultural memory is a prime example of the way poetry has helped turn an abstraction called honor into a reason to die.

"To Lucasta, Going to the Wars" is so familiar that it takes an effort to see it freshly. Although I have known it by heart for over forty years, I now believe that the commonplace sentiments of this famous lyric conceal some troubling contradictions. Like other literary mistresses, Lucasta may have been imaginary, and the speaker of the poem may not be identical to the poet. For convenience, however, I will call him Lovelace.

He begins abruptly:

> Tell me not (sweet) I am unkind,
>   That from the nunnery
> Of thy chaste breast and quiet mind,
>   To war and arms I fly.

Perhaps the poem is a letter; perhaps it starts in the middle of a conversation. In either case, Lovelace is silencing Lucasta; she will not be allowed to tell him he is unkind. Not only is ordering one's mistress not to speak an odd way to begin a love poem, but the complaint he is trying to forestall is entirely natural. If she loves him, it makes sense for her to call him unkind for abandoning her and putting himself in danger. And because the primary meaning of *unkind* at this time was *unnatural*, Lucasta is not merely complaining of her own mistreatment; she is telling Lovelace that his actions are inhuman.

Even the sounds of this stanza suggest the unease of the speaker. Although the Cavalier poets are famous for their smooth lyricism, the rhythm here is quite awkward. The parenthetical address to Lucasta – *(sweet)* – breaks up the flow of the first line, not just because of the punctuation, but because the cluster of consonants – *not sweet* – is difficult to pronounce quickly. If you read the stanza out loud, similar clusters – *That from, chaste breast, quiet mind* – will slow down your reading until the last line of the stanza. Lovelace sounds hesitant, even tongue-tied, until the thought of war and arms frees up his speech.

Like the rhythm, the metaphors are strange. Although Lovelace invokes Lucasta's breast, a female feature often celebrated in Cavalier verse, he calls it a *chaste* breast, as if trying to suppress the erotic dimension. Although he mentions her mind, a feature rarely praised in poems addressed to women at this time, he calls it a *quiet* mind, perhaps in the hope that her natural calmness will keep her from complaining about his desertion. But before he names either her breast or her mind, he likens both to a nunnery, a metaphysical gesture linking flesh and spirit with religious faith – and also a striking anachronism. Henry VIII had seized all the monasteries and convents in England in the 1530s; those religious houses, like the Catholic faith they served, were a thing of the past. Perhaps Lovelace is invoking the medieval idea of the nunnery as part of the process by which he casts himself as a medieval knight and refuses to face the realities of the present. But he does not merely place Lucasta *within* a convent; he turns her into one. Her flesh becomes stone, and the strongest image is the idea of enclosure, with Lucasta imagined as the nunnery from which Lovelace needs to *fly*. A scene replayed again and again in poems about war, the hero's tender parting from his sweetheart or wife, turns into a scene of escape, with the Cavalier eagerly withdrawing from the confining embrace of a woman pictured as a walled convent.

He is leaving her for someone else:

> True; a new mistress now I chase,
> The first foe in the field;
> And with a stronger faith embrace
> A sword, a horse, a shield.

Medieval and Renaissance poets often described their mistresses as enemies with the power to slay them, but these lines reverse the convention. Instead of describing a woman's erotic power in military language, Lovelace uses the language of desire to describe encountering an armed male opponent. He shows no embarrassment about the metaphors that depict him pursuing another man. Instead of embracing Lucasta, the poet now proposes to embrace a sword, a horse, and a shield. Except for the horse, these were not modern weapons. Shields were useless against artillery, and many cavalrymen in the Civil Wars carried pistols, but firearms were too modern for Lovelace to include in this deliberately backward-looking poem. Mentioning only those weapons that might allow him to imagine himself as a knight confronting a single foe, he ignores the realities of seventeenth-century warfare, with its mass troop movements and deadly cannon. By censoring gunpowder, he hopes to stifle the explosive noise of the present world.

Religion and sex, frequent themes in war poetry of all periods, were central motivations in the English Civil Wars. The Puritan soldiers of Oliver Cromwell's New Model Army believed they were fighting to bring in the Kingdom of God, while the Cavaliers liked to imagine they were fighting for the honor of their ladies. When Lovelace embraces his knightly trappings with a stronger *faith*, his language connects the religious imagery of the first stanza to the admission of sexual faithlessness in the second. His love of honor, oddly expressed by the grotesque image of the warrior embracing his horse and weapons, is clearly stronger than his love for his mistress or his God.

In the final stanza, disarmingly admitting his inconstancy, Lovelace claims that Lucasta must adore it:

> Yet this inconstancy is such
> As you too shall adore; . . .

The word *shall* conveys constraint; "you gotta love it" might be a colloquial modern equivalent. *Adore*, with its religious connotations, suggests that Lucasta must not only accept but even worship her lover's inconstancy. Yet the most remarkable word in these lines is the little adverb *too*. It must mean that someone besides Lucasta adores Lovelace's inconstancy, and the only plausible candidate is Lovelace himself. With that little word, the speaker reveals that his apology to Lucasta is really a way of convincing himself that choosing honor rather than love is the right course.

The conclusion, which is supposed to resolve all the tangled uncertainties of the previous stanzas, comes in the most beautifully balanced lines of the whole poem:

> I could not love thee (dear) so much,
> Lov'd I not Honour more.

There is lyrical music here – the delicate reordering of *I, love,* and *not*; the subtle alliteration of _much_ and _more_; the murmuring *r* sounds in

Deare, Honour, and *more.* Seductive and memorable, these lines are still alive; I recently found them quoted on a website created by a woman of my generation to honor her husband, a Vietnam veteran. But without intending any disrespect for the thousands of English-speaking soldiers and sweethearts who have found comfort in these words, I have to confess that I find their message deeply troubling. Drawing on centuries of chivalric language about honor, Lovelace argues that his willingness to desert his mistress and risk death increases and proves his love for her. He does not claim to be showing his love for Lucasta by shielding her from violence. Nor does he make her a metaphor for a homeland he has sworn to protect. He says, quite baldly, that he embraces violence, adores his own inconstancy, and loves an abstraction called Honor more than he loves Lucasta – yet he asks her to experience the poem as a compliment.

In light of the poet's treatment of his lady, it is remarkable that even women poets have appropriated these lines. Katharine Tynan, mourning the death of a soldier in the early months of the Great War, explicitly names Lovelace as a model:

> Percy, golden-hearted boy,
> In the heyday of his joy
> Left his new-made bride and chose
> The steep way that Honour goes.
>
> Took for his the deathless song
> Of the love that knows no wrong:
> Could I love thee, dear, so true
> Were not Honour more than you?
>
> (Oh, forgive, dear Lovelace, laid
> In this mean Procrustean bed!)
> Dear, I love thee best of all
> When I go, at England's call.[17]

As Tynan's apology suggests, she knew she was flattening and distorting Lovelace's lines. She cannot have known that her sugges-tion that Lovelace, like Percy, had gone to the wars at England's call was historically incorrect. Despite the date, the wars to which Lovelace was going were *not* the English Civil Wars. After presenting a Royalist petition to Parliament, he languished under house arrest from 1642 until 1646, when he became a colonel in the French army, fighting against Spain in the final phase of the Thirty Years' War. Seriously wounded at Dunkirk, he returned to England in 1648. His contemporaries believed that Lovelace sought this overseas service to vindicate his honor after being prevented from fighting for the Royalist cause.[18] If this poem reflects that decision, the honor it celebrates is not duty to family, King, or country, but personal status as a noble warrior. Lucasta should not have accepted it as an expression of love. Her complaints about his unkindness take on even more urgency when we realize that Lovelace was actually going to the wars in France. Although it masquerades as a love poem, "To Lucasta" is really a poem of self-love, as are many poems invoking honor.

The long afterlife of Lovelace's poem is as much a part of my story as the particular circumstances of its composition. "To Lucasta" is so beautifully made that it has been an anthology piece for 350 years, but its aesthetic excellence has helped to conceal its deep dishonesty. The possibility of the poet's death – an important fear for Lucasta – never becomes explicit. The polished verse serves to distance the poem from the realities of seventeenth-century combat, directing Lucasta's attention away from sweat, pain, danger, and death toward the abstract notion of honor. In the process, Lucasta is told to keep silent, treated as if she had no desire, and invited to approve of her lover's unfaithfulness. She may be called sweet and dear, but the poet's self-regarding celebration of his own honor renders her more a rhetorical convenience than a person.

In remembering the intricate music of Lovelace's poem, most readers remember the elegant, clever poet and his devotion to honor. They forget Lucasta and her abandonment; they forget which wars the poet was going to; and they forget the hard reality of death in battle. By writing the poem, Lovelace may have been engaging in a similar exercise. He may have been whistling in the dark, keeping up his courage by invoking honor and inventing extravagant images: the woman imagined as a nunnery, the foe imagined as a mistress. In the end, he may have needed more than anything else to convince himself that he loved honor (and therefore the risk of pain and death) more than he loved Lucasta.

When Lovelace died in 1658, his friends issued a posthumous edition of his poems. The frontispiece shows the poet in armor, draped in a classical toga, with a laurel wreath hovering over him.

Figure 5. Frontispiece to *Posthume Poems of Richard Lovelace, Esq.* (London, 1659).

Lucasta appears as a name on the urn that serves as his pedestal. The picture perfectly captures the poet's studied disregard for his lady.

Most readers in the centuries that separate Lovelace from us have taken "To Lucasta" and similar poems at face value, believing that the poet's stoical invocation of honor was sincere and admirable. One striking exception is Anne Finch, Countess of Winchilsea, born just three years after Lovelace died. The wars of her lifetime were continental campaigns fought by professional armies: the Nine

Years' War (1689–1697) and the War of the Spanish Succession
(1701–1714). In a memorable section of a longer poem on vanity,
published during the final year of the War of the Spanish
Succession, Finch describes a young man seduced by the finery of
an officer's uniform. Splendid in his gold embroideries and feath-
ered hat, the youth

> Walks haughty in a Coat of Scarlet Die,
> A Colour well contriv'd to cheat the Eye,
> Where richer Blood, alas! May undistinguisht lye.
> And oh! too near that wretched Fate attends;
> Hear it ye Parents, all ye weeping Friends!
> Thou fonder Maid! won by those gaudy Charms,
> (The destin'd Prize of his Victorious Arms)
> Now fainting Dye upon the mournful Sound,
> That speaks his hasty Death, and paints the fatal Wound!
> Trail all your Pikes, dispirit every Drum,
> March in a slow Procession from afar,
> Ye silent, ye dejected Men of War!
> Be still the Hautboys,* and the Flute be dumb!
> Display no more, in vain, the lofty Banner;
> For see! Where on the Bier before ye lies
> The pale, the fall'n, th' untimely Sacrifice
> To your mistaken Shrine, to your false Idol Honour![19]

The officer's dashing uniform is a cheat, a gaudy charm that
wins a foolish maid. Although this latter-day Lucasta is supposed to
be the prize of his victorious arms, the soldier, slain by arms of
steel, will never hold her in his arms of flesh. In Finch's sad version
of a military parade, pikes trail in the dust, banners flutter in vain,
and honor is exposed as a false idol. She insists on the realities that
Lovelace sought to banish from his poem: the hero's death and the
grief of his loved ones.

Unfortunately, the Cavaliers passed into the anthologies, while
Anne Finch faded into obscurity and has only recently begun to be
read again. Unaware of the strenuous critique of honor offered by
Finch and a few others, English-speaking children in later times
memorized "To Lucasta" and other such poems, inheriting the

---

* Oboes.

chivalric vocabulary, the unquestioning respect for honor, and the disregard for those left behind. The Great War provides ready examples, including Katharine Tynan's explicit imitation of Lovelace. Like the scarlet coat of Finch's officer, many poems written during the early years of the war were contrived to cheat the eye, using a nostalgic vocabulary drawn from earlier poets to camouflage the bloodshed of the present. "The Volunteer," by the minor poet Herbert Asquith, son of the Prime Minister, is an all-too-typical example:

> Here lies the clerk who half his life had spent
> Toiling at ledgers in a city grey,
> Thinking that so his days would drift away
> With no lance broken in life's tournament:
> Yet ever 'twixt the books and his bright eyes
> The gleaming eagles of the legions came,
> And horsemen, charging under phantom skies,
> Went thundering past beneath the oriflamme.*
> And now those waiting dreams are satisfied;
> From twilight to the halls of dawn he went;
> His lance is broken; but he lies content
> With that high hour, in which he lived and died.
> And falling thus, he wants no recompense,
> Who found his battle in the last resort;
> Nor needs he any hearse to bear him hence,
> Who goes to join the men of Agincourt.[20]

Once again, the poet invokes a weapon not actually used in the war he is describing. Cavalry units were issued lances in 1914, but machine guns soon demonstrated the futility of edged weapons or mounted troops in modern war. As Lovelace, by embracing his sword, horse, and shield, denies the reality of muskets and cannon, so Asquith, by referring to the gleaming eagles of Roman legions and the oriflamme of medieval France, denies the reality of machine guns and barbed wire, with which he was surely familiar as an officer in the Royal Artillery. The hazy myths of ancient and medieval warfare, bound up in Asquith's mind with the notion of honor, serve to distance the pain

---

* "The sacred banner of St. Denis, . . . attached to a lance, which the early kings of France used to receive from the hands of the abbot of St. Denis, on setting out for war" *(Oxford English Dictionary).*

and loss of death. The poet imagines a soldier with a broken lance dying in a high hour because he cannot describe a soldier with a rifle and a gas mask dying with thousands of others.

By deflecting the reader's attention from the carnage of the Great War and directing it toward such empty notions as "the halls of dawn," Asquith attempts to disown the present. He may have believed that he was honoring the memory of his clerk-volunteer by likening him to the men of Agincourt, the English archers who fought with Henry the Fifth in 1415. But by being compared to a medieval archer, the volunteer loses his particularity as a rifleman of 1915 and disappears from our memory. Like Lovelace's Lucasta, silenced in the poem that bears her name, the volunteer has no voice in his poem, and Asquith's fanciful account of his motives and feelings looks dubious. There were plenty of City clerks who enlisted in the Army, but I wonder how many of them knew much about Agincourt, or the Roman legions, or the oriflamme. Those details point to Asquith himself, with his Oxford education and his flair for poetry. Asquith evidently projected his own romantic yearnings for glory onto the clerk, then imagined the clerk as content in death, with his waiting dreams satisfied by falling heroically. The poet may have felt better about the volunteer's death because he had magically given him the education – and thus the class status – that he never had. But the resulting poem is flat and false.

After the Battle of the Somme and the Battle of Verdun in 1916, each of which cost the Allies more than 600,000 casualties, it became difficult to pretend that the mechanized slaughter between the trenches had anything to do with knighthood, honor, or glory. The hero of Ernest Hemingway's *A Farewell to Arms* speaks for his generation when he bitterly rejects the official vocabulary of the war:

I was always embarrassed by the words sacred, glorious, and sacrifice and the expression in vain. We had heard them, sometimes standing in the rain almost out of earshot, so that only the shouted words came through, and had read them, on proclamations that were slapped up by bill posters over other proclamations, now for a long time, and I had seen nothing sacred, and the things that were glorious had no glory and the sacrifices were like the stockyards at Chicago if nothing was done with the meat except to bury it. There were many words that you could not stand to hear. . . . Abstract words such as glory, honor, courage, or hallow were obscene beside the concrete names of villages, the numbers of roads, the names of rivers, the numbers of regiments and the dates.[21]

Adopting Hemingway's ideas as metaphor, I would argue that poetry has sometimes been a way of shouting words like *sacred, glorious,* and *sacrifice* and making them heard in the rain. It has given abstractions like honor such memorable expression that readers forget to scrutinize their meaning. The question, as I have already suggested, is whether the power of poetry, like the shouting of patriotic slogans, amplifies something empty and questionable or something deep and admirable. It is depressing but true that all the abstract words that Hemingway declared obscene in 1928 – *glory, honor, courage,* and *hallow* – appear again in MacArthur's speech of 1962. Although the old general preferred remembering the vapid myths of poets like Richard Hovey and Herbert Asquith to confronting the tougher vision of a Wilfred Owen, great poets as well as weak ones have played a role in the process I am describing. The central canon of western poetry, from Homer to Lovelace and beyond, has provided politicians and generals with ample material for celebrating the idea of honor.

Hemingway's other image, the idea of bill posters slapping their proclamations over other proclamations, is a useful metaphor for the power of tradition, in this case the long tradition of poems about war. By imitating or evoking earlier poems, poets invite their readers to view the present from the perspective of the past. When allusion and imitation create a simultaneous awareness of the poet's own times and some earlier period, the new poem gains new layers of richness. In visual terms, a new poster of this kind does not obliterate the old one; it creates a *palimpsest,* a piece of writing in which several layers are visible.

The practice of the Cavaliers was different. By patterning their work on lyrics by earlier poets, Lovelace and the other Cavaliers were trying to suppress the facts of their own times, denying the reality of the forces that were threatening monarchy and tradition, covering up the present with a thick layer of the past. Their poetic nostalgia expresses their political nostalgia, though I like to believe they were sometimes aware of their own motives. When Lovelace speaks of embracing a horse or taking a foe as a mistress, his comic extravagance may betray his awareness that striking a chivalric pose in 1648 was faintly absurd. Poets like Katharine Tynan and Herbert Asquith lack even that saving grace. Refusing to face the present, they claim continuity with earlier and better poets without gaining complexity, irony, or depth from their borrowings.

Parody is another way of dealing with tradition. By retaining some parts of the original and distorting others, the writer of parody reveals the weaknesses of the original and gains an oblique way of expressing his own views. As later poets recognized, "To Lucasta" invited parodic imitation. Rudyard Kipling's bitter, laconic collection, *Epitaphs of the War* (1919), includes a sharp, effective parody. Kipling's speaker, identified in the title as a bridegroom, also admits to unfaithfulness, but this time the new mistress is not the first foe or honor, but death:

> Call me not false, beloved,
>   If, from thy scarce-known breast
> So little time removed,
>   In other arms I rest.
>
> For this more ancient bride,
>   Whom coldly I embrace,
> Was constant at my side
>   Before I saw thy face.
>
> Our marriage, often set –
>   By miracle delayed –
> At last is consummate,
>   And cannot be unmade.
>
> Live, then, whom Life shall cure,
>   Almost, of Memory,
> And leave us to endure
>   Its immortality.[22]

Kipling exposes some of the contradictions of Lovelace's poem in the very act of imitating it. All the other creatures Lovelace proposes to embrace – the first foe in the field; a sword, a horse, a shield; and most of all, honor – are ultimately euphemisms for death. Kipling's poem, written after a war in which he lost his own son, makes explicit the cold embrace of the ancient bride that Lovelace's skillful verse attempts to conceal from his sweetheart – and from himself.

Although Kipling's parodic critique of Lovelace scores some accurate points, his poem remains connected to the world of its model. The diction is old-fashioned, dignified, abstract; and in urging his bride to live on, the soldier-bridegroom affects a stoic gallantry that resembles the pose struck by Lovelace. More honest about death than its model, this poem still rests on some similar assumptions about honor. Kipling was correcting Lovelace, not rejecting him. There is a considerable distance between his attitude toward the literary past and the sweeping dismissal of high poetic language in Owen's preface or Hemingway's novel.

Thanks to meter, verse is more readily memorable than prose, but the formal power that gives a poem its entrance into our hearts may be used for good or ill. By inducing readers to remember one aspect of war, the poet may simply, and falsely, encourage them to forget another. But if he makes use of poetry's capacity for multiple meanings, he may both deepen and complicate the process of memory. When Kipling's bridegroom speaks of enduring immortality, his immediate reference must be to the pain of his permanent separation from his bride. For the poet, however, these words may have held another meaning. The old Kipling of 1919, sobered and saddened by the loss of his son and indeed of his son's generation, had to endure the immortality of his own imperialistic and patriotic poetry from the Victorian era, which had helped to shape the attitudes that led to the War. I like to think that some sort of regret, some sense of responsibility, quietly deepens these lines.

Sometimes a parodist includes himself explicitly in the criticism he levels at the original. In 1917, Robert Graves published "To Lucasta, On Going to the Wars – For the Fourth Time," a jaunty little poem that provides a shrewd and penetrating reading of Lovelace's original. Graves gains some detachment by describing the soldier going to the wars in the third person, but preserves some intimacy by speaking directly to Lucasta:

> Lucasta, when to France your man
> Returns his fourth time, hating war,
> Yet laughs as calmly as he can
>   And flings an oath, but says no more,
> That is not courage, that's not fear –
> Lucasta he's a Fusilier,
>   And his pride sends him here.[23]

Graves exposes the weakness of Lovelace's gallant claims about honor by suggesting more plausible motives for going to the wars: the group pride of a regiment (here the Royal Welch Fusiliers) and the individual pride of the soldier. What Lovelace calls honor, Graves identifies as male bonding, self-love, and pride. He even cautions Lucasta against supposing that she is important:

> Don't plume yourself he fights for you;
> It is no courage, love, or hate
> That lets us do the things we do;
>   It's pride that makes the heart so great;
> It is not anger, no, nor fear –
> Lucasta he's a Fusilier,
>   And his pride keeps him here.

Notice the pronouns. The soldier may be *he*, but he is a part of *us*, and with that little gesture, Graves includes himself in the company of those who do the things *we* do. The officers of the Fusiliers included three noteworthy poets – Graves, Sassoon, and Charles Hamilton Sorley, who was already dead by the time Graves wrote this poem. They were fighting a war they knew was pointless, and although both Graves and Sassoon displayed remarkable physical courage, Graves dismisses courage, fear, love, anger, and hate as motives, claiming that the soldier fights only because of his pride. By including himself among those susceptible to such folly, Graves quietly softens his criticism of Lovelace, who now appears as one more in a long line of soldiers going to the wars for dubious motives.

It is difficult, perhaps impossible, to make poetry solely from the concrete names of villages, the numbers of roads, the names of rivers, the numbers of regiments and the dates. But that does not mean that the only alternative is to invoke the halls of dawn, the steep way of Honor, or the ghostly roll of immaterial drums. True poetry honors the dead by bringing the present into a dynamic relation with the past. The parodies by Kipling and Graves achieve that richness in a satiric mode. Wilfred Owen's "Anthem for Doomed Youth" does so in the tones of elegy:

> What passing-bells for these who die as cattle?
> – Only the monstrous anger of the guns.
> Only the stuttering rifles' rapid rattle

> Can patter out their hasty orisons.
> No mockeries now for them; no prayers nor bells;
>   Nor any voice of mourning save the choirs, –
> The shrill, demented choirs of wailing shells;
>   And bugles calling for them from sad shires.[24]

Unlike Asquith or Lovelace, Owen acknowledges the reality of guns, rifles, and shells, but he brings these realistic details of the modern battlefield into a metaphoric relationship with the older practices of religious ritual. The rattle of the rifles is a hasty orison, a rapidly spoken prayer, and the wailing shells are a choir, albeit a *demented* choir. Owen avoids the false nostalgia of those who deny the suffering of the present by describing it only with oriflammes and eagles, swords and shields, glorious hazy images from a past imagined as heroic fantasy. With a compact, painful lyricism, he shows how present realities overwhelm the rituals of the past, which prove inadequate in the face of slaughter. His bugles, calling for the dead from sad shires, sing a truer, sadder music than the loud bugles celebrating the rich dead in Brooke's naïve sonnet, the ghostly bugles of Hovey's banal lines, or the faint bugles of MacArthur's derivative and dishonest speech.

Deep in Owen's memory, feeding the darkness of this poem, lies one of the great English meditations on death, Thomas Gray's "Elegy Written in a Country Churchyard" (1751). In Gray's opening line – "The curfew tolls the knell of parting day" – the bell sounding for the end of the day suggests the bell tolling for the end of a life. Another sign of sunset is the return of the cattle, as "The lowing herd wind slowly o'er the lea."[25] Owen creates *his* opening line by radically reshaping these melancholy rural details. His troops die as cattle, and the passing-bells that should toll their deaths are silent, drowned out by the noises of modern war. I believe Owen drew upon Gray's elegy – perhaps even unconsciously – because Gray's pessimism about glory and honor was so similar to his own. Gray's lines on the futility of human pride may stand as an answer to those poets and generals who would soften death by invoking honor:

> The boast of heraldry, the pomp of pow'r,
>   And all that beauty, all that wealth e'er gave,
> Awaits alike th' inevitable hour.
>   The paths of glory lead but to the grave.

Although Gray was not writing directly about war, his first readers immediately grasped the relevance of these lines to military action. The British general James Wolfe was among them, as the great American historian Francis Parkman reveals in a poignant anecdote. In the boat that carried him to the battle of Quebec and his own death, Wolfe recited these lines from Gray's poem, "which had recently appeared and which he had just received from England."

Perhaps, as he uttered those strangely appropriate words – "The paths of glory lead but to the grave," the shadows of his own approaching fate stole with mournful prophecy across his mind. "Gentlemen," he said, as he closed his recital, "I would rather have written those lines than take Quebec tomorrow."[26]

As both Wolfe and Owen evidently recognized, Gray's melancholy poem points to the limits of any ideology of honor. The fundamental issues of this chapter appear in his poem as pointed questions:

> Can storied urn or animated bust
>> Back to its mansion call the fleeting breath?
> Can Honour's voice provoke the silent dust,
>> Or Flatt'ry soothe the dull cold ear of Death?

The answer, of course, is no. The animated bust of Lovelace, sitting atop an urn bearing his sweetheart's name, represents a dead man. The seductive voice of Honor means little to Owen's doomed youth, who die as cattle, without even a passing-bell to mark their deaths. The flowery flattery MacArthur lavished upon the American man-at-arms could not soothe the dull cold ears of the 80,000 men he left behind on the Bataan peninsula.

CHAPTER 2

Shame and slaughter

A month before the Armistice that finally ended World War I, the British critic Arthur Waugh, father of the novelist Evelyn Waugh, wrote a survey of the war poetry of the previous four years. He especially admired the increasing realism of the poems of 1917 and 1918:

Poetry has now, for the first time, made War – made it in its own image, with all the tinsel and gaud of tradition stripped away from it; and so made it perhaps that no sincere artist will ever venture again to represent War in those delusive colours with which Art has been too often content to disguise it in the past.[1]

Waugh was recording a shift in style that had partly happened: the supplanting of the gaudy tinsel of poets like Asquith by the tougher realism of poets like Owen. But he was quite wrong about the place of this shift in the larger histories of poetry and war. Later artists, perhaps even sincerely, would venture again to represent war in the delusive colors of tradition, and World War I was not the first time that poetry had made war in its own image. For sheer, unblinking realism, there is no poem from the Great War that can surpass these typical lines from the *Iliad*:

> Idomeneus skewered Erymas straight through the mouth,
> the merciless brazen spearpoint raking through,
> up under the brain to split his glistening skull –
> teeth shattered out, both eyes brimmed to the lids
> with a gush of blood and both nostrils spurting,
> mouth gaping, blowing convulsive sprays of blood
> and death's dark cloud closed down around his corpse.[2]

Homer's brutal honesty about warfare is apparent in the physical details of every combat death in the *Iliad*. A similar toughness informs his treatment of the system of values that drives his heroes, a system anthropologists call *shame culture*. Shame is the dark underside of honor. Beneath the high-sounding clichés about glory and honor lurks the fear of being ridiculed or dishonored. Mycenaean culture built an elaborate system on the power of shame, and Homer, during the course of the *Iliad*, reveals the rules of this system and subtly exposes its limitations. But because he lets his characters do most of the talking and rarely offers explicit judgments of their actions, later readers, translators, and teachers have often lost sight of his critical attitudes – or deliberately distorted them. In the boarding schools and universities that trained the European elite, especially during the nineteenth century, the teaching of ancient epic turned Homer's shrewdly observant account of individual chieftains struggling to claim honor and avoid shame into a nationalistic and didactic story stressing the duties and obligations of the upper classes.

Consciously or unconsciously, these later readers reshaped the stark, retributive world of the *Iliad* to make it more like the chivalric, Christian, and nationalistic worlds in which they lived. Their distortions of Homer inevitably affect the way we read his poem, and continuing cultural changes have made Homer's world more and more distant from ours, yet the fear of shame remains a potent motive for warfare. In a fine, poetically charged meditation on the war in Vietnam, Tim O'Brien speaks of shame as the greatest of all burdens:

They carried all the emotional baggage of men who might die. ... They carried the common secret of cowardice barely restrained, the instinct to run or freeze or hide, and in many respects this was the heaviest burden of all, for it could never be put down, it required perfect balance and perfect posture. They carried their reputations. They carried the soldier's greatest fear, which was the fear of blushing. Men killed, and died, because they were embarrassed not to. It was what had brought them to war in the first place, nothing positive, no dreams of glory or honor, just to avoid the blush of dishonor. They died so as not to die of embarrassment.[3]

Although more than 2,600 years separate O'Brien from Homer, his comrades in Vietnam had feelings much like those of Hector, the doomed Trojan champion in the *Iliad*, who tells his wife that he would feel terrible shame before the Trojan warriors and the Trojan women if he were to shrink from battle.

As generations of readers in many languages have recognized, the *Iliad* is a poem of astonishing power. Its influence has been vast, even though some later poets, unnerved by Homer's honesty, have censored or altered his language. Its characters and story have passed into the common memory of our culture, most recently recalled in an expensive motion picture called *Troy* (2005). Yet the *Iliad's* most important virtue is that it tells terrible truths about shame.

In his opening lines, Homer announces his subject as the anger of the Greek warrior Achilles, but he immediately makes it clear that the cause of that destructive anger is an act of shaming. Mycenaean culture represented honor in the form of material goods: tripods, horses, brass vessels, captured women. The honor or respect that the Greeks called *timê* was thus inextricably connected to the prizes or booty (*geras*) that made it concrete.[4] *Timê* was quite unlike the more abstract honor that poets like Lovelace and Brooke would later invoke through lyrical eloquence. To honor someone normally meant giving him a ceremonial gift; more gifts meant more honor; and having a gift taken away meant unbearable shame.

The story of the Trojan War bears out this pattern. The Trojan prince Paris dishonors the Greek king Menelaus by abducting Helen, Menelaus' wife. In Homer's version of the story, Paris also steals shiploads of treasure. To defend the honor of Menelaus, the Greeks go to war, led by his brother Agamemnon. During a siege that lasts ten years, they quarrel bitterly among themselves about who should receive the most honor – represented by the richest spoils – for his feats in battle. The *Iliad* opens with just such a quarrel. Agamemnon, the top commander, has in his tent a woman named Chryseis, whom he has claimed as a battle prize. Her father, a priest of the god Apollo, offers a splendid ransom to redeem her, but Agamemnon refuses. Shamed and dishonored, the father prays to Apollo. Homeric gods, like Homeric men, resort to violence in face of any real or imagined slight, so Apollo promptly sends a deadly plague upon the Greek camp. When it becomes clear that the deaths of men and animals will cease only if he returns Chryseis, Agamemnon reluctantly does so. To avoid being dishonored, however, he insists on having a replacement, and reclaims a woman named Briseis, whom he had previously awarded to Achilles. Now Agamemnon has a woman in his tent and Achilles does not. Angry at the insult to *his* honor, Achilles withdraws from battle, and the tide of war turns against the Greeks.

In its emphasis on material reward, Homeric shame culture is fundamentally different from later cultures. In theory, at least, any seventeenth-century warrior could claim honor, as Lovelace did, by abandoning his sweetheart and going heroically to the wars. In World War I, according to Rupert Brooke, any soldier who fell in the trenches could make rarer gifts than gold to his fellow-citizens. For Brooke, Honour is a king with an inexhaustible treasury, but for Homer, honor is finite because war spoils are finite. Achilles makes that point when he accuses Agamemnon of taking more than his share of the plunder:

> "My honors* never equal yours,
> whenever we sack some wealthy Trojan stronghold –
> my arms bear the brunt of the raw, savage fighting,
> true, but when it comes to dividing up the plunder
> the lion's share is yours, and back I go to my ships,
> clutching some scrap, some pittance that I love,
> when I have fought to exhaustion."[5]

Achilles' assertion here is straightforward: he is the best fighter, the strongest man in a war where physical strength counts for everything, and he should therefore receive the most booty. When he gets only a scrap or a pittance while Agamemnon takes more, Achilles feels dishonored. When Agamemnon arbitrarily takes back Briseis, a prize already awarded, the shame is unbearable, and generates the destructive anger that Homer announces as his theme.

Agamemnon is also a good fighter, skilled at throwing the javelin, but he never claims to be stronger or faster than Achilles. Instead, he discounts the importance of physical prowess and asserts his superiority as an act of sheer will:

> "What if you are a great soldier? That's just a gift of god.
> Go home with your ships and comrades! . . .
> But I . . . will take Briseis in all her beauty, your own prize –
> so you can learn just how much greater I am than you."[6]

---

* The Greek word is *geras*, prize.

Agamemnon evidently considers it unnecessary to specify a reason for his angry assertion that he is the greater or more powerful man, but Homer provides an explanation in the words of the wise old warrior Nestor, who urges Achilles to respect Agamemnon's political power:

> "No one can match the honors dealt a king, you know,
> a sceptred king to whom Zeus gives great glory.
> Strong as you are – a goddess was your mother –
> he has more power because he rules more men."[7]

According to this formula, political status – in this case being a king over more men – means that Agamemnon can demand greater rewards than Achilles, even though Achilles has an immortal mother and prodigious fighting strength. Violently rejecting this claim, Achilles calls Agamemnon a "king who devours his people."[8] This is an effective insult. If Agamemnon is claiming superior honor based on ruling more men – an idea slightly more abstract than physical prowess – Achilles will make his claim grotesquely physical by accusing him of eating his subjects.

In cultural terms, the personal struggle between Achilles and Agamemnon dramatizes a conceptual struggle between two ideas of honor – one based on might in battle, the other on kingship. Achilles claims honor and booty based on his individual, heroic strength. Although he is the younger man, his view appears to represent an earlier, more basic stage in the development of the idea of honor. Agamemnon, according to Nestor, can claim more honor because of his kingship, which gives him the power to send others into battle. By that logic, part of the booty won by anyone under his command belongs to him.

The conflict between these two characters foreshadows later conflicts between bungling strategists and suffering soldiers, but in the world of the *Iliad*, there is no sharp separation between leaders and fighters. In Benét's fine phrase, Agamemnon is a "spear-handling king," not a general at a desk behind the lines. His language about his honor, despite Nestor's rational explanations, is angry and personal. When finally forced to return Chryseis, he makes a gesture toward what is "best for all," but his emotional emphasis falls on his refusal to accept personal shame:

"I am willing to give her back, even so,
If that is best for all. What I really want
is to keep my people safe, not see them dying.
But fetch me another prize, and straight off too,
else I alone of the Argives go without my honor.
That would be a disgrace. You are all witness,
look – *my* prize is snatched away!"[9]

This speech neatly illustrates the basic distinction that anthropologists make between shame cultures and guilt cultures. People in shame cultures care deeply about what others see them do and say about them, while those living in guilt cultures feel guilty about failings and weaknesses that go unseen by others. The classicist E. R. Dodds, who was the first to apply this distinction to Homer, describes it as the difference between "the enjoyment of *timê*, public esteem" and "the enjoyment of a quiet conscience."[10] Like other useful binaries, this formula simplifies a cultural history that is often complex and contradictory; people in most cultures have probably felt both shame and guilt. But the formula is still helpful for understanding what the *Iliad* meant to its first audience and how that meaning has shifted over time. As participants in a shame culture, Homer's warriors feel little guilt about running away from battle – as long as no one sees them doing so. Later readers of the poem, however, often felt compelled to supply Homer's characters with guilty consciences, and rewrote ancient compulsions in the language of later systems of belief and behavior.

A society placing strong emphasis on *timê*, which we might translate as honor, status, glory, or esteem, but which has much to do with how one *looks* to others, will produce men likely to turn angry and violent when they experience shame. If Agamemnon recognizes, however reluctantly, that giving back Chryseis is necessary, he gains no satisfaction from having done good for others. Instead, he feels acute shame at having lost a prize, a physical representation of his status. His insistence on seizing Achilles' prize is an outrageous act, made more hurtful by the power of shame in the culture. When men like Agamemnon "break the norms" of the culture, says the classicist Hans van Wees, "they do so in order to humiliate others."[11] Although

Achilles will ultimately recognize the limits of a system that represents honor with material goods, he cannot find a way to escape that
system. Both the gifts and the honor they symbolize are scarce
commodities, and the competition for them is therefore intense,
even deadly.

From the fall of Rome until the fourteenth century, very few
people in Western Europe read Greek literature, and when
Renaissance scholars rediscovered the Homeric epics, they naturally
interpreted the behavior of the heroes by their own norms. The
consequences of this process are apparent when we compare what
Homer's Agamemnon says as he reluctantly agrees to return Chryseis
with Alexander Pope's translation of the same speech, published in
1715:

> "Yet if the Gods demand her, let her sail;
> Our Cares are only for the Publick Weal:
> Let me be deem'd the hateful Cause of all,
> And suffer, rather than my People fall.
> The Prize, the beauteous Prize I will resign,
> So dearly valu'd, and so justly mine.
> But since for common Good I yield the Fair,
> My private Loss let grateful Greece repair;
> Nor unrewarded let your Prince complain,
> That He alone has fought and bled in vain."[12]

Homer's Agamemnon, a pure product of a shame culture,
demands another prize immediately. His loss is public, not private.
Pope's Agamemnon, by contrast, has become a Christian monarch,
willing to accept responsibility and suffer for his people. He uses the
royal *we* and claims to be more concerned for the common good than
for his own prestige. Pope has recast the whole speech in the language
of a guilt culture. His Agamemnon is content to "be deem'd the
hateful Cause of all, / And suffer, rather than my People fall" –
sentiments for which there is no basis in the Greek, and which only
make sense if Agamemnon is seeking to assuage his private conscience.
The real Agamemnon appraises Chryseis as an object; this one calls her
"beauteous," "dearly valu'd," and "the Fair" – phrases that hint at
something like chivalric love. The petulant demand of the original –
"fetch me another prize, and straight off, too" – becomes, in Pope's
version, a diplomatic request that the Greeks "repair" their monarch's

private loss. Students reading Homer through the lens of Pope, whose translation was standard for two hundred years, were unlikely to see the stark, primitive world of the *Iliad* very clearly. Homer's harsh realities lay buried under layers of Christian, chivalric, and refined words and ideas.

Even those who could read Greek encountered the poem in classrooms offering similar distortions. Well-informed classical scholars struggled to reconcile the stark realities of Homer's culture with the norms of their own world. In 1886, R. C. Jebb, Regius Professor of Greek at Cambridge, described "the Homeric Greeks" as

... a gentle and generous race in a rude age. There is no trace among the Homeric Greeks of oriental vice or cruelty in its worst forms. Their sense of decency and propriety is remarkably fine – even in some points in which their descendants were less delicate.[13]

It may help us interpret this odd passage to know that "oriental vice" is Victorian code for homosexuality. Jebb's reference to the later Greeks as "less delicate" is his embarrassed way of acknowledging that Greeks of later centuries accepted a wide and colorful range of expressions of affection between members of the same sex. And while Homer is indeed reticent about all sexual matters, Jebb surely knew that those later Greeks interpreted some relationships in the *Iliad* as homosexual. In his insistence that the entire culture exhibited "decency and propriety," we may detect his need to give Homer's characters the virtues of Victorian gentlemen. He goes on to describe the feelings provoked by a breach of propriety among Homeric Greeks as "righteous indignation" – a tame phrase indeed for the curses and insults that Homer's shame-driven characters hurl at one another.

Later on the same page, Jebb retreats from his own claims, speaking of the Homeric period as "an age of transition."

Luxuries and splendours of an eastern cast are mingled with elements of squalid barbarism. Manners of the noblest chivalry and the truest refinement are strangely crossed by traits of coarseness or ferocity. There are moments when the Homeric hero is almost a savage.

It is difficult to reconcile this description with the earlier insistence that the heroes show no trace of cruelty. Jebb's knowledge of Greek was far more professional than Pope's, and he had the benefit of 170 more years of linguistic and archaeological scholarship. In the contradictions of his description, however, we may watch his accurate knowledge of the ferocity and savagery of Homer's heroes struggling against his cultural need to see them as exemplars of noble chivalry and true refinement.

For Homer's warriors, shame is personal and painful, a reason to lash out at others. In later centuries, fanciful translations and misleading interpretations slowly detached the idea of shame from the individual and attached it to groups and nations. Pope is pushing in this direction by recasting Agamemnon's angry speech so that the Greek king's insistence that he wants to keep his own people safe turns into a selfless, almost democratic concern for the "Publick Weal" and the "common Good." By the end of the nineteenth century, the transformation was complete. Soldiers were supposed to fight not so much from individual pride as to save their nations from shame. A. E. Housman, writing in 1919, imagined the numerous English dead in the Great War articulating just that view. Significantly, the dead men speak in the plural:

> Here dead lie we because we did not choose
>> To live and shame the land from which we sprung.
> Life, to be sure, is nothing much to lose;
>> But young men think it is, and we were young.[14]

Housman was not only a great poet but a learned classicist, and this epitaph resembles the lines Simonides wrote to commemorate the Spartan heroes who died defending the mountain passes at Thermopylae against a vastly larger Persian army in 480 BC:

> Stranger, carry a message to the Spartans,
> That here we lie, obedient to their commands.[15]

But where the Spartan dead simply and nobly assert their obedience, Housman's dead claim to have chosen death to avoid shaming England.

Once shame becomes a matter of national pride, abstract symbols like flags gain prominence in poetry. The American poet Alan Seeger, who enlisted in the French Foreign Legion at the beginning of World

War I and died in action on 3 July 1916, provides a poignant example. In a diary entry of April, 1915, Seeger records his respect for the French troops who were defending their homeland: "here it is practically the entire able bodied male population who make a living wall across the country that they are there to protect or perish for."[16] But when he expresses these ideas in poetry, he describes one French soldier, part of that living wall, as saving future generations from shame and his flag from dishonor:

> That other generations might possess –
>   From shame and menace free in years to come –
> A richer heritage of happiness,
>   He marched to that heroic martyrdom.
>
> Esteeming less the forfeit that he paid
>   Than undishonored that his flag might float
> Over the towers of liberty, he made
>   His breast the bulwark and his blood the moat.[17]

The unspecified national shame from which Seeger's soldier has supposedly freed other generations is much more abstract than the sharp personal shame Menelaus feels when Paris absconds with Helen. In order to accept the idea of fighting so that future generations might enjoy a heritage of happiness, the soldier needs to believe that the pursuit of happiness is a fundamental right. This belief, first articulated in the eighteenth century, would have baffled any Homeric warrior, as would the Christian concept of martyrdom. The vague dishonor from which the French soldier strives to protect his flag has little in common with the acute dishonor Achilles feels when Agamemnon seizes Briseis. While the hotheaded Homeric warrior writhes in painful shame, the French soldier makes a cool calculation that esteems the loss of a human life as less important than the preservation of a flag's symbolic honor – a clear instance of the workings of guilt culture. But the forfeit Seeger's Frenchman must pay – his life – is the same tragic price that many a warrior in the *Iliad* pays for the sake of avoiding public shame.

Seeger's struggle to reconcile democratic and Christian ideology with the brutal and unchanging fact of death in battle is especially apparent in the strained expressions of the second stanza. His syntax

is awkward and tangled, with almost every word in the first two lines
wrenched out of its normal prose order:

> Esteeming less the forfeit that he paid
> Than undishonored that his flag might float . . .

Seeger places heavy metrical emphasis on the odd word *undishonored*,
a double negative implying that the need to avoid shame is a more
powerful motive than the desire to gain honor. Elaborating the idea
of the living wall, he pictures the dead man as a medieval fortress –
"His breast the bulwark and his blood the moat." These metaphors
remind me of the way Lovelace turns Lucasta into a nunnery, but
with a terrible difference. Lovelace calls Lucasta a nunnery to avoid
thinking about her as a real woman with flesh and needs. Seeger treats
his dead soldier as a fortress in order to place *more* emphasis on the
battering of his body and the pouring forth of his blood.

And here, despite the sweeping cultural changes that separate Seeger
from the ancient world, there is a tragic continuity. When Achilles
defeats the Trojan champion Hector in the decisive battle of the *Iliad*,
Homer offers a rare and explicit moral judgment. He tells us that
Achilles has devised shameful treatments for the noble Hector, and the
insult Achilles enacts is dreadful: he ties his opponent's lifeless corpse to
his chariot by the heels and drags it around the city walls. The Trojans,
forced to see their hero not only dead but dirty and dishonored, wail in
grief. Modern Americans will have some appreciation for the shame and
horror felt by the Trojans if we remember the personal and national
emotions we experienced when television showed the bodies of slain
American soldiers dragged through the streets of Mogadishu, Somalia in
1993. Homer makes the Trojans' grief more powerful by imagining the
death of one man as the destruction of a whole city. It was, he says,

> for all the world as if Troy were torched and smoldering
> down from the looming brows of the citadel to her roots.[18]

The fall of Hector makes the fall of Troy inevitable, so Homer
brilliantly collapses the two: the fall of Hector *is* the fall of Troy. In
Seeger's belated version of the same idea, the fall of the unnamed
soldier becomes the destruction of an ancient stone fortress. The slow
shift from personal shame to collective or national shame is an

important difference between Homer and Alan Seeger, apparent in Seeger's refusal to name the dead man, his evocation of the undishonored flag, and his general veneer of patriotic abstraction. But whether they are motivated by fierce personal shame or by a patriotic belief system that makes such shame collective and transforms it into guilt, men still die so as not to die of embarrassment.

I was studying the *Iliad* in Greek during my last semester as an undergraduate, the spring term of 1968. American cities had exploded in riots the previous summer, and a frustrating, unpopular war was dividing the nation. During one short semester, draft deferments for graduate study ended, President Johnson declined to seek a second term, and assassins ended the lives of Martin Luther King and Robert Kennedy. Perhaps because of those circumstances, certainly because of a superb teacher, I learned to read the *Iliad* as a tragic poem describing men driven to their deaths by a system they could not change. Four decades later, I still believe that reading is true.

Homer understands the tragedy. As scholars have begun to realize during the last fifty years, he does not merely *describe* ancient Greek shame culture; he *criticizes* the culture. Because the only language available to Homer as a narrator is the traditional language he inherited from centuries of oral poets before him, a language of prefabricated phrases called formulas, his capacity to express this criticism is limited. But as the classicist Adam Parry explains, "Homer uses the epic speech a long tradition gave him to transcend the limits of that speech." He does so in part by giving Achilles speeches that point toward "the awful distance between appearance and reality."[19] Through the contradictions and confusions of these speeches, Homer shows us that Achilles is a victim of his society's assumptions about shame – assumptions that limit his options and lead to disaster. Embracing this reading means adding another dimension to the already remarkable accomplishments of Homer. It means believing that the poet was not only capable of composing a poem of some fifteen thousand lines, but also capable of building into its structure a subtle critique of the very code of honor he so carefully describes. Poetry is the ideal vehicle for expressing such moral complexity.

The best evidence of Homer's critical attitude toward shame culture comes in the breakdown of the connection between gifts and honor. At the beginning, Achilles insists that honor must be rewarded by treasure. As the story moves forward, however, Homer records a steady erosion of faith in the notion that physical objects are a complete and sufficient representation of honor. With Achilles out of action, Hector devastates the Greeks, and Agamemnon has no choice but to send ambassadors to ask Achilles to rejoin the fight. As an incentive, he offers an impressive catalogue of gifts: seven tripods, ten bars of gold, twenty burnished cauldrons, twelve stallions, and seven women skilled in crafts. In addition to these expensive items, Agamemnon promises to give Briseis back to Achilles, and to reward him with a huge share of the booty when Troy falls. If the Greeks reach home, he goes on, Achilles will have his choice of Agamemnon's daughters, as well as seven citadels "filled with people."[20] That last phrase is especially significant in light of Nestor's earlier claim that Agamemnon has more power because he rules more men. By offering Achilles towns filled with people, Agamemnon appears to be offering him a larger share of power. But as Achilles evidently realizes, there is a "hidden hook": by making Achilles his son-in-law, Agamemnon would assure his subordination.[21] Despite the sumptuous rewards he offers, Agamemnon is still asserting his superiority. When giving instructions to his ambassadors, he follows his extravagant list of gifts by insisting that Achilles must end his anger, and by repeating his claim to be more kingly and older in years than Achilles.

When the shrewd counselor Odysseus repeats the list of gifts to Achilles, he omits the conclusion of Agamemnon's speech, and Achilles, sensing the omission, angrily refuses the offer. "I loathe his gifts," he says, insisting that he will not return to the fight for ten or twenty times the offered bounty. He will not come back until Agamemnon pays "full measure" for dishonoring him.[22] Clearly, "full measure" now has little to do with material goods, just as Agamemnon's insistence on submission continues despite his offer of goods. At this point, neither man regards the gifts as an equivalent of the honor they supposedly signify. Homer is probably dramatizing the moment in cultural history when the concept of honor began to detach itself from material goods. He is certainly describing characters whose need for honor can no longer be satisfied by mere objects.

In the heat of his anger as he spurns Agamemnon's offer, Achilles goes even further, valuing life above all treasures:

> Cattle and fat sheep can all be had for the raiding,
> tripods all for the trading, and tawny-headed stallions.
> But a man's life breath cannot come back again –
> no raiders in force, no trading brings it back,
> once it slips through a man's clenched teeth.[23]

If treasure were a pure equivalent to honor, Achilles would be implying here that honor matters less than life, and he toys with that idea by threatening to return home to a long and peaceful life in Greece, rather than the short but glorious life that will be his lot in the war. Finally, however, he declares that he will stay out of the fight until Hector reaches his own ships. Concern for his immediate comrades is now a stronger motive for Achilles than booty or glory. When Hector threatens to burn the Greek ships, which provide their only means of retreat, Achilles allows his friend Patroclus to enter the battle, wearing Achilles' own armor. After turning the tide and slaying many, Patroclus falls to Hector, who falls in turn to Achilles, driven back into combat by the death of his friend. In every case, Homer's choice of details as he narrates the battle shows an acute awareness of the fate of the victim. His focus is on loss, not glory. Hector, dragged in the dust, demands our sympathy; Achilles, exulting in his power, calls forth our fear – and perhaps our disgust.

When Agamemnon finally delivers the gifts, they appear to have lost their power to give or even stand for honor. The whole ceremony is rushed and perfunctory, as Achilles is now anxious to return to battle to avenge the death of Patroclus. After Agamemnon declares his intention to set things to rights, Achilles dismisses the gifts as unimportant:

> "Produce the gifts if you like, as you see fit,
> or keep them back, it's up to you. But now –
> quickly, call up the wild joy of war at once!"[24]

At this moment, the wild joy of war matters more to Achilles than the formal giving of gifts. Odysseus, acting as a spokesman for tradition, urges both men to perform the proper ceremonies of gift-giving, sacrifice, formal apology, and feasting. Agamemnon embraces the plan, but Achilles' mind is elsewhere.

> "Now our men are lying mauled on the field –
> all that Hector the son of Priam overwhelmed
> when Zeus was handing Hector his high glory –
> but you, you and Odysseus urge us to a banquet!
> I, by god, I'd drive our Argives into battle *now*,
> starving, famished, and only then, when the sun goes down,
> lay on a handsome feast – once we've avenged our shame."[25]

A part of the shame Achilles feels has a material equivalent: Hector has stripped his armor from the corpse of Patroclus. But Achilles does not emphasize recovering the armor. (His goddess mother has given him a splendid new set.) He speaks of redressing the balance of glory, too much of which has come to Hector, and he speaks of avenging shame, which now seems to be more a matter of losing men than of losing material spoils.

As Hector later waits – alone, outside the walls – for the dreadful onslaught of Achilles, he considers using gifts to buy off the Greeks:

> "I could promise to give back Helen, yes,
> and all her treasures with her, all those riches
> Paris once hauled home to Troy in the hollow ships –
> and they were the cause of all our endless fighting –
> Yes, yes, return it all to the sons of Atreus now
> to haul away, and then, at the same time, divide
> the rest with all the Argives, all the city holds . . ."[26]

In this fanciful, perhaps desperate interpretation of events, Hector treats the treasure as the cause of the war, suppressing the adultery and the insult to Menelaus. If the war were being fought about mere treasure, returning the treasure with interest might stop the war. Hector is imagining a world in which material goods, rather than serving as a direct reward for fighting, would function as a substitute for fighting, but he knows full well that Achilles will not listen to any such proposal:

> "I must not go and implore him. He'll show no mercy,
> no respect for me, my rights – he'll cut me down
> straight off – stripped of defenses like a woman
> once I have loosed the armor off my body."[27]

A few minutes later, with Achilles' spear through his throat, Hector offers a princely ransom of bronze and gold if the victor will allow his friends and family to bury his body. The speech Achilles gives in reply is as terrifying as anything in the *Iliad*:

> "Beg no more, you fawning dog – begging me by my parents!
> Would to god my rage, my fury would drive me now
> to hack your flesh away and eat you raw –
> such agonies you have caused me! Ransom?
> No man alive could keep the dog-packs off you,
> not if they haul in ten, twenty times that ransom
> and pile it here before me and promise fortunes more –
> no, not even if Dardan Priam should offer to weigh out
> your bulk in gold! Not even then will your noble mother
> lay you on your deathbed, mourn the son she bore . . .
> The dogs and birds will rend you – blood and bone!"[28]

Already behaving like a savage in his fury, Achilles dares to wish that he might become a cannibal, that he might regress to an even more primitive state. In refusing the ransom, he repeats Agamemnon's original offense against the priest who sought to ransom his daughter. In wishing he could devour Hector's flesh, he imagines becoming an eater of people – the very thing he accused Agamemnon of being.

It may be comforting to believe that such feelings only appear in primitive societies, but there are many points of contact between the emotions expressed in the stark, violent world of the *Iliad* and the emotions expressed by much later poets. Siegfried Sassoon, in a passage already quoted, says that "lust and senseless hatred make me glad." Alan Seeger, in his last letter, declares himself "glad to be going in the first wave. If you are in this thing at all it is best to be in to the limit. And this is the supreme experience."[29] Julian Grenfell, writing a few weeks before his death in 1915, celebrates the "Joy of Battle" in lines that sound quite close to Achilles' longing for the wild joy of war:

> And when the burning moment breaks,
> And all things else are out of mind,
> And Joy of Battle only takes
> Him by the throat and makes him blind –

> Through joy and blindness he shall know,
> Not caring much to know, that still
> Nor lead nor steel shall reach him so
> That it be not the Destined Will.[30]

I wish it were possible to argue that Grenfell felt some ironic distance from the soldier he describes here, some capacity to judge his frenzied subject as I believe Homer judges his heroes. But the historical record does not support that conclusion. In a letter written at the same time, Grenfell celebrates his own joy of battle: "Here we are in the burning centre of it all, and I would not be anywhere else for a million pounds and the Queen of Sheba."[31] In his playful bravado, the doomed poet rejects imagined gifts of treasure and exotic flesh. At some level of consciousness, he is modeling himself on Achilles. Agamemnon's gifts cannot bribe Achilles to return to battle, but once he has returned, Hector's gifts cannot bribe him to provide a decent burial. A million pounds and the Queen of Sheba could not persuade Grenfell to seek a safer post. Two weeks later, he was dead.

Like the Greeks in the *Iliad*, British and American soldiers in France were cut off from their homes and families, trapped in a harsh, masculine, and primitive world where shame assumed massive importance. So, too, were the Germans on the other side, who were also fighting on foreign soil, or the Americans in Vietnam, who killed, and died, because they were embarrassed not to. But shame can be just as powerful a motive for men fighting on their own soil, defending their homelands and families. Seeger invokes it in praising his anonymous French soldier, who supposedly fights not for his own farm or children, but so that his nation may be free from shame in the future. Homer recognizes it in his Trojans, who are determined to protect their wives and children, and therefore less interested in booty than the Greeks, but who are no less driven by the fear of shame.

In a poignant scene dramatizing this compulsion, Hector returns to Troy, where his mother Hecuba, his brother's mistress Helen, and his own wife Andromache try in turn to persuade him to stay with them in the city, or at least to draw back into a defensive posture. Hector's conversation with Andromache in this scene is the ultimate model for Lovelace's poem to Lucasta, but Homer does not silence the woman. As she weeps and clings to his arm, Andromache appeals to Hector:

> "Reckless one,
> my Hector – your own fiery courage will destroy you!
> Have you no pity for *him*, our helpless son? Or me,
> and the destiny that weighs me down, your widow,
> now so soon? Yes, soon they will kill you off."[32]

Andromache reminds Hector that Achilles has already killed her father and her brothers. With her mother also dead, her husband is everything to her. Although she begs him to think of his family, fear of shame will drive him back to attack the Greeks, as he tells her:

> "All this weighs on my mind too, dear woman.
> But I would die of shame to face the men of Troy
> and the Trojan women trailing their long robes
> if I would shrink from battle now, a coward."[33]

Unlike the self-absorbed Lovelace, who gives Lucasta good reasons to doubt his devotion, Hector loves his family and grasps how great his loss will be to them. He is even honest enough to imagine Andromache being hauled off to Greece as a slave-woman after his death. But as he explains, he has been trained from birth to fight in the front ranks to earn glory for his father and himself. His need to avoid shame is more powerful than his need to protect his loved ones. In this very scene, Homer dramatizes how families enforce the power of shame, how fathers teach sons to seek honor and glory at all costs. Removing his bronze helmet, which has frightened the boy with its gleaming metal and horsehair crest, the hero lifts and tosses his son in his powerful arms. But even in this moment of domestic pleasure, made more poignant by the setting aside of the terrifying helmet, Hector prays that Astyanax will become a warrior, "first in glory among the Trojans, / strong and brave like me, . . .

> and one day let them say, 'He is a better man than his father!' –
> when he comes home from battle bearing the bloody gear
> of the mortal enemy he has killed in war –
> a joy to his mother's heart."[34]

All the elements of shame culture come together in this speech. Hector takes pleasure in imagining what future Trojans will say about his son; he makes the boy's future honor concrete in the image of bloody gear stripped from a mortal enemy.

Although readers and translators of Homer in later periods often softened or suppressed the savagery of his heroes, adding a veneer of chivalric gallantry, they transmitted this scene quite faithfully. In Pope's version of these lines, the booty that Hector imagines Astyanax bringing home is called "the reeking spoils," and "His Mother's conscious Heart o'erflows with Joy."[35] Readers of Homer from the Renaissance until the First World War had no need to distort this part of the *Iliad* because it was so familiar. In all those centuries, parents sent their sons to war with similar hopes and invoked the fear of shame as a motive for fighting. The American Civil War poet George Henry Boker, for example, dealt with the Union defeat at Bull Run in 1861 by arguing that the dead were more fortunate than those caught up in the retreat, who would be marked forever by shame:

> O happy dead, who early fell,
> Ye have no wretched tale to tell
> Of causeless fear and coward flight,
> Of victory snatched beneath your sight,
> Of martial strength and honor lost,
> Of mere life bought at any cost,
> Of the deep, lingering mark of shame
> Forever scorched on brow and name,
> That no new deeds, however bright,
> Shall banish from men's loathful sight!

Here the mark of shame falls on the Union troops, but Boker soon transfers the idea to the nation and himself:

> O, let me not outlive the blow
> That seals my country's overthrow!

Imagining a scene that reverses Hector's tender parting from Andromache, he asks Northern women to urge their men into battle:

> Fair matrons, maids, and tender brides,
> Gird weapons to your lovers' sides;
> And, though your hearts break at the deed,
> Give them your blessing and God-speed.[36]

Figure 6. George Henry Boker.

Shame multiplies its power as a motivation when applied not only to individuals, but to nations. In September 1914, the British journalist C. F. G. Masterman, newly appointed to a Cabinet post to supervise war propaganda, called together a large group of well-known writers – including James Barrie, Arthur Conan Doyle,

John Galsworthy, Thomas Hardy, and Rudyard Kipling – and got
them to sign the following "Declaration of Authors":

The undersigned writers, comprising amongst them men and women of the
most divergent political and social views, some of them having been for
years ardent champions of good will towards Germany, and many of them
extreme advocates of peace, are nevertheless agreed that Great Britain could
not without dishonour have refused to take part in the present war.[37]

The string of negatives in the convoluted verb form – "could *not
without dis*honour have *refused*" – betrays a struggle between Edwardian
manners and ancient passions. The writers reveal the same unease that
Alan Seeger shows by using the word *undishonored*. But in essence, both
might as well be Hector telling Andromache that he would die of shame
if he did not go forth to fight.

A few horrific years later, Wilfred Owen was able to treat the
ancient tradition of preferring death to dishonor with scornful irony.
In "S. I. W.," an account of a soldier's death from a self-inflicted
wound, the young man gets the conventional send-off:

> Patting goodbye, doubtless they told the lad
> He'd always show the Hun a brave man's face;
> Father would sooner him dead than in disgrace, –
> Was proud to see him going, aye, and glad.[38]

Eventually the "torture of lying machinally shelled" wears the soldier
down, and courage leaks out of him "as sand / From the best
sandbags after years of rain." He begins to consider wounding
himself, but his father's voice rings in his mind:

> He'd seen men shoot their hands, on night patrol.
> Their people never knew. Yet they were vile.
> 'Death sooner than dishonour, that's the style!'
> So Father said.

When he can no longer stand the "days of inescapable thrall," the
soldier kills himself, but no one treats him as vile. His comrades
protect his reputation:

> With him they buried the muzzle his teeth had kissed,
> And truthfully wrote the mother, 'Tim died smiling.'

And the poet explains his suicide as "the reasoned crisis of his soul," worn down by

> Slow grazing fire, that would not burn him whole
> But kept him for death's promises and scoff,
> And life's half-promising, and both their riling.

Homer's warriors live in constant fear of the real or imagined taunts of other men. There is a distant but distinct echo of their fears in the belief that "Britain could not without dishonour have refused to take part in present war." Owen's soldier, by contrast, is driven mad by slow grazing fire, which seems to promise release in death, and by the half-promising of life, which teases him with hope. Owen has transferred the idea of scoffing and riling, the terrible fear of being shamed or dishonored, from real or imagined people to death and life themselves. To be at war in these horrific circumstances is to carry each day what O'Brien calls "the emotional baggage of men who might die," to feel each day the crippling power of shame.

Owen pictures his soldier as a youth from the working class, subject to the stock beliefs and imperatives of his culture. " 'Death sooner than dishonour, that's the *style!* " says the father, invoking that lethal cliché as if it were merely a matter of fashion. For the officer corps, however, there was a more direct link between ancient epic and societal expectations – an education that included classical languages and teachers who insisted on treating ancient heroes as moral exemplars. In the schooling of these men, a favorite model was Homer's Sarpedon, the King of Lycia and son of the god Zeus, who fights as a Trojan ally. With no goods or cattle at stake in Troy, Sarpedon fights for glory. In a famous speech, he argues that kings must put themselves on the line in battle, not to gain more riches, but to justify their inherited honor and wealth,

> "so a comrade strapped in combat gear may say,
> 'Not without fame, the men who rule in Lycia,
> these kings of ours who eat fat cuts of lamb
> and drink sweet wine, the finest stock we have.
> But they owe it all to their own fighting strength –
> our great men of war, they lead our way in battle!'"[39]

Filtered through centuries of chivalric and aristocratic lore, this belief that the upper classes had a special obligation to lead the way in warfare, later called *noblesse oblige*, became an operative force in European and even American culture. The sense of obligation applied to kings as late as 1743, when George II led his troops into battle at Dettingen, though he was the last English monarch to do so. It continued to apply to titled aristocrats for two more centuries. Alexander Pope's translation of Sarpedon's speech (1715) illustrates the process by which the simple equation between kingship and fighting strength was recast in the language of social class:

> Why on those Shores are we with Joy survey'd,
> Admir'd as Heroes, and as Gods obey'd?
> Unless great Acts superior Merit prove,
> And Vindicate the bounteous Pow'rs above:
> 'Tis ours, the Dignity They give, to grace;
> The first in Valour, as the first in Place:
> That while with wondring Eyes our Martial Bands
> Behold our Deeds transcending our Commands,
> Such, they may cry, deserve the Sov'reign State,
> Whom those that Envy dare not Imitate![40]

What Homer had described as charging into the blaze of war Pope calls, more vaguely, "great Acts." The slashing blows of combat become unspecified "Deeds." Although deftly balanced in Pope's fine couplets, these abstract nouns are euphemisms, much like the hollow terms Hemingway's hero disliked hearing shouted in the rain. The fundamental idea – that those enjoying rank and affluence incur a military obligation – remains the same, but in Pope's version, there is a wider gap between the powerful man and the common soldier. Homer's anonymous Lycian citizen, marching side by side with Sarpedon and Glaucus, takes a comrade's pride in the fame, courage, and physical strength of his kings. Pope's martial bands, now conveniently plural, behold the deeds of their kings from a distance, with emotions including wonder and envy. Unable or unwilling to imitate the prowess of their superiors, they concede that such men deserve to rule. In Pope's version, the crucial function of the soldiers is to give dignity to the kings, who graciously prove they deserve such honor by being "The first in Valour, as the first in Place."

Pope's suppression of Homer's emphasis on physical strength reflects eighteenth-century expectations. In the War of the Spanish Succession, which England and France were fighting at the time Pope wrote these lines, victory depended on artillery and musket fire; soldiers needed skill and courage, but not prodigious physical strength. Like his society, Pope substitutes superior merit, dignity, and social place for the muscle power of the ancient heroes. By the end of the eighteenth century, the metamorphosis was complete. The historian George Lyttelton, writing in 1767, describes "the idea of honor" as "something distinct from mere probity, and which supposes in gentlemen a stronger abhorrence of perfidy, falsehood, or cowardice, and a more elevated and delicate sense of the dignity of virtue, than are usually found in vulgar minds."[41]

The notion of honor as elevated and delicate would have astonished Achilles and Sarpedon, who were just emerging from the notion of honor as material goods. Yet this class-driven version of honor, linked to Homer but actually quite distant from either his culture or his critique of his culture, sustained Europeans for centuries of internecine and imperialist warfare. It took the wholesale slaughter of a generation of affluent, well-educated young officers in World War I to lay *noblesse oblige* to rest. The American modernist poet Ezra Pound, who lost close friends in the war, captures the moment in a few caustic lines:

> There died a myriad,
> And of the best, among them,
> For an old bitch gone in the teeth,
> For a botched civilization,
>
> Charm, smiling at the good mouth,
> Quick eyes gone under earth's lid,
>
> For two gross of broken statues
> For a few thousand battered books.[42]

What defines the best among the myriad of war dead is no longer the fighting strength of Achilles or the dictatorial kingship of Agamemnon but the conventional attributes of class: "Charm, . . . the good mouth, / Quick eyes" – and sufficient education to imagine fighting for the sake of statues and books. In the minds of many lost in that carnage, the statues and books were Greek, and the privilege of knowing the ancient world, especially as interpreted in English or German schools, required the educated man to model himself on characters like Sarpedon.

Rupert Brooke, whom Churchill praised for his "classic symmetry of mind and body," provides a poignant example. Despite his famous lines imagining his richer dust at peace in a corner of Flanders, where fierce trench warfare left so many dead, his grave is on the tiny Greek island of Skyros, which Homer mentions in the *Iliad*. When he died of blood poisoning, the result of an infected mosquito bite, Brooke's unit was on its way to Gallipoli, one of the most wasteful battles of the Great War, fought not far from the site of ancient Troy. Among the books he had with him was an *Iliad* in Greek.[43] In an incomplete poem written on that last voyage, Brooke's awareness of his own mortality comes cloaked in a reference to Sarpedon:

> Death and Sleep
> Bear many a young Sarpedon home.[44]

He is remembering how Zeus sends Apollo to remove Sarpedon's body from the battlefield and magically transport it home. In these lyrical lines, Apollo

> . . . bore him far from the fighting, off and away,
> and bathed him well in a river's running tides
> and anointed him with deathless oils . . .
> dressed his body in deathless, ambrosial robes
> then sent him on his way with the wind-swift escorts,
> twin brothers Sleep and Death, who with all good speed
> set him down in Lycia's broad green land.[45]

But neither in the *Iliad* nor in World War I was such a burial common. Homer's opening lines tell how the bodies of great fighters became feasts for the dogs and birds. The remains of half a million British soldiers in France, including Kipling's son, were never found.

Many voices at the time – some more explicitly than Pound – argued that the Great War, with its millions of anonymous, unheroic deaths, would spell the end not only of *noblesse oblige* but of the whole idea of inherited titles. But in 1923, we find C. F. G. Masterman, the same man who persuaded those famous writers that Britain could "not without dishonour have refused to take part" in the war, writing a lament not merely for the British dead, but specifically for the fallen aristocrats:

In the retreat from Mons and the first battle of Ypres perished the flower of the British aristocracy, 'playing the game' to the last, as they had been taught to play it all through their days of boyhood. . . . These boys, who had been brought up with a prospect before them of every good material thing that life can give, died without complaint, often through the bungling of Generals, in a foreign land. And the British aristocracy perished, as they perished in the Wars of the Roses, or in fighting for their King in the great Civil War, or as the Southern aristocracy in America, in courage and high effort, and an epic of heroic sacrifice, which will be remembered as long as England endures.[46]

The allusions are telling. Masterman wants his readers to link the recent massive losses of young aristocrats to losses in other wars that might more easily be imagined as heroic: the late medieval Wars of the Roses, the English Civil Wars of Lovelace's era, and even the American Civil War, here described as the last stand of the plantation aristocracy. But he also refers to an *epic* of heroic sacrifice, a phrase that suggests the presence of Homer – or at least of Homer as interpreted in Edwardian schools.

Homeric warriors do not speak of death as a sacrifice, but it was not difficult for later readers to map the fate of Sarpedon, the beloved son of Zeus, onto the fate of Jesus Christ, the beloved son of God, the ultimate model for selfless sacrifice. The Victorian artist William Blake Richmond painted *Sleep and Death Carrying the Body of Sarpedon into Lycia* as if it were a descent from the cross, with Sleep and Death appearing as Christian angels and a handsome, heroic, and intact Sarpedon slumping in their arms. By focusing on this part of the story of Sarpedon, painters like Richmond and poets like Brooke were making death in battle beautiful. Scholars like Jebb aided this process by speaking fondly of the Greeks as gentle and generous.

The semi-divine Sarpedon, suffused in Christian imagery, is a perfect illustration of a phrase from Horace much memorized in Victorian schools: *dulce et decorum est pro patria mori* ("it is sweet and proper to die for one's country").[47] But Homer, who recounts Sarpedon's burial in especially beautiful verse, does not describe his

Figure 7. William Blake Richmond, *Sleep and Death Carrying the Body of Sarpedon into Lycia* (1875–1876).

death as sweet or proper or patriotic. When Sarpedon falls at the hands of Patroclus, struck by a spear to the heart, he lies "sprawled and roaring, clawing the bloody dust,"[48] one more in an endless sequence of wasted warriors.

Pound's account of the reasons why men enlisted for World War I shows his acute awareness of the importance of ancient poetry in the minds of those who fought:

> Some quick to arm,
> some for adventure,
> some from fear of weakness,
> some from fear of censure,
> some for love of slaughter, in imagination,
> learning later . . .
> some in fear, learning love of slaughter;
>
> Died some, pro patria,
>   non "dulce" non "et decor" . . .

Although he quotes – in Latin – the tag from Horace, Pound takes pains to deny both adjectives, and thus to cast doubt on patriotism as a motive for war. The motives he recognizes are "fear of weakness," "fear of censure," and "love of slaughter" – the same forces that impel Homer's heroes toward their cruel deaths. Despite Homer's clear-eyed exposure of the tragic workings of ancient shame culture, shame retains its power. In fear of censure, men learn to love slaughter.

CHAPTER 3

The cost of empire

In the aftermath of the terrorist attacks of 11 September 2001, the word *empire* has reappeared in political discourse. Anxious for control over rogue states, some commentators now openly advocate an imperialist revival. The British columnist Sebastian Mallaby, one of the first to take this position, expresses fond nostalgia for the good old days of imperialism.

The war on terrorism has focused attention on the chaotic states that provide profit and sanctuary to nihilist outlaws, from Sudan and Afghanistan to Sierra Leone and Somalia. When such power vacuums threatened great powers in the past, they had a ready solution: imperialism. But since World War II, that option has been ruled out. After more than two millennia of empire, orderly societies now refuse to impose their own institutions on disorderly ones.[1]

Predictably, Mallaby goes on to argue that America *should* impose its institutions on other states. In the immediate afterglow of the military campaign in Iraq, his opinion gained ground, with some hawkish voices advocating invasions of Syria or Iran. But as the continuing unrest in post-conquest Iraq has shown, carrying out such a policy requires more than simple military force, and raises moral questions that have often interested poets.

Advocates of a new American empire will continue to face resistance, in part because of a modern habit of mind linking empire and evil. Many Americans vividly remember President Reagan's calling the Soviet Union and its allies an evil empire, implying that his own nation had no imperial ambitions. Those who were children in the 1980s will forever associate the word *empire* with evil because of the *Star Wars* movies, in which the heroic Rebel Alliance struggles to gain freedom from the wicked and dominant Galactic Empire. And as Arab responses to the campaign in Iraq have shown, memories of the humiliations colonial peoples suffered under European imperialism remain sharp. Aware of these associations, which have made it difficult to advocate imperialism openly, the American neoconservative journalist Robert Kaplan dreams of an empire that need not speak its name. "The power of this new *imperium*," he writes, using the Latin word instead of its English equivalent *empire*, "will derive from its never having to be declared, saving it from ... self-delusive, ceremonial trappings."[2] On the same page, however, Kaplan admits that "a single war with significant loss of American life ... could ruin the public's appetite for *internationalism*" – a word he misuses in order to avoid writing the dreaded word *imperialism*.

Even when anticipating opposition, the new imperialists assume that the public has a short and limited memory. Yet anyone who remembers how nations in America, Africa, and Asia emerged from colonialism should be suspicious of the coy passive Mallaby uses to explain that the option of imperialism "has been ruled out." As Americans took the initiative in their own revolution against Great Britain in the eighteenth century, subject peoples in more recent times have taken active steps to combat imperialism. Their strategies have ranged from the non-violent resistance to British rule led by Mahatma Gandhi in India to the revolutionary warfare against French rule led by Ho Chi Minh in Indochina, but their success has served to make the masters of empire aware of how futile it was to impose their own institutions on other cultures. Even after the departure of the European colonizers, imperialism left a bitter legacy. The Vietnam War, which led to our distaste for "significant loss of American life," was a belated result of French colonialism. Many of the intractable problems of modern Iraq are results of the way the British drew national borders. Those now proposing a new imperialism must hope that their readers have forgotten not only these currently relevant pieces of history, but all the other unhappy consequences of the European urge to acquire colonial empires.

They must also hope that the public has no memory of the insights into imperialism offered by poets. Of course, some poets have praised empire, just as some poets have celebrated honor and invoked the power of shame. Alfred, Lord Tennyson, Queen Victoria's Poet

Laureate, is an obvious example. His poem on "The Defence of Lucknow," a fortress besieged during the Indian Mutiny of 1857, celebrates the discipline of a small British garrison that held off a much larger rebel force:

Ready! Take aim at their leaders – their masses are gapp'd with our grape –
Backward they reel like the wave, like the wave flinging forward again,
Flying and foil'd at the last by the handful they could not subdue;
And ever upon the topmost roof our banner of England blew.[3]

Enjoying the technological advantage of grapeshot – small, cast-iron balls fired in clusters from cannons – the British troops create gaps in the masses that oppose them, but Tennyson does not focus on the fact that those gaps are made by killing native people. Instead, he invokes the Union Jack and celebrates the victorious troops as "English in heart and in limb / Strong with the strength of the race to command, to obey, to endure." Many of the troops at Lucknow were actually Scottish and Irish, but even if Tennyson means to include them in the broad category he calls *English*, his language about the "strength of the *race* to command" remains shocking. There were almost as many loyal Indian troops inside the garrison as Europeans, but when Tennyson praises those men, he calls them "faithful and *few*" and mentions their skin color twice in two lines:

Praise to our Indian brothers, and let the dark face have his due!
Thanks to the kindly dark faces who fought with us, faithful and few,

The rescue column that relieved the siege after eighty-seven days was a company of Scots, duly praised as "glorious Highlanders," but Tennyson suppresses the fact that they mistakenly bayoneted some of the loyal Indians when they entered the fort. His claim that the strength "to command, to obey, to endure" is a racial trait unique to the English, made in the face of these inconvenient facts, is an overtly racist version of the doctrine that Mallaby and Kaplan are still asserting, the supposed prerogative of orderly societies to impose their own institutions on disorderly ones.

Other poets have seen these issues differently. Samuel Taylor Coleridge, writing more than eighty years before Tennyson, condemned his countrymen for imposing their vices on their growing Empire:

> We have offended, Oh! My countrymen!
> We have offended very grievously,
> And been most tyrannous. From east to west
> A groan of accusation pierces Heaven!
> The wretched plead against us; multitudes
> Countless and vehement, the sons of God,
> Our brethren! Like a cloud that travels on,
> Steamed up from Cairo's swamps of pestilence,
> Even so, my countrymen! Have we gone forth
> And borne to distant tribes slavery and pangs,
> And, deadlier far, our vices, whose deep taint
> With slow perdition murders the whole man,
> His body and his soul![4]

Drawing on the very prejudice that assumed the superiority of European customs and climates, Coleridge follows his lines on the wretched multitudes with a description of a steaming cloud from Cairo's swamps. Then he springs the trap, linking that pestilent cloud not to foreign natives but to the supposedly civilized English. The contrast with Tennyson is telling: one poet applauds the rapid destruction of masses by grapeshot; the other deplores the slow destruction of native peoples by the deep taint of English vices.

Tennyson and Coleridge exemplify two opposing strains in Western poems of empire, one glowing with confidence, the other troubled by guilt. Both strains have their roots in Rome, specifically in the work of Virgil. Thanks to its high degree of military and political organization, the Roman Empire was the fundamental model for later European empires, whose apologists often invoked Roman originals. Even contemporary neo-imperialists, by speaking of two millennia of empire, evidently include Rome among their positive models, though they slyly decline to name it. Roman writers of prose, such as the orator Cicero or the historian Livy, were important sources for later imperialists. Cicero, for example, articulated the belief that it was just and right for the civilized Romans to rule over the barbarians. Being in servitude, he argued, improved the welfare of the conquered.[5] Centuries later, European imperialists and

American slaveholders repeated that pernicious doctrine. But it was the poet Virgil – taught in schools from his own time to ours and often claimed as a Christian prophet – who proved the richest source for those seeking to invoke Roman models to justify later empires.

Written at the request of the emperor Augustus, the *Aeneid* is a model for poems in praise of national destiny. Virgil's heroic history celebrates the Romans as a civilized people fated to rule the world. But the *Aeneid* is also a poem of loss and sorrow, filled with trenchant warnings about the dangers of conquest. That this morally subtle poem, as attentive to the fate of victims as to the glory of victors, so often became a pretext for expansive aggression by later imperialists strikes me as a distressing example of misreading. I take comfort, however, in the fact that the greatest poems opposing empire draw strength from more sensitive readings of Virgil.

Ancient and modern empires have sometimes installed a central figure – an Augustus Caesar or a Queen Victoria – as a symbolic icon, but creating and sustaining an empire requires collective action. Roman institutions made collective action possible. The Senate brought eloquent men together to debate national policy. Religion as practiced in the temples of the gods sought heavenly guidance for national goals. And in the army, what had once been merely personal motives for violence began to operate collectively, multiplying their force. The old impulse to seize excessive booty as a symbol of honor – a personal imperative for the warriors of the *Iliad* – was played out in Rome on a national scale. In the enormous parades called *triumphs*, staged at the end of successful campaigns, Roman generals displayed the exotic goods and people they had captured, symbolically extending their own prestige to the crowds who watched. The army and the nation thus collectively enacted what had once been the pride of the single warrior. They also enacted his anger. Homer tells us that the personal wrath of Achilles touched thousands, which is his poetic way of emphasizing the scale of the disaster. A reliable historical record tells us that the collective wrath of the Roman Empire slaughtered *millions*, and those bodies are facts.

Imperial violence is excessive by definition; it goes beyond the force needed to achieve national goals. Warrior nations, in the words of the economic historian Joseph Schumpeter, "seek expansion for the sake of expanding, war for the sake of fighting, victory for the sake of winning, dominion for the sake of ruling."[6] A comparison of Greek and Roman conventions of war may help to explain why Rome was the most influential Western example of a warrior nation. In the *Iliad*, the force attacking Troy is a loose confederation of warriors from various regions. They barely consider themselves a unified army, let alone a unified country. Only two brief passages describe groups of men in organized combat;[7] thousands of lines describe heroic confrontations between single, named warriors. By the fifth century BC, when written texts of Homer were widely circulated and eagerly studied, Greek warfare had changed. Heavily armed infantrymen called *hoplites* now fought in a formation called a *phalanx*, in which overlapping shields and deep ranks provided protection of a kind not available to Homer's solo warriors, who range across the battlefield seeking individual opponents. Hoplites, by contrast, were packed tightly into the phalanx, with each man's shield, held in his left hand, protecting the right side of his neighbor. All were forced forward by the momentum of the group. If the battles they fought were necessarily brief, the bloodshed was often terrible.

The classicist Victor Hanson, who has reconstructed the experience of hoplite combat, describes it as conventional, even stylized, but intensely violent. He pictures

heavily armed and armored farmers filing into a suitable small plain – the usual peacetime workplace of all involved – where brief but brutal battle resulted either in concessions granted to the army of invasion, or a humiliating, forced retreat back home for the defeated. ... Greek hoplite battles were struggles between small landholders who by mutual consent sought to limit warfare (and hence killing) to a single, brief, nightmarish occasion.[8]

This method of combat required teamwork and bred a spirit of collective honor. But there was still no country. As Plato once remarked, the normal state of relations between Greek cities was war,[9] and most of the wars fought by hoplites pitted various Greek cities against each other. Only when the Persians threatened all of them were the Greeks able to form brief alliances among themselves, and even those proved fragile.

The Romans, by contrast, had both a highly organized army and a *patria*, a fatherland for which Horace believed it was sweet and proper to die. Early records show a large army on the hoplite model, manned entirely by those able to purchase their own weapons. Propertied males between the ages of seventeen and forty-six owed sixteen years of military service to the state. Even after the government began to supply uniform equipment, only property owners were drafted, so that the army consisted of men who believed they had a collective stake in Rome's success. Unlike the Greek hoplites, these Roman soldiers fought sustained campaigns. They had no trace of the desire to limit warfare that apparently shaped Greek modes of battle. Their army, writes the historian Michael Grant, was "a terrible weapon . . . capable of atrocious cruelty." Yet as Grant points out, Roman leaders also displayed "a talent for patient political reasonableness that was unique in the ancient world."[10] As Rome built the Empire for which its citizens made such frequent and painful sacrifices, treaties and bargains were at least as important as wars. Time after time in the early history of Rome, diplomats forged separate treaties with cities that might otherwise have banded together in opposition. In making these agreements, the Romans typically absorbed the cults of local deities into their religion, encouraged intermarriage, and offered their new allies whole or partial Roman citizenship.

Because they had a far more corporate and national sense of the motives for war than the ancient Greeks, the ancient Romans were eventually able to gain an empire stretching from Spain to Jerusalem. Thanks to shrewd diplomacy and administration, they retained that empire for centuries. With the larger political organization of Rome came a sense of war as a collective enterprise. Personal honor became less important than one's place in a family, duty to a civil structure, and obligation to a nation. Transmitted to future generations by historians and poets, these values – self-discipline, patriotism, and diplomacy – became the positive elements of the idea of empire. For Romans, they were summed up in the concept of *pietas*, not merely religious piety as we understand it, but a broader idea of *"dutiful conduct"* towards the gods and towards one's parents, relatives, benefactors, and country.[11]

Roman virtues, however, are not an adequate explanation for Roman aggression. Some historians have argued that the wars fought to extend the Empire served the interests of large landholders, who gained a supply of slaves from those captured in battle, and who may have avoided serious questions about domestic politics by keeping the nation focused on war.[12] But the fact that wealthy patricians profited by war does not explain the destructive excess of Roman soldiers. The ancient historian Polybius reports widespread atrocities when cities fell to the Romans after being besieged, and describes the carnage not as an exception, but as a *custom*. The purpose of this custom, he explains, is "to inspire terror, so that when towns are taken by the Romans one may often see not only the corpses of human beings, but dogs cut in half."[13] As Polybius' tone suggests, such acts were routine. "Almost every year," writes the modern classical historian William Harris, "the Romans went out and did massive violence to someone."

Harris has the courage to acknowledge the primitive impulses that were undeniably a part of Roman conquest. "Roman imperialism," he writes, "was in large part the result of quite rational behaviour, . . . but it also had dark and irrational roots."[14] Because poetry begins, as Yeats puts it, "in the foul rag and bone shop of the heart,"[15] it is one of our best ways of getting at these darker motives, whether they drive individuals or nations. Virgil celebrates Roman patriotism and diplomacy, but places equal emphasis on the violence expended in the cause of empire and the damage done to both victims and victors in the course of imperial expansion. His *Aeneid* is a deeply felt meditation on the very contradiction that has so puzzled modern historians, many of whom have wondered how the Romans could have simultaneously shown "an extreme degree of ferocity in war" and "a high level of political culture."[16] By taking full advantage of poetry's capacity to sustain two moral or political ideas at the same time, Virgil explores and exposes the fundamental contrast between Roman virtue and Roman cruelty.

Virgil approaches Roman attitudes toward war and empire indirectly. In his nostalgic account of events that supposedly occurred a thousand years before his own time, a defeated band of Trojans searches for a new home, fighting single combats like those of the *Iliad*. Remembering and partly inventing Rome's mythic origins, Virgil models his work closely on Homer's two epics: Aeneas' wandering adventures in the first half closely resemble those of Odysseus in the *Odyssey*; the bitter war he fights in the second half recalls the *Iliad*. But Virgil is more overtly present in his poem, more palpable as an engaged, questioning narrator, than Homer is in his. The tragic sensibility that is largely implicit in Homer is often explicit in Virgil, in part because of the circumstances of composition. While Homer worked within an oral tradition, drawing on formulaic language, Virgil wrote his poem down, refining and revising as he went along. Even when he closely imitated specific Homeric episodes, Virgil was therefore able to reshape them. For readers aware of Homer, as most of his original readers would have been, Virgil's work gained layers of meaning not as easily produced in a primary, oral epic like Homer's. His poem is an early example of the way poems on war engage not only the historical past but the poetic past, with consequences that are not merely literary. By simultaneously imitating Homer and rewriting him, reminding his readers of his model while calling attention to his departures from it, Virgil learned how to manage other kinds of poetic tension, including the political and moral tension between the values of his characters and the pressure of their imperial destiny.

Homer's heroes have gigantic passions and cause massive destruction. They act as individuals, not as agents of a nation, and their actions rarely point to the future. Virgil's hero Aeneas, son of the mortal Anchises and the goddess Venus, is supposed to be different. The opening lines define him not by his conquests, but by his sufferings and his place in a national history:

> Arms and the man I sing, who first from the shores
> of Troy, sent forth by fate, arrived in Italy,
> and reached Lavinia's banks; thrown all around
> on land and the deep by the force of the gods and the anger,
> relentless, of savage Juno; suffering much
> in war as well, he finally founded a city,
> and brought in his gods to Latium, whence the race
> of Latins, the Alban fathers, and even the towering
> walls of Rome.[17]

In this account, war is a necessary evil, something through which Aeneas suffers in order to found a city and father an empire. There is nothing here about the personal honor for which Achilles and Agamemnon struggle, nothing about fighting to avoid shame. The emotion of anger, a defining trait for the hero of the *Iliad*, appears here in connection with the savage goddess Juno, whose resentment against the Trojans repeatedly blocks Aeneas in his search for a homeland. If Achilles is driven by personal anger, Aeneas is driven by a sense of national destiny that often requires him to suppress his emotions. He undergoes the buffeting of fate and the gods, including the challenge of war, in order to lead a collective effort that will spawn a new nation. He is also "a man marked out by *pietas*,"[18] defined by his duties to the gods, the community, and the nation rather than his personal honor. "I am the pious Aeneas,"[19] he says, apparently without embarrassment, when introducing himself to a beautiful maiden who turns out to be his goddess mother in disguise. In the same speech, he mentions saving his household idols from the sack of Troy, announces his hope to settle in Italy, and claims to be famous above the sky. Although his military prowess, described in several episodes of the *Iliad*, must be one source of that fame, he does not explicitly evoke his skill in battle.

Aeneas' reticence about his war record contrasts sharply with the way heroes in the *Iliad* define themselves by the spoils they have stripped from slain foes. It is one of many signs that point to Virgil's ambivalence about war. *Arms* may be one of his subjects, but he often associates them with fury, savagery, and cruelty. The first extended treatment of war, early in the epic, is Aeneas's heartbreaking account of the fall of Troy, told from the viewpoint of the losing side and focusing on scenes of pathos and destruction. His story wins the heart of Queen Dido, his hostess; it also reminds Virgil's reader of what is lost when a great city falls. Throughout the poem, the Latin adjectives from which we derive the English words *dire, horrible*, and *horrid* appear frequently with *bellum*, the noun for war. As the second half of the *Aeneid* begins, and the tale of travels becomes a tale of war, the poet invokes the Muse Erato, who presides over erotic and passionate poetry, to help him tell about "horrid wars" and "fierce kings driven to their graves by passions." "A new order of things is born for me," he announces. "I am starting a larger work."[20] If the work of writing on war is larger than the work of narrating the Trojan wanderings, it is also more painful and difficult. Virgil undertakes war poetry with a sense of obligation, not unlike the attitude his hero brings to war itself.

As the narrative of the war in the *Aeneid* makes clear, the Trojans gain the land on which to build their longed-for city by conquering the people who are already there. In modern terms, theirs is a campaign of colonization. When Virgil's Trojans arrive in Italy after years of wandering, they beach their ships, build wooden palisades, fight to gain a foothold, and ultimately intermarry with the Latin people. Treaties, marriages, and alliances – all of which Aeneas initially seeks – are the harbingers of the Roman way. War comes about when people on both sides cannot control their passions.

While recounting the ancient myth of a Trojan remnant coming to Italy, Virgil also creates and seizes opportunities to praise the emperor Augustus, who had requested the poem, and Augustus' uncle Julius, whose victories in the civil wars of the first century BC ended the Roman republic and led to the Empire. The poet's praise of the Caesars, however, invariably couples pride at Roman conquest with hope for a lasting peace. Like other citizens of his time, Virgil was grateful to his patron Augustus for ending decades of civil war, settling the Roman economy, and presiding over a long period of relative peace. But he was also acutely conscious of the cost of that peace. Using every device at his command, he therefore constructed a poem that Augustus might read as a patriotic celebration of Roman power and destiny, but that alert readers would recognize as a meditation on the moral cost of empire. Adam Parry has put this truth in memorable terms:

Virgil continually insists on the public glory of the Roman achievement, the establishment of peace and order and civilization. But he insists equally on the terrible price one must pay for this glory. More than blood, sweat and tears, something more precious is continually being lost by the necessary process; human freedom, love, personal loyalty, all the qualities which the heroes of Homer represent, are lost in the service of what is grand, monumental and impersonal: the Roman State.[21]

Unfortunately, the *Aeneid* has not often had readers as acute as Parry, though it has always been a canonical text. It was well known in the Middle Ages, a period in which Homer was virtually forgotten, and it was revered in the Renaissance as the master poem of antiquity. Aspects of its style and versification provided models for poets in many languages. Yet poets, readers, and teachers in later periods missed, ignored, or suppressed the unease about war and empire that now seems so palpable in Virgil. Despite the fact that Virgil died before the birth of Jesus, medieval readers interpreted the poem as a Christian allegory. In this reading, the real people whom Aeneas and the Trojans kill during their invasion of Italy become representations of the sins and weaknesses that the true Christian must conquer in his own soul. Renaissance readers, despite their increased knowledge of the ancient world, cast Aeneas as a chivalric Crusader, conquering barbaric forces in the cause of civilization. During the centuries of European colonial expansion, the same schoolmasters who rewrote Homeric shame as *noblesse oblige* encouraged their students to view the *Aeneid* as a straightforward celebration of national piety, patriotism, sacrifice, duty, and the manifest destiny of Rome (or Spain or England or Holland or France). Poets celebrating these new empires were shrewdly selective in their use of Virgil. They often took important passages out of context, treating them as proof texts for their own ideologies. By emphasizing the official or patriotic surface of Virgil's national epic, they managed to suppress the questioning and tragic aspects of his work, rewriting Virgil as a positive model for their own colonial and imperial wars.

In my first engagement with Virgil, I encountered a belated version of this approach. My high-school Latin teacher, Mary Stewart Duerson, had been teaching the *Aeneid* for forty years when I entered her class. Her knowledge of the poem was impressive. She knew long stretches of it by heart, and she never faltered in explaining the complexities of Virgil's syntax or the beauties of his meter. Her account of Roman politics, however, was flat, simple, and highly patriotic. She sought in Virgil support for her own conservative views on American politics, including her deep distrust of the Kennedy administration. When most Americans – certainly most high-school students – were rejoicing at the peaceful resolution of the Cuban missile crisis, Miss Duerson longed for decisive imperial action. I especially remember one class in the fall of 1963, when our exercise on Latin derivatives included the adjective *patent*. "It is a *patent* truth," said Miss Duerson, "that the Russians still have missiles in Cuba, and that we should have asserted our control of this hemisphere by destroying them." In explaining *pietas*, she insisted that the dutiful Aeneas was a positive model throughout Virgil's poem, and that he should be a model for us. I think she imagined him as a Presbyterian elder who voted Republican.

Like earlier imperialistic misreadings, Miss Duerson's patriotic simplification of Virgil required suppressing the fact that the main narrative line of the second half of the *Aeneid*, the part devoted to war, shows how even pious men prove unable to conform to their ideals when thrown into combat. In battle, the noble Trojans become thrall to the emotions of anger, honor, and shame – now felt collectively as well as personally. Even Aeneas finally fails to achieve the balance, forgiveness, and discipline in which he believes, and seeks his imperial destiny through violence. In showing his hero's helplessness in the face of the impersonal forces of empire, Virgil reveals his awareness of the danger of those forces in his own time. During the period stretching from the first Punic War against Carthage (264–241 BC) to the consolidation of the Western Empire under Augustus Caesar (30 BC), the Roman army fought in Spain, North Africa, Greece, Asia Minor, Gaul, and Egypt. Slave revolts and civil wars led to fighting in Sicily and even in mainland Italy. Under the pressure of nearly constant warfare, republican institutions collapsed, as did the idea of an army of property-holding citizens. Conscription now included men without property, who predictably demanded land and other rewards after their service. Later, the Romans replaced the draft with a system of cash payments in lieu of service, which allowed them to hire foreign mercenaries, who were of course less loyal than the citizen-soldiers of the Republic. From the time of Augustus until the final fall of the Empire in AD 476, the army regularly deposed, killed, and appointed emperors. By gaining an empire, the Romans lost their political freedom.

Politicians, including those now in power, have always found it difficult to acknowledge the inevitable loss of freedom that follows the embrace of imperial ambitions. To help us stare that terrible irony in the face, we need poets, and we may need them most at moments of national enthusiasm. As America entered World War II, outraged by the attack on Pearl Harbor and filled with a sense of moral urgency, the poet Robinson Jeffers predicted that the war would turn a republic into an empire:

> It is war, and no man can see an end of it. We must put freedom
> away and stiffen into bitter empire.
> . . . .

Now, thoroughly compromised, we aim at world rule, like Assyria,
    Rome, Britain, Germany, to inherit those hoards
Of guilt and doom. I am American, what can I say but again,
    "Shine, perishing republic?"... Shine, empire.[22]

Jeffers was writing directly about the present moment, but his is
not the only strategy available to poets skeptical about empire. Virgil,
working obliquely, tells an ancient, mythic story, but uses that story
to comment indirectly on events of his own time. He self-consciously
emphasizes the emotions he feels in the present as he writes about the
past. His description of horrid wars in the invocation to Erato, for
example, applies to the Roman civil wars of his own lifetime as well as
the semi-mythical wars between the Trojans and Latins. His epic
similes – extended comparisons between an event in the main narrative and some different but similar event familiar to his readers –
often link the past and the present. In the first simile in the poem, for
example, he establishes a contrast between piety and *furor*, his word
for those dark and irrational passions that fueled Roman violence.
The main narrative describes Neptune calming a storm that has
scattered Aeneas's fleet. Then Virgil compares the god controlling
the winds to a Roman citizen controlling a street mob:

> And just as in a crowd there often arises
> sedition, the rude mob raging in their minds,
> and now the sticks and stones will fly – for furor
> furnishes weapons; then, should they happen to see
> a serious man well-known for service and piety
> they hush, and stand around with ready ears;
> with words he rules their minds, and calms their hearts.[23]

This is a wonderfully compact formulation of a Roman ideal. One
distinguished man calms a large mob; words prove more powerful
than weapons; piety overcomes furor. But Virgil is never simple, and
the passage is open to another reading. Although the effective orator
is a generic figure, Romans of Virgil's period would surely have
remembered the orator Cicero, who was a victim of the civil wars.
After the assassination of Julius Caesar in 44 BC, Cicero delivered
speeches in the Senate opposing Mark Antony, who was among those
jockeying for power. A year later, Antony joined forces with Caesar's
nephew Octavian (later called Augustus). Together they marked for

death three hundred Senators, including Cicero. Antony ordered the assassins who went to carry out the sentence to bring him the old man's head – and the hands with which he had written his works. Such, too often, was the fate of the serious man well known for service and piety.

I believe Virgil understood and encouraged both readings of this passage, and thus both readings of his poem. One Roman reader might take comfort in this example of pious control, remembering that Augustus himself had identified clemency and piety as his principles. Another, more mindful of the terrible violence of the recent civil wars and the destruction of republican ideals, might find in this passage an implicit criticism of the Caesars, who had at least as much in common with the furious, vengeful heroes of the *Iliad* as they did with the pious Aeneas.

Another device for linking past and present is prophecy. Homer never alludes to the centuries of history between the Trojan War and his own period, but Virgil, by including several extended prophecies detailing how Aeneas' descendants will rule, fills in the centuries of Roman history between the arrival of the mythical Aeneas and the real acts of the Caesars. From the perspective of the characters in the *Aeneid*, these prophecies are inspiring or mystifying visions of the future, but from the perspective of Virgil and his readers, they are accounts of the recent past, or even the present. Near the beginning of the poem, Jupiter assures the goddess Venus that her mortal son Aeneas will father a great people, who will be called Romans. "For them I set no limits of actions or times," he tells her; "I have given them an empire without end."[24] Sketching the future history of the Romans, Jupiter explains that Aeneas will "wage a huge war in Italy, and subdue fierce peoples." After the war, he can "build walls and customs for his men."[25] The emphasis falls not on courage or victory but on the larger purpose of war: to gain peace and stability, with an inherent contrast between the fierce peoples whom Aeneas will find in Italy and the Roman civilization he will make possible.

Julius Caesar liked to trace his ancestry to Ascanius (sometimes called Iülus), Aeneas' son by his Trojan wife Creüsa. When Jupiter's prophecy reaches Caesar, Virgil endorses that genealogy, carefully emphasizing Caesar's beauty, his conquests, and his transformation into a star in the heavens:

From this handsome line will be born a Trojan Caesar,
who will bound his rule by the sea, his fame by the stars.
Julius, a name sent down from great Iülus.
Him in time, now safe, you will welcome to heaven,
weighed down with the spoils of the East; he too will be summoned
with prayers.[26]

Although Virgil's contemporaries were surely supposed to feel pride
in this assertion of wide dominion, Jupiter gives no details of the
military victories by which Caesar will extend Roman rule. His bland
formulas of praise conceal some ugly historical truths, well known to
Virgil's first readers. The historian Plutarch, who wrote not long after
Virgil, believed that Caesar's conquest of Gaul involved killing at
least one million of the enemy, and modern historians describe this
campaign as a "human, economic, and ecological disaster probably
unequalled until the conquest of the Americas."[27] Although Miss
Duerson would never have used such language to describe Caesar's
victories in Gaul, the term *genocide* is surely no exaggeration for death
on this scale.

Virgil does not mention the wars in Gaul, but he does show a keen
awareness of the ironies of empire. Immediately after the lines in
praise of the handsome Julius, Jupiter's prophecy shades into praise
for the reign of Augustus as an age of peace:

With wars set aside, the rugged ages will soften;
old Faith, and Vesta,* Quirinus** and his brother Remus
will give out laws; with iron and welded joints,
the dire gates of War will be closed; and impious Furor
sitting inside on his savage weapons, and bound
with a hundred knots of brass behind his back,
will groan grotesquely from his bloody mouth.[28]

Here Virgil embodies the anger that proves so destructive in the *Iliad*
as the minor deity *Furor*, and calls him *impius* (irreverent, ungodly,
undutiful, unpatriotic),[29] an implicit contrast with the gods and men
who give out laws, and thus with the pious Aeneas.

---

* Goddess of home and the hearth.
** The name given to Romulus when he became a god.

The triumph of law and peace over Furor represents a true ideal. But Virgil is never naïve. In the allusive texture of his verse, he has left clues that show his awareness of how hard it is to conquer Furor. Here the ominous signal is the naming of the twin brothers Romulus and Remus. Anyone familiar with their story would have known its sad ending. As Romulus, who believed the gods had designated him to found Rome, was starting to build the city wall, Remus jumped playfully over it. Furious at the insult, Romulus killed him. Remembering that part of the myth, astute readers might have seen a parallel with the fratricidal struggles of the recent civil wars, which had pitted Julius Caesar against his son-in-law Pompey, then Augustus Caesar against his brother-in-law Mark Antony. Reconciled in heaven, Romulus and Remus are now invoked as giving laws and assuring peace. But the Furor they help to bind is a god whose power they felt in life.

Always attentive to pain and loss, Virgil deplores the human costs of empire. He also recognizes the cultural costs, as he shows in his best-known prophetic passage. At the center of the epic, Aeneas visits the underworld, where his father Anchises shows him a vision of his still unborn descendants. This line of future rulers includes Romulus and Augustus Caesar, who will "stretch his empire to the stars and constellations."[30] In a narrative of Roman victories, Anchises then praises future military heroes, with special attention to those who would conquer Greece in the second century BC. Although Virgil surely meant to appeal to the patriotic pride of his Roman audience, his close study of Homer had made him keenly aware of the excellence of Greek culture. Unable to argue for Roman superiority in sculpture or science, he allows Anchises to make a gracious compliment to Greek aesthetic and intellectual accomplishments while defining conquest and diplomacy as Roman arts:

> Others will cast bronze works that breathe more subtly
> (indeed I believe it), and draw living faces from marble,
> plead better at law, and mark the paths of heaven
> with rods, and name the circling stars; but you,
> Roman, remember to rule the peoples with power
> (these will be your arts), to establish the custom of peace,
> to spare your subjects, and to disarm the proud.[31]

For the Romans, says Anchises, political administration will become an art form, and by associating imperial rule with the arts, Virgil makes the exercise of power look like a sign of civilization. This benign view of imperial power conceals a much uglier reality. The Roman consul Mummius, praised in this passage for conquering Corinth, actually treated his vanquished foes with savage cruelty. In retaliation for the ill treatment of some Roman ambassadors, he burned the city to the ground, sold all the survivors into slavery, and shipped the remaining art works to Rome.[32] If the survivors of Corinth included sculptors, astronomers, and orators like those admired in Virgil's fine lines, their works were seized and their bodies sold for slave labor. Mummius and his troops do not seem to have been very interested in sparing their new subjects.

Virgil's prophecy, with its emphasis on the positive effects of Roman rule, was far better known in later times than the facts of the conquest of Corinth. Although his original readers were surely aware of the distance between the benign view of empire presented by Anchises and the stern reality of Roman warfare, later readers lost the irony. Interpreting passages like this one in ways that suited their needs, they made the linkage between empire and art a part of the standard ideology and stock vocabulary of imperialism. In 1883, for example, the Victorian classicist W. Y. Sellar quoted the prophecy of Anchises and concluded that "Virgil softens and humanises the idea of the Imperial State, representing her as not only the conqueror but the civiliser of the ancient world, and the transmitter of that civilization to the world of the future."[33]

In treating empire as a benign and nurturing force, poets have often employed personification, the trick of representing a nation or concept as a person or god. By portraying nations as people, personification can also make abstract, collective motives for war – nationalism, patriotism, and imperialism – seem emotional and personal. Virgil is a master of personification; his picture of Furor bound in chains is an example. Despite Sellar's claim, however, Virgil never treats the imperial state as female. That process begins with the fourth-century Roman poet Claudian, who pictures Rome as the "mother of arms and law,"[34] exerting her power over all. Later poets suppressed the emphasis on arms and used the female image of Empire to connect imperial power with beauty, peace, justice, mercy, order, honor, and even freedom.

The fundamental myth of empire, in which a great and civilized city, gleaming at the center of an extensive empire, receives the grateful tribute of exotic peoples from the far corners of the world, finds its most memorable expression in poems personifying Empire as a woman. In 1667, long before Britain became an imperial power, John Dryden imagined London, which was then recovering from a devastating fire, as "a City of more precious mold; ... With Silver pav'd, and all divine with Gold."

> Now, like a Maiden Queen, she will behold,
>   From her high Turrets, hourly Sutors come;
> The East with Incense, and the West with Gold,
>   Will stand like Suppliants to receive her Doom.[35]

In this fanciful, courtly version of the imperial myth, representatives of distant lands appear as suppliant suitors, voluntarily bringing precious metals and rare spices to enrich the maiden queen who represents London. A portrait of a royal mistress, painted not long after Dryden's poem, provides a close visual analogue. The French artist Pierre Mignard shows the Duchess of Portsmouth, mistress to Charles II, receiving a shell filled with pearls and a branching red coral from an African slave dressed in European finery, whom she embraces. Behind her left shoulder, he paints a stormy sea, which suggests the dangerous voyages undertaken to gain spices and jewels for the privileged of Europe. It is surely no accident that the column behind her right shoulder is Roman in style.

By treating Empire as a female figure, Dryden and Mignard expand the idea of nurture implicit in Virgil's description of Rome sparing the conquered and taming the proud. In a poem of 1892 called "The British Empire," Sir Edwin Arnold takes the next step, personifying the Empire as a nurturing mother:

> She alone knew, of victors first and best,
> To fold the vanquished to her pardoning breast:
> To gather 'neath her wings, in one great brood,
> The tribes of Man, by might, then love, subdued,
> Mother, not Queen, calling those sons by birth
> Whom she had conquered – linking ends of Earth.[36]

Figure 8. Pierre Mignard, *Louise Kéroualle, Duchess of Portsmouth* (1682).

Although the long reign of Queen Victoria, who was on the throne at the time, may have influenced Arnold's choice of female imagery, he was loosely translating lines from Claudian that praise Rome with maternal imagery, calling her the only nation to "take conquered people into her embrace."[37] English readers might also hear echoes of

Jesus' comparison of himself to a mother hen – "O Jerusalem, Jerusalem, ... how often would I have gathered thy children together, even as a hen gathereth her chickens under her wings, and ye would not!"[38] – and of Milton's invocation of the Holy Spirit in the opening lines of *Paradise Lost*:

> Instruct me, for Thou know'st; Thou from the first
> Wast present, and, with mighty wings outspread,
> Dove-like sat'st brooding on the vast Abyss,
> And mad'st it pregnant.[39]

By encouraging his readers to imagine the Empire as a brooding mother, a suffering savior, and a Holy Spirit, Arnold was downplaying the armed might by which Britain had subdued the native tribes and emphasizing instead the pardoning process by which the Empire supposedly turned those vanquished peoples into sons.

This soft, Christian, feminine image of the Empire was fraudulent, and Arnold knew it. He had translated the *Bhagavad-Gītā* into English, along with sacred texts from many Asian languages. His poems draw upon Hindu, Muslim, and Buddhist traditions, so he had expert knowledge of the cultural variety he was suppressing by lumping all those peoples together into one great brood of imperial subjects. During the Indian Mutiny, he was working as a schoolmaster in Bombay, and was thus an eyewitness to the savage reprisals, atrocities, and tortures by which the British put down that early attempt to gain self-determination. "At Peshawar," writes the modern historian Niall Ferguson, forty mutineers were "strapped to the barrels of cannons and blown apart. ... The King of Delhi's three sons were arrested, stripped, and shot dead by William Hodson – the son of a clergyman. ... The route of the British retaliation could be followed by the scores of corpses they left hanging from trees along the line of their march."[40] Modern estimates put the death toll at 15,000 – surely stronger evidence of might than love.

By giving a nation personal qualities, imperial poets could emphasize some aspects of empire while suppressing others. By personifying empire as a goddess or queen, they could avoid discussing the plundering voyages and bloody wars by which the central state gained and kept its far-flung possessions. Eventually this process allowed some poets to treat conquest as liberation. The Australian poet

George Essex Evans, celebrating the coronation of Edward VII in 1902, pictured the centralized power of the British Empire as a "Throne of Freedom":

> Free is the wind that lashes into foam
> The fortress waves that gird the Sea-King's home;
> And free the war-worn Flag that is our fame –
> That fear, nor treason, nor the Storm-God's might,
> Nor the leagued banners of the World can shame
> When Britain arms for Honour and the Right.
> And free the hearts that on this golden day
> Bear willing witness to the Sea-King's sway:
> From world-wide realms washed by the world-wide sea
> They turn, O Throne of Freedom, unto Thee.[41]

Despite the rhetoric of willing allegiance to the Sea-King's sway, violent imagery leaks into this poem. The free wind is a force of nature, and Evans links it to the fortress of waves, the natural defense that protects the island nation of England. But the verb he uses to describe the action of the wind, *lashes*, makes me think of the discipline of the British Navy, enforced by the flogging of sailors. Military imagery becomes explicit when Evans invokes the war-worn flag as free, though freedom here is not democratic liberty, but freedom from *shame*, a word Evans emphasizes by rhyming it with *fame*. The largest leap is the last one: the wind is free, the flag is free, and the hearts of those governed by the Empire are allegedly free. Such sentiments may have been common in Australia, but I suspect that British subjects in Kenya, South Africa, and Ireland were less eager to bear willing witness to the Sea-King's sway on Coronation Day. Economically exploited, politically powerless, and defeated by armies supposedly fighting for honor and the right, they had ample reason to doubt the notion that Edward was ascending to a throne of freedom.

Fondly imagining that they had given primitive or savage peoples a higher degree of civilization, nurture, or freedom, European apologists for empire rarely admitted that the quest for wealth and power could make supposedly civilized people savage. If they had been better readers of Virgil, however, they might have recognized his awareness of another cost of empire: its harmful effects on the imperialists themselves. As introduced at the beginning of the

Aeneid, the devotion to familial, religious, and civic duties captured by the Roman concept of *pietas* seems admirable, but as events unfold, Aeneas' attention to duty deprives him of his emotional life. The women Virgil brings into his poem with sympathy are those whom imperial destiny forces Aeneas to leave behind. When he loses his wife Creüsa in the flames of Troy, he races back to find her, only to have her ghost appear and assure him that his losing her is part of the plan of the gods, who will lead him to a new kingdom. When he falls in love with the beautiful Dido, queen of Carthage, the gods insist that he abandon her. Jupiter sends his messenger Mercury to tell Aeneas that he must leave Dido and sail onward, fulfilling his destiny to rule Italy. While instructing Mercury, Jupiter describes Italy as "pregnant with empires and raging with war."[42] Instead of fathering a child by Dido, Aeneas must father an empire through war. The price of empire is the loss of human love.

Aeneas' painful parting from Dido is another sad variant of the scene of the hero's farewell. Unlike Hector, who can express his love for Andromache while admitting his fear of shame, unlike Lovelace, who can express his love of honor as if it were a compliment to Lucasta, Aeneas stands dumb before Dido's fury at being abandoned. He cannot appeal to honor or shame; he can only cite his imperial destiny and duty. Pointing to the cost of that duty, Virgil calls him *pious* as he leaves her:

> But pious Aeneas, much as he desires
> to sweetly ease her grieving, and to turn
> her cares aside with words, now groaning much
> and tearful in his mind from his great love
> still follows nonetheless the gods' commands
> and goes back to the fleet.[43]

I believe Virgil hoped his best readers would understand these human costs of empire. Later apologists for empire, however, treated the dutiful, self-denying Aeneas as a model for the colonial soldiers and administrators of their own times. In Tennyson's racist model, the English were born not only to command, but also to obey and to endure. British soldiers sent to India or Hong Kong had to leave their wives and families behind – often for years. Young men who took up administrative posts abroad did so in the certain knowledge that they were delaying or forgoing marriage. Victorian educators tried to make such emotional privation legitimate by insisting that Aeneas was doing the right thing in abandoning Dido. With great subtlety and sympathy, Virgil shows us the painful struggle between imperial duty and human feeling. Too many of his later readers saw only the power of duty.

A sad example is Kipling's notorious poem, "The White Man's Burden," written on the occasion of the American conquest of the Philippines. Here Kipling, a veteran of the English colonial establishment, sets out to instruct Americans in the costs of empire. His words, intended as a stirring call to duty, would fit half the tunes in a Victorian hymnal:

> Take up the White Man's burden –
> Send forth the best ye breed –
> Go bind your sons to exile
> To serve your captives' need;
> To wait in heavy harness,
> On fluttered folk and wild –
> Your new-caught, sullen peoples,
> Half-devil and half-child.[44]

Virgil had pictured Furor bound and imprisoned, controlled by imperial laws. Kipling applies similar imagery to the supposed agents of civilization, the best young men America can breed, bound to exile and strapped in heavy harness to serve the needs of the sullen peoples who are now their captives. By emphasizing the burdens borne by the conquerors, he deliberately misappropriates imagery more fitting for the conquered. In the Philippines as in other colonies, it was the subject peoples who bore the real burdens, and who worked in heavy harness to support a faraway power.

In order to emphasize the suffering involved in taking up the White Man's burden, Kipling describes colonial administration as hard physical labor. His image of empire as work contrasts starkly with Virgil's claim that the administrative and diplomatic skills of empire would become *arts* for the Romans, perhaps comparable to the Greek arts of sculpture, oratory, and astronomy. Not all of the peoples conquered by Rome were as advanced as the Greeks, and Virgil sometimes notices the exotic costumes and customs of alien peoples. But Kipling's description of the conquered as "new-caught, sullen peoples, / Half-devil and half-child" assumes not merely cultural difference, but racial inferiority.

The contrast with Rome is worth pondering. The Roman ideal articulated by Virgil, though not always carried out in practice, honored the cultural accomplishments of other peoples. Roman policy sought to identify local deities with Roman gods, to bring distant peoples into fruitful contact with the center, to award Roman citizenship to talented people, and to encourage intermarriage. Trajan, who became emperor in AD 98, was the son of a Roman settler in Spain and a Spanish mother. So far, no person of Indian descent has become the Prime Minister of Britain, and no African-American has become President of the United States.

Kipling had a classical education; in other poems, he invokes details of the Roman occupation of Britain. But his account of empire, at least in this poem, bears scant resemblance to Virgil's. The burden falls wholly on the conqueror, the blame on the victim:

> Take up the White Man's burden –
> The savage wars of peace –
> Fill full the mouth of Famine
> And bid the sickness cease;
> And when your goal is nearest
> The end for others sought,
> Watch sloth and heathen Folly
> Bring all your hopes to nought.

There are terrible ironies here, but I am not sure the poet intended all of them. I wonder, for example, how best to interpret "the savage wars of peace." In reality, the wars of empire often pitted disciplined armies equipped with machine guns against tribal warriors armed with spears and courage. Mechanically mowing down their foes, the forces of empire were at least as deserving of the term *savage* as those they fought.

By calling these colonial campaigns wars of peace, Kipling presumably meant to claim that the victors were bringing order and stability to those they defeated. Feeding and healing their new subjects, the conquerors doubtless believed that their motives were altruistic, even Christian. They thought they had a selfless desire to improve the lot of the natives. As the bitter legacy of colonialism shows, however, the desire to make others more civilized usually took the form of imposing alien beliefs and practices on conquered peoples, a strategy the new imperialists want to revive. Resistance to Western institutions and beliefs may have seemed like heathen folly to Kipling and his contemporaries, but the determined effort by which colonized people have since cast off their conquerors has surely disproved the notion that they were guilty of sloth.

Yet even in this short-sighted and racist poem, there are moments of insight – perceptions that might give pause to those now advocating an imperialist revival. In a later stanza, Kipling hints at the loss of freedom inevitable in nations that seek empire, and recognizes that conquered peoples, even when they appear to be silent and sullen, are in a position to judge their rulers:

> Take up the White Man's burden –
> Ye dare not stoop to less –
> Nor call too loud on Freedom
> To cloke your weariness;
> By all ye cry or whisper,
> By all ye leave or do,
> The silent, sullen peoples
> Shall weigh your gods and you.

In the recent campaign in Iraq, coalition forces were willing to *do* almost anything to secure the oil fields, but content to *leave* the museums and libraries to be looted and burned. Considering that choice, what conclusions must the formerly colonized peoples of the world – no longer sullen or silent – draw about our gods and us?

Although some poets have been complicit in furthering a simplified myth of empire, others have shown a deeper understanding of its costs. Dryden, perhaps the most Virgilian of English poets, skillfully celebrates the idea of empire in his picture of London as a maiden queen receiving incense and gold from her suitors. But in *The Indian Emperour*, a poetic drama staged *before* he wrote those lines, he shows a full awareness of the political and moral costs of empire. In a memorable scene, the Spanish conquistador Cortez discovers two of his officers and a priest torturing the Indian ruler Montezuma in order to find where he has hidden his gold. Angrily releasing the crippled victim, Cortez curses the greed of his men – and the European urge to empire:

> Accursed Gold, 'tis thou has caus'd these crimes;
> Thou turn'st our Steel against thy Parent Climes!
> And into *Spain* will fatally be brought,
> Since with the price of Blood thou here art bought.[45]

Acted in 1665 and printed in 1667, this play is remarkably prescient. If it sometimes suited Dryden to portray the gold and other treasures brought from the wider world as gifts of tribute from willing suppliants to a nurturing empire, he was also able to imagine the fatal consequences of riches bought with the price of blood.

Alexander Pope's *Windsor-Forest* (1713) displays similar Virgilian depth. Writing at the request of a friend in the government, Pope applauds the Peace of Utrecht, which ended decades of land war in Europe. As the poem draws to a close, Father Thames, the spirit of London's great river, rises from the waves to celebrate peace. His language closely echoes Virgil's prophecies:

> Hail Sacred *Peace*! hail long-expected Days,
> That Thames's Glory to the Stars shall raise!
> Tho' Tyber's streams immortal Rome behold,
> Tho' foaming Hermus swells with Tydes of Gold,
> . . . .
> These now no more shall be the Muse's Themes,
> Lost in my Fame, as in the Sea their Streams.[46]

In this vision, the Thames becomes the new Tiber, his fame and glory, like Caesar's, reaching to the stars. Like the deified Caesar of Virgil's prophecy, Peace has the power to disarm the forces of evil:

> Exil'd by Thee from Earth to deepest Hell,
> In Brazen Bonds shall barb'rous *Discord* dwell:
> Gigantick *Pride*, pale *Terror*, gloomy *Care*,
> And mad *Ambition*, shall attend her there.
> There purple *Vengeance* bath'd in Gore retires,
> Her Weapons blunted, and extinct her Fires:
> There hateful *Envy* her own Snakes shall feel,
> And *Persecution* mourn her broken Wheel:

> There *Faction* roar, *Rebellion* bite her Chain,
> And gasping Furies thirst for Blood in vain.[47]

As the detail of the brazen bonds suggests, Discord is Pope's female version of Virgil's bound and imprisoned Furor. Expanding the allegory, Pope lists other personified motives for warfare: Pride, Terror, Care, Ambition, Vengeance, Envy, Persecution, Faction, and Rebellion. By picturing all these passions as female and irrational, he links them to the bloodthirsty Furies of ancient myth.[48] Like Virgil, Pope hoped that Peace could lay those destructive furies to rest. He also knew how difficult it was to keep them chained. As a Roman Catholic whose family had been forced to leave London by punitive legislation, he had an especially acute sense of the continuing power of persecution.

Happy that his sons will no longer "dye" foreign rivers "with British Blood," Father Thames describes peace as an idyllic pastoral:

> Safe on my shore each unmolested Swain
> Shall tend the Flocks, or reap the bearded Grain;
> The shady Empire shall retain no Trace
> Of War or Blood, but in the Sylvan Chace,
> The Trumpets sleep, while chearful Horns are blown,
> And Arms employ'd on Birds and Beasts alone.[49]

In the shady empire of Windsor Forest, military skills will be practiced only in hunting. But the Peace of Utrecht actually brought Great Britain new possessions including Hudson Bay, Nova Scotia, Newfoundland, St. Christopher, Gibraltar, and Minorca – a real empire that required increasing military garrisons. A related agreement gave the British control over the slave trade with Spanish America, a lucrative commerce in human commodities.

Father Thames's vision of peace reflects these developments by prophesying a global mercantile empire, created and guaranteed by the British Navy. Extending the reach of the empire, ships will bring to England the coral, pearls, and other luxuries depicted in Mignard's portrait:

> Thy trees, fair Windsor! now shall leave their Woods,
> And half thy Forests rush into my Floods,
> Bear Britain's Thunder, and her Cross display,

> To the bright Regions of the rising Day;
> Tempt Icy Seas, where scarce the Waters roll,
> Where clearer Flames glow round the frozen Pole;
> Or under Southern Skies exalt their Sails,
> Led by new Stars, and borne by spicy Gales!
> For me the Balm shall bleed, and Amber flow,
> The Coral redden, and the Ruby glow,
> The Pearly Shell its lucid Globe infold,
> And Phoebus warm the ripening Ore to Gold.[50]

As the passage on hunting displaces trumpets and arms from war to the forest, this passage recasts imperial violence and conquest as natural forces. Pope fancifully pictures the ships of the Navy as the trees that provided their planks and imagines their cannon as thunder. He disguises the rapacious violence of imperialism as the seasonal violence of spring floods and summer storms. By pointing to the Christian cross displayed on the Union Jack, he even implies that imperial conquest is part of God's plan. (Its natural equivalent, the Southern Cross, was one of the new stars British sailors could see in southern skies.) Pope does not describe the destruction that the thunder of the Navy's vessels was sure to produce, such as the burning and sinking of the ships of European rivals. In his vision of world empire, the only flames are the Northern Lights seen near the frozen Pole. He does not mention the bleeding of conquered peoples, but the precious balm brought from their countries does bleed, and the valuable amber is said to flow. Although Pope skillfully displaces violent imagery, substituting a mercantile vision of empire for a purely military one, his language reveals that the peace and prosperity he celebrates will ultimately depend upon force of arms.

Like his master Virgil, Pope shows a deep understanding of the moral ambiguity of empire. He follows this prophecy of world exploration and trade with a vision of world peace that is truly remarkable for a poet writing in the early eighteenth century:

> The Time shall come, when free as Seas or Wind
> Unbounded Thames shall flow for all Mankind,
> Whole Nations enter with each swelling Tyde,
> And Seas but join the Regions they divide;
> Earth's distant Ends our Glory shall behold,
> And the new World launch forth to seek the Old.

> Then Ships of uncouth Form shall stem the Tyde,
> And Feather'd People croud my wealthy Side,
> And naked Youths and painted Chiefs admire
> Our Speech, our Colour, and our strange Attire![51]

This vision of the world flocking to London resembles Dryden's, but the ultimate source again is Virgil. Among the scenes depicted on the highly-wrought shield that Venus gives to her son Aeneas is a Roman triumph presided over by Augustus. Aeneas cannot understand the meaning of the shield because the events shown on it will happen after his life, but describing the shield gives Virgil another chance to comment on recent history. He shows the conquered tribes marching in long lines, "as different in tongues as in costume and arms," and lists such exotic groups as "Africans with flowing robes" and "arrow-bearing Geloni."[52] In Pope's version, however, the exotic peoples are not captives brought in chains to the center of empire, but willing travelers, free to marvel at the strange attire and foreign speech of their English hosts.

As the passage continues, Pope explicitly expresses his hope that peace and freedom will be the ultimate results of empire:

> Oh stretch thy Reign, fair *Peace!* From Shore to Shore,
> 'Till Conquest cease, and Slav'ry be no more:
> 'Till the freed Indians in their native Groves
> Reap their own Fruits, and woo their sable Loves.[53]

Pope imagines a world free from conquest and slavery. His freed Indians, unlike the African servant in Mignard's portrait, will be at liberty to follow the customs of their own culture, living in their own land. When he returned to this topic twenty years later, in *An Essay on Man*, Pope portrayed the Indians' version of Heaven as a place where they might escape the lust for gold deplored by Dryden's Cortez:

> Some safer world in depth of woods embrac'd
> Some happier island in the watry waste,
> Where slaves once more their native land behold,
> No fiends torment, no Christians thirst for gold![54]

The ironic pressure Pope places on the word *Christians* is a powerful indictment of colonial greed.

The Peace of Utrecht gave England new colonial possessions and control of the slave trade, and Pope was close to some of the politicians who negotiated the treaty. In light of those facts, his praise of the Peace might seem either naïve or disingenuous. But Pope had before him the model of Virgil, who knew how to temper his praise for his patron with a recognition of some of the unfortunate consequences of power. Like many others, Pope was genuinely grateful to Queen Anne and her ministers for bringing an end to decades of warfare on the Continent. His poetic account of the coming of peace, however, says very little about the War of the Spanish Succession (1701–1714), which the Peace of Utrecht concluded, or about the Nine Years' War (1689–1697), which preceded it. Instead, Pope describes recent history as

> A dreadful Series of Intestine Wars,
> Inglorious Triumphs, and dishonest Scars.[55]

For Pope's readers, "Intestine Wars" could only refer to the English Civil Wars of the previous century. Pope was quietly suggesting that the costly recent wars on the Continent were a long-term consequence of the English Civil Wars – as indeed they were. King William, who started those continental campaigns, came to power by deposing his father-in-law, James II. The Revolution that placed him on the throne was the concluding act in the long struggle between Parliament and the Stuart kings, an intestine conflict that had already caused a decade of civil war and another decade of rule by a military dictatorship. William retained his crown by aggressively pursuing military adventures abroad, trusting that the pride taken in his successes would induce his subjects to overlook his shaky claim to the throne. By invoking "Intestine Wars," Pope was reminding his readers of recent history and inviting them to compare the English Civil Wars with the Roman civil wars.

A specific echo of Virgil's language provides the link. In one of his most explicit passages of criticism and regret, Virgil pictures the Roman civil wars as an attack on the *viscera*, the *intestines* of his country. Shrewdly, he uses Anchises, Aeneas's dead father, as a spokesman. A few lines before the passage in praise of Greek culture, Anchises looks sadly forward to the struggles of Virgil's own time. He shows Aeneas a vision of the unborn spirits of Julius Caesar and

Pompey, bitter opponents who were related to each other by marriage, like James and William:

> But those you see shining in equal arms,
> spirits in concord now, held back by night,
> Alas what war will they wage against each other,
> if they reach the light of life, what slashing and carnage,
> the father-in-law* coming down from the top of the Alps
> and the fort of Monoecus, the son-in-law** opposed,
> his Eastern forces drawn up in formation![56]

Although the geographical details and the emphasis on the kinship relation would have allowed his readers to identify Caesar and Pompey, Virgil suppresses their names. But then Anchises directly addresses both men, urging his descendant Caesar to be merciful:

> My children, do not accustom your minds to wars
> or turn your strength against your country's bowels,
> and you, be merciful first, who draw your birth
> from Olympus, cast the darts down from your hand,
> child of my blood![57]

Virgil's first readers, who had lived through years of civil war, knew that Anchises' pleas to his descendants would prove futile. At the battle of Pharsalus (48 BC), Julius Caesar showed no mercy to Pompey. The battle was a decisive defeat for Pompey, and when he sought refuge in Egypt, his hosts promptly beheaded him. Virgil's patron Augustus owed his power to his uncle's victory over Pompey, and had recently won a civil war of his own by defeating his rival (and brother-in-law) Mark Antony. To recite these lines before him was an act of considerable courage on Virgil's part. To allude to these lines in a poem on Queen Anne's peace, written at a time of deep uncertainty about the succession, was a similar act of courage on Pope's part.

Virgil's prophetic plea for mercy, spoken by a dead man addressing his unborn descendant, is not a digression. It sets up the ending of the poem, in which Aeneas himself fails to be merciful. In the war between the Trojans and the Latins, the Latin leader is the handsome and honorable Turnus, who is outraged not only by the invasion of

---

*   Julius Caesar.
** Pompey.

his country but by Aeneas' claiming the princess Lavinia, whom he had intended to marry himself. After much bloodshed, the armies agree to settle the war by a single combat between Aeneas and Turnus. Wounded by a spear that Aeneas hurls through his seven-fold shield, Turnus falls to the ground and makes a noble speech admitting defeat, yielding Lavinia, and asking Aeneas to let him return to his father, or at least to send back his body. Aeneas hesitates, until he sees on the shoulder of his rival a piece of war-booty, a belt Turnus has taken from the Arcadian prince Pallas, sent by his father to aid the Trojans and slain by Turnus a few days earlier. Enraged by the sight of that belt, Aeneas cannot achieve mercy. The closing lines are terrible. Inflamed with anger, boiling with rage, Aeneas plunges his sword into the chest of Turnus, whose limbs dissolve in a deathly chill. "His life, dishonored, flies with a groan to the shadows below."[58]

By ending his epic with this stark killing, Virgil points in two directions. In one sense, Aeneas has regressed. He is no longer the pious leader whose only concern is for the larger polity. He has returned to the behavior of a vengeful hero from the world of the *Iliad*. Yet his language here is not quite the language of an Achilles, taunting his victim and exulting in his strength. Aeneas tells Turnus that it is really Pallas who is sacrificing him, who is taking just payment in blood. In acting to avenge the death of an ally's son, Aeneas might appear to embody the Roman virtues of alliance and diplomacy, but Virgil stresses his primitive emotions, telling us that his hero is burning with terrible fury. At this moment, Aeneas enacts the basic conflict in Roman imperialism: measured by the standards of diplomacy and the requirements of empire, his act is rational, but in its emotional intensity, it entails a return to the dark and primitive world of vengeance and shame.

Poetry, it bears repeating, is an art of memory, and poets some-times remember what journalists and politicians forget. Before embarking on further imperialist adventures, our leaders might profit by reading Virgil, and by reading one of the best poems of the Vietnam era, Philip Appleman's "Peace with Honor," which main-tains a constant parallel between modern America and ancient Rome. In the opening stanza, Roman terms ("outer provinces," "Legions," "barbarians") clash ironically with familiar modern phrases ("the late-late news," "minds and hearts"):

> The outer provinces are never secure:
> our Legions hold the camps, their orders
> do not embrace the minds
> and hearts of barbarians. So, when the late-
> late news reported the outlandish
> screams in that distant temple,
> the great bronze Victory toppled,
> red stains in the sea, corpses
> stranded by the ebb tide – all of that,
> and only four hundred
> armed men at the garrison – why,
> of course it had to come, the massacre,
> the plundering.[59]

The same devices continue as Appleman sketches the national response to the distant threat:

> Reports from the field
> were cabled not to the Emperor but
> to the Joint Chiefs, to filter
> through at last, edited
> and heavy with conclusions.

Even numbers contribute to the effect, with the 101st Airborne Division imagined as a Roman legion:

> They sent our toughest
> veterans, the Ninth Legion, the Fourteenth,
> the Hundred-and-First, their orders un-
> ambiguous: teach the barbarians respect.

When the battle comes, it is a composite of all the imperial wars from Caesar in Gaul to the My Lai massacre:

> And then the charge, the clash of arms,
> cavalry with lances fixed, the glorious
> victory: a hundred thousand tons of TNT
> vaporized their villages, their forests were
> defoliated, farmland poisoned forever,
> the ditches full of screaming children,
> target-practice for our infantry.

The conclusion, dripping with sarcasm, depends upon the reader's knowing that the outcome of the Vietnam War was not a glorious victory.

> A glorious victory, of course,
> but in a larger sense, a mandatory act
> of justice: the general peace
> was kept, the larger order held; . . .
> the honor of Empire
> is saved.

The whole effect of this poem comes from Appleman's skill in echoing the standard vocabulary of imperialism – a system of language poetry helped to build. When celebrating European empires, poets too often invoked without irony the abstractions Appleman's conclusion calls into question – justice, peace, order, honor.

Sensitive poets, however, may correct not only the excesses of emperors but those of other poets. In 1892, an obscure Victorian poet, Robert Williams Buchanan, marked the death of Alfred, Lord Tennyson, by gently chiding the Poet Laureate for his readiness to celebrate imperial conquest. Addressing his fellow poet as "Dear singing Brother," Buchanan gave due respect to Tennyson's "faultless diamonds of song," but ruefully noted that he had used his gifts in the service of empire,

> And praised the Christ as God and Man
> That wars were made and trumpets blown;
>
> Yea, deem'd this later greater Rome
> Supremely just and surely wise,
> And shut [his] ears against the cries
> Of races slain beyond the foam.[60]

Like Appleman, Buchanan recognizes the terrible arrogance of empire and its poetic apologists. When nations come to believe that they are supremely just and surely wise, that it is their racial destiny to command, other races will be slain.

CHAPTER 4

The myth of chivalry

On 31 May 1897, the city fathers of Boston unveiled a monument to Robert Gould Shaw, who died in a Civil War battle in 1863. Reared by a family of committed abolitionists, Colonel Shaw recruited and commanded the Massachusetts Fifty-Fourth, the first regiment of freed slaves raised in the North. He was killed, along with nearly half his troops, in a doomed assault on a Confederate battery in South Carolina. The motion picture *Glory* (1989) tells their story.

Shaw's monument, executed by the American sculptor Augustus St. Gaudens, still stands on Boston Common. It is a highly realistic piece, accurately depicting the uniforms, weapons, and faces of the young colonel and his determined soldiers. The Harvard philosopher William James, who spoke at the dedication, praised the monument for its realism and the regiment for its sacrifice in the cause of racial justice:

Look at the monument and read the story; – see the mingling of elements which the sculptor's genius has brought so vividly before the eye. There on foot go the dark outcasts, so true to nature that one can almost hear them breathing as they march. State after State by its laws had denied them to be human persons. The Southern leaders in congressional debates, insolent in their security, loved most to designate them by the contemptuous collective epithet of "this peculiar kind of property." There they march, warm-blooded champions of a better day for man. There on horseback, among them, in his very habit as he lived, sits the blue-eyed child of fortune, upon whose happy youth every divinity had smiled. Onward they move together, a single resolution kindled in their eyes, and animating their otherwise so different frames. The bronze that makes their memory eternal betrays the very soul and secret of those awful years.[1]

Figure 9. Augustus St. Gaudens, Monument for Robert Gould Shaw and the
Massachusetts Fifty-Fourth on the Boston Common.

St. Gaudens was keenly interested in realism, and later explained
that the creases in one soldier's trousers had cost him months of
effort. His passion for accuracy, however, did not prevent him from
alluding to the ancient world; the female figure who flies above the
soldiers looks like a classical goddess. James was at pains to praise the
monument as true to nature, but could not resist a classical touch of
his own. By claiming that every divinity had smiled on Shaw's happy
youth, he indulged in the fiction that a pantheon of pagan deities had
endowed the young man with various talents. For both the sculptor
and the orator, these bits of classical imagery were ornamental
touches. Both men were fundamentally concerned to depict Shaw
and his regiment as actors in their own time, those awful years
of bloodshed over the question of whether the dark outcasts
were property or human persons. If hints of ancient myth hang
over their heads, the men in the monument are marching towards a
real death.

In his "Ode on the Unveiling of the Shaw Memorial on Boston Common," written for the same occasion, the Boston poet Thomas Bailey Aldrich took a very different approach. Drawing upon centuries of poetic tradition, Aldrich described Shaw as a medieval knight, treating his death as if it had happened in another era:

> He fell as Roland fell
>   That day at Roncevaux,
> With foot upon the ramparts of the foe!
> . . . .
>   See where he rides, our Knight!
>   Within his eyes the light
> Of battle, and youth's gold about his brow;
> Our Paladin, our Soldier of the Cross,
>   Not weighing gain with loss –
> . . . .
> Not his to hesitate
> And parley hold with Fate,
> But proudly to fling down
> His gauntlet at her feet.[2]

These lines invoke some of the oldest, most powerful emblems of the myth of chivalry. Aldrich names an early medieval hero, Roland, and his final battle, Roncevaux. He calls Colonel Shaw a Paladin, a title originally reserved for King Charlemagne's personal knights, the Twelve Peers of France, of whom Roland was one. Although the historical Roland lived over 300 years before the Crusades, Aldrich also calls Shaw a soldier of the cross, alluding to the red crosses worn by the Crusaders in their campaigns to secure Jerusalem. He imagines Shaw refusing a parley with a personified Fate and challenging her by flinging down his gauntlet at her feet. If Aldrich had designed the monument, Shaw would have been in armor, the flying goddess would have taken up the foreground, and the foot soldiers would have been left out.

Conventional and empty, Aldrich's poem pales by comparison with James's stirring prose or St. Gaudens's eloquent sculpture. I have introduced it here to show that a professional poet in the closing years of the nineteenth century could still have faith in the power of chivalric language. Of all past forms and ideologies of warfare, medieval chivalry has had the most persistent hold on the

imagination of poets. For Lovelace in 1648 or for Aldrich in 1897 –
even for General MacArthur in 1962 – a chivalric vocabulary was the
surest way to evoke the mystique of honor, and the surest way to
connect the ugly work of war with noble birth, Christian faith, and
the purity of women.

Alluding to earlier parts of the long history of war has sometimes
helped poets gain a clearer perspective on the wars of their own times.
I have already praised Philip Appleman for imagining the 101st
Airborne in Vietnam as a Roman legion, an ironic comparison that
casts a searching moral light on both periods. But when poets have
appealed to chivalry, they have usually done so to *avoid* uncomfor-
table questions. With its specialized vocabulary and disdain for
reality, chivalry is a closed system. Working within the fictional
frame of chivalry has often allowed modern poets to censor or
suppress unpleasant realities. By writing about paladins, parleys,
and gauntlets, elements having nothing to do with the Civil War,
Aldrich was able to ignore the appalling efficiency of modern
mechanized warfare, which enabled the Confederate battery to anni-
hilate Shaw's troops. By shifting the time-frame to a vaguely medieval past, he was able to evade the issue of race, still urgent in 1897 (and
now), but acknowledged in his poem only by a passing reference to
Shaw's troops as "dusky braves."

For Aldrich as for many other writers, chivalry was a way to treat
war as if it were a distant fantasy, not a present reality. And as even a
cursory account of its origins will show, the idea of chivalry has
always been a fraud, a system of polite and honorable ideals masking
shameful and violent acts. Poetry, I am sorry to say, played a crucial
part in creating the myth of chivalry and has been largely responsible
for sustaining it. The persistence of chivalric myth is a sobering
instance of poetry's capacity to make fantasy seem real, and thus to
efface the bloody truths of war.

Mounted on horseback and clad in elaborate armor, his face
concealed by a visor, his purpose a sacred Crusade or a gallant defense
of a lady's honor, the storybook knight is a creation of poets living
from the Renaissance forward, poets writing *after* artillery had ended
the era of the actual knight. The myth as it has come down to us more
truly reflects the nostalgic and romantic fantasies of these later writers
than the stark and violent practices of the real Middle Ages. With its

knights in shining armor and damsels in distress, its turreted castles and scaly dragons, the fairy-tale version of chivalry bears scant resemblance to actual conditions in early medieval Europe, where the strong central government and efficient administration of the Roman Empire had completely collapsed, leaving a small population to eke out a perilous living on tiny pockets of soil reclaimed from the encroaching forest.

In those dark days, warfare was more or less constant, but it was utterly unlike the massed, collective campaigns of the Roman legions. Muslim raiders from the South attacked coastal cities like Marseilles, then penetrated as far as the Alps, sacking monasteries and churches. Pagan Vikings from the North used their longboats to mount devastating raids on towns as far-flung as Kiev, Florence, and Rouen.[3] Although they were usually content to seize goods rather than territory, some of the Vikings settled in France and became the Christian Normans who conquered England in 1066. In the absence of strong kings, French and German dukes and counts waged war on their immediate neighbors. If successful in imposing their rule on larger parcels of land, they built castles to defend their holdings. Though cruel and destructive, early medieval warfare was local and limited, more focused on the surprise raid or decisive battle than on longer, more organized campaigns.

The collective sense of responsibility to a nation honored in Roman culture and exemplified by Aeneas appears to have disappeared from early medieval culture, which celebrated the power of the strong individual. Although only a few scholars knew about Homer, some of the motives for violence in early medieval culture closely resemble the passions that drive the warriors in the *Iliad*: greed for booty, fear of shame, and the "wild joy of war." In the fragmented, vulnerable world of the early Middle Ages, as the modern historian Michael Foss points out, "military prowess seemed the only worthwhile virtue. Continuous struggle engendered a lust for war; and the sternness of the contest demanded ferocity and anger equal to those of the invaders. These became the ordinary qualities of knighthood faithfully recorded in the old epic poetry of Europe."[4] Foss is thinking of the *chansons de geste* (songs of exploits), vigorous narrative poems about real warriors written in the early Middle Ages. In these poems, he explains, "pride, foolhardiness, greed," and "shameless brutality" appear as "the authentic lineaments of early western knighthood."

Historical documents describing early knights confirm the picture given in poetry. In a sermon preached in 1095 outside the unfinished cathedral at Clermont, Pope Urban II leveled serious charges at the whole class of knights:

> You, girt about with the badge of knighthood, are arrogant with great pride; you rage against your brothers and cut each other in pieces. . . . You, the oppressors of children, plunderers of widows; you, guilty of homicide, of sacrilege, robbers of another's rights; you who await the pay of thieves for the shedding of Christian blood – as vultures smell fetid corpses, so do you sense battles from afar and rush to them eagerly.[5]

Urban had a purpose in denouncing the knights: he was hoping to redirect their violent impulses toward the liberation of Jerusalem from its Muslim rulers, a quest that became the First Crusade. But his description of knights as bloodthirsty destroyers was a sober reflection of reality. Shortly after embracing the cause of the Crusade, a titled German knight, Count Emich of Leiningen, massacred the Jewish communities of Mainz and several other cities, directing his wrath against all who were not Christians.[6] The knights who eventually reached Jerusalem left a shocking trail of slaughter and rapine behind them. When they took the Holy City in 1099, they slew Muslims and Jews indiscriminately. Even when fighting other Christians, as they did in the feudal wars of Europe, knights engaged in ruthless violence. Despite routine invocations of Christian values, early medieval history and literature provide ample evidence of "the prickly sense of honour," the "insistence on autonomy," and "the quick recourse to violence" that the medievalist Richard Kaeuper has identified as the distinguishing traits of actual knights.[7]

The values later associated with chivalry – courtesy, Christian piety, magnanimity to defeated enemies, chaste adoration of ladies, and appreciation for poetry – are difficult to detect in either the historical record or the early *chansons de geste*. These rough and ready narrative poems, typically constructed by grouping together long stanzas in which every line ends with the same rhyming sound, relate real events. The *Song of Antioch*, for example, describes a pivotal episode in the First Crusade. Christian armies on their way to

Jerusalem laid siege to the city of Antioch in October of 1097 and took it in June of 1098. Although the *Song* as we have it was written in about 1180, experts believe that its author worked from an earlier poem by an eyewitness. He describes the final battle for the city with a freshness that gives the impression of real experience:

> Down from the major castle descended Garsion,*
> he entered into battle and led 10,000 Turks;
> each one was holding fast a Turkish bow and arrows.
> There in the widest street, Garsion made his stand,
> just where the opposing French were making a strong fight;
> And to do well each Turk was taking special pains,
> Back to the head of one street our Frenchmen soon recoiled,
> the Turks on the towers above severely wounded some.[8]

The claim that there were ten thousand Turkish archers in the city is dubious, and other sources report that the city fell without much resistance once the walls were breached. Although he may be exaggerating the number of soldiers and the length of the fight, the poet vividly pictures the press and confusion of men in armor fighting in city streets. As the Frenchmen urge each other on, their voices ring with the pride of early knighthood:

> Then Godfrey of Boulogne** cried out a shrill command:
> "Barons, noble Christians, push yourselves forward there,
> because right now their force – too great – is breaking us."
> . . . .
> And when they saw the combat, each Frenchman burned with rage;
> they shouted, "Holy Sepulchre! Barons, it is clear,
> he never will have honor who does not do well here;
> let us award to each whatever he can win;
> much good will come to barons who slay these pagans now."[9]

The Holy Sepulchre in Jerusalem, supposedly the ultimate goal of the Crusade, appears here as a formulaic battle-cry, but the motives the poet emphasizes are hardly Christian. Appealing to the usual principles of shame culture, the Crusaders declare that the man who does not fight well on this day will never have honor. Mindful of booty,

---

* The Turkish ruler of Antioch, who was actually named Yaghi Siyan.
** The leader of the Frankish Crusaders.

they agree to award whatever he can win to every soldier. Although neither the poet nor the knights he praises could possibly have known Homer, the resemblances to the brutal world of the *Iliad* are striking.

The Song of Roland, best known of all the *chansons de geste*, was written at a much greater distance from the events it describes. The ambush on which the story is loosely based took place in 778, and the poem as we have it was not finished until about 1100, so the anonymous poet had more freedom to exercise his imagination than the author of the *Song of Antioch*. There are some obviously fictional features: King Charlemagne, in this poem, is said to be 200 years old, and the Basques who were Roland's historical foes have conveniently become Muslims. But the central plot displays again the prickly sense of honor and insistence on autonomy characteristic of real knights. Thanks to a kinsman's treachery, Roland is in command of the rearguard of Charlemagne's army, which is making its way back to France from Spain. When attacked by a large force of Saracens in a pass in the Pyrenees, he wants all the glory for himself and his small band of noble fighters. His friend Oliver, whose wisdom contrasts with Roland's headlong courage, repeatedly asks him to sound his horn, the signal that will summon Charlemagne and the main French force. But Roland delays too long and dies with all his comrades.

Roland's disastrous need to hoard all the glory for himself and a few companions closely resembles the pride of Achilles or Agamemnon. In a crucial exchange, he explicitly invokes shame as a reason for rejecting Oliver's sensible advice:

> "Roland, Companion, now sound the olifant,
> Charles will hear it, he will bring the army back,
> The King will come with all his barons to help us."
> Roland replies: "May it never please God
> that my kin should be shamed because of me,
> or that sweet France should fall into disgrace."[10]

Despite his nominal Christianity, Roland expresses emotions much like those of a warrior from an ancient shame culture. If he blows his horn to summon help, he fears that his family and his country will be dishonored. Yet Thomas Bailey Aldrich, who knew enough about *The Song of Roland* to name the last battle correctly, saw fit to invoke Roland as an analogue to Robert Gould Shaw, who did not fight from shame, greed, or personal pride, but because of his fervent opposition to slavery and his enlightened belief in the capacity of his troops. Though intended as high praise, the comparison to Roland dishonors the memory of Shaw.

When Aldrich compared Shaw to Roland, he was not thinking about the violent, shame-driven practices of early knights. He was drawing instead on the idealized version of chivalry developed by poets in later periods, in which noble, courteous knights do penance for personal failings, undertake arduous quests on behalf of wronged ladies, spare their defeated foes, and collectively advance the cause of Christendom. There is some faint historical basis for these ideals in the later Middle Ages. From the twelfth century forward, the rise of kings and courts helped soften the rapacious shame culture of early medieval knights, adding an emphasis on courtliness and courtship more reflective of a Christian guilt culture. Large ransoms induced some knights to take their defeated rivals as prisoners rather than killing them at once. An increased emphasis on love may even have encouraged some of them to behave with more delicacy.

Yet primary sources from the later Middle Ages still record many episodes of savage brutality. When his sappers successfully undermined the walls of Limoges in 1370, Edward, Prince of Wales, led a slaughter of civilians in which the death toll may have reached 3,000. The French poet Jean Froissart, whose prose *Chronicles* describe the Hundred Years' War, gives a chilling account of the massacre:

The prince, the duke of Lancaster, the earls of Cambridge and of Pembroke, Sir Guiscard d'Angle and the others, with their men, rushed into the town. You would then have seen pillagers, active to do mischief, running through the town, slaying men, women, and children, according to their orders. It was a most melancholy business; for all ranks, ages and sexes cast themselves on their knees before the prince, begging for mercy; but he was so inflamed with passion and revenge that he listened to none, but all were put to the sword, wherever they could be found.[11]

As this stark record suggests, the ideas and values that later poets have commonly invoked as chivalric owe very little to historical practice. They derive instead from three kinds of poetry that succeeded the *chansons de geste*: the lyric songs of the troubadours, the chivalric romances recounting the legends connected with King Arthur, and the elaborate chivalric epics of the Renaissance.

In an influential study of chivalry, the Oxford historian Maurice Keen has compactly described it as "an ethos in which martial, aristocratic and Christian elements were fused together."[12] A fourth element, which grows in importance as the cult of chivalry develops, is the notion of service to women, which turns heterosexual desire into a motive for warfare. Although the origins of chivalry are obscure, it is possible to sketch a general picture of how these four elements came together, a process in which poetry played a large part. The word *chivalry* comes from the French word for horse; like the simpler term *cavalry*, it initially referred to mounted soldiers. With the invention of the stirrup, probably during the eighth century, warriors on horseback became more stable in the saddle, more capable of handling heavy weapons while riding. Their armor also became heavier, more complete, and much more expensive. By the eleventh century, a single charge by a relatively small number of knights, holding their lances under their armpits and aiming their points at the front lines of the enemy, could decide a battle, so kings and dukes were eager to invest in knights. One effective method of giving knights the means to purchase horses and armor was to cede them pieces of land, and some knights became landholding aristocrats as a result of such gifts. When the mounted warrior, originally distinguished by his courage and physical strength, became the noble retainer of the king, capable of passing his property and titles on to his children, the link between knighthood and aristocracy was in place.

That link, however, was much stronger in poetry than in reality. Some medieval knights were simply mercenaries, whose noble masters supplied them with expensive weapons in the expectation that they would return their arms after battle. The process by which knights became nobles also differed considerably from region to region. By the thirteenth century, knights and nobles in France had become a single class, but in Germany, knights were technically serfs until the later Middle Ages, and actually had to seek permission from their masters to get married.[13]

In poetry, however, knights are invariably of noble birth. The twelfth-century French poet Chrétien de Troyes, whose rhyming chivalric romances are our earliest sources for the stories of King Arthur, routinely explains great exploits by pointing to noble blood.

His hero Perceval, raised by his mother in the forest, is a teenager when he first sees a knight. He instantly sets off to become a knight himself, ignoring his mother's attempts to dissuade him. She tells him that his father and uncles were slain in combat, but he still insists on seeking knighthood. Despite his comical naïveté, he shows remarkable skill, killing his first opponent with a wooden spear, then quickly learning the use of chain mail, spurs, lances, and swords. Instructed by kindly nobles, he learns to defend helpless women as quickly and precociously as he learns to handle weapons. Both his skill at arms and his virtuous behavior, Chrétien implies, stem from his gentle blood.

When Perceval appears at King Arthur's court, his demand for instant knighthood and his country manners betray his ignorance and expose him to rude comments from the grumpy Sir Kay. Although he has no idea of the young man's name or parentage, King Arthur intuits his nobility and rebukes Sir Kay:

> "Kay, you are very wrong to jeer.
> No gentleman should taunt and sneer.
> As for the young man, you may find,
> although he has a simple mind,
> he is of noble family still,
> and though he has been trained so ill
> by a rough master, yet he can
> become a valiant nobleman."[14]

Perceval, according to this accurate prophecy, can become not only a successful knight, defeating formidable foes, but a valiant *nobleman*. Arthur expresses not only confidence in his physical strength, but belief in his noble character.

Later poets so closely fused the concepts of gentility and knighthood that the phrase *a gentle knight* became a cliché. The description of the Knight in Geoffrey Chaucer's *Canterbury Tales* (c. 1386–1400) concludes by calling him "a verray, parfit, gentil knight."[15] The opening lines of Edmund Spenser's *The Faerie Queene* (1590–96) describe a "gentle Knight ... pricking on the plaine."[16] And the definitions of *gentle* in the *Oxford English Dictionary* include:

Well-born, belonging to a family of position; originally used synonymously with *noble*. ... Having the rank or status of 'gentleman', the distinguishing mark of which is the right to bear arms. ... Having the character appropriate to one of good birth; noble, generous, courteous.

The language of this dictionary entry records a number of curious and significant historical developments – not only in the meaning of the word but in the social expectations connected to the word. In the early Middle Ages, the *ability* to bear arms allowed some knights to become nobles. A few generations later, only those of "noble" or "gentle" birth had the *right* to bear arms. Men born into such families were supposed to exhibit "gentle" behavior, to be generous, courteous, and protective toward the weak, especially women. Eventually, the right to bear arms and the privileges that came with it turned into an *obligation*, still powerfully felt as late as World War I, in which titled aristocrats and university graduates on both sides died in disproportionate numbers.

In some modern poems invoking chivalric language, gentility functions as a substitute for military valor. Laurence Binyon's elegy for his friend George Calderon, published in 1917, is an extreme example. Calderon, a respected writer, scholar, and translator, was in his late forties when the Great War began, but he had a strong sense of obligation and enlisted in the British Army. Wounded in France, he recovered, returned to active service, and was killed at Gallipoli in 1915. Although these facts offered an elegist great opportunities for praising Calderon's courage under fire, Binyon chose instead to celebrate his noble character, avoiding direct references to battle. His poem begins with a list of capitalized chivalric virtues:

> Wisdom and Valour, Faith,
> Justice, – the lofty names
> Of virtue's quest and prize, –
> What is each but a cold wraith
> Until it lives in a man
> And looks thro' a man's eyes?[17]

The rhetorical question is an implicit promise that the poem will show how the lofty virtues named in its opening lines found life in Calderon's actions, but it takes Binyon three more stanzas to name the dead man:

> On Chivalry as I muse,
> The spirit so high and clear

> It cannot soil with aught
> It meets of foul misuse;
> It turns wherever burns
> The flame of a brave thought;
>
> And wheresoever the moan
> Of the helpless and betrayed
> Calls, from near or far,
> It replies as to its own
> Need, and is armed and goes
> Straight to its sure pole-star; –
>
> No legendary knight
> Renowned in an ancient cause
> I warm my thought upon.
> There comes to the mind's sight
> One whom I knew, whose hand
> Grasped mine: George Calderon.

In this abstract account, chivalry is a high and clear spirit – impervious to soil, burning with brave thoughts, and quick to defend the powerless. Binyon acknowledges that chivalry is armed, but he does so with the palest possible verb. He might have spoken of chivalry *wielding* arms or *taking up* arms, but his emphasis does not fall on the weapons knights use to defend the weak; it falls instead on their selflessness. Chivalry, according to Binyon, instinctively replies to the cries of others. There is a huge distance between this high-minded version of chivalry and the destructive selfishness of Roland or the acquisitive violence of the Crusaders in the *Song of Antioch*. Even Chrétien, whose fictional heroes exhibit their gentility by defending the weak and helpless, pointedly describes the speeding horses, splintered lances, and slashing swords they use to perform those noble acts.

Calderon had shown exemplary courage by volunteering to take part in the Great War, but Binyon postpones discussing his service to speak of the dead man's social graces:

> Him now as of old I see
> Carrying his head with an air
> Courteous and virile,
> With the charm of a nature free,
> Daring, resourceful, prompt,
> In his frank and witty smile.

Some of these adjectives – such as "virile," "daring," and "resourceful" – describe traits that might shine forth in combat, but Binyon locates all of them in Calderon's handsome appearance. Instead of picturing the dead man in uniform, he places him in a college setting and praises his skills in debate and foreign languages, then poses a rhetorical question:

> Was all that accomplishment,
> Wit, alertness, grace,
> But a kind of blithe disguise?

By asking this question, the poet reveals a fleeting unease about the process his poem enacts, the celebration of gentility as a substitute for martial courage. Perhaps the real Calderon *was* a soldier. Perhaps his social and literary skills masked his true nature, which only appeared in wartime. Binyon moves in that direction by celebrating Calderon's Spanish ancestry and representing that heritage as a gleaming weapon:

> Restless in curious thought
> And subtle exploring mind,
> He mixt his modern vein
> With a strain remotely brought
> From an older blood than ours,
> Proud loyalties of Spain.
>
> Was it the soul of a sword?
> For a bright sword leapt from sheath
> Upon that August day
> When war's full thunder stored
> Over Europe, suddenly crashed,
> And a choice upon each man lay.

This is as close as Binyon can come to praising his friend's courageous decision to volunteer. The image of the bright sword magically leaping from its sheath recalls similar episodes in chivalric romance, and for that very reason, deflects our attention from the real and deadly consequences of Calderon's brave choice. To the extent that the poem succeeds in casting Calderon as a chivalric hero, it fails in describing him as a modern hero. The men who fell at Gallipoli may have imagined themselves as modern-day Crusaders fighting the Turks, but they did not carry swords.

When Binyon finally gets to Calderon's death, his focus turns even more fuzzy and distant:

> In that long battle afar,
> Fruitless in all but fame,
> Athos and Ida saw
> Where sank his gallant star.

Gallipoli, a disastrous defeat, is called "Fruitless in all but fame" – as if the notoriety of the battle might balance its terrible results. Athos and Ida, the mountains of ancient Troy, observe Calderon's death as the sinking of a gallant star, but neither the poet nor the reader can look upon that death. By conflating feats of arms with nobility of character, the chivalric tradition licensed this sort of poetic and moral dishonesty.

In this case, the failure is puzzling because the poet who chose a chivalric mode for this poem was capable of a much tougher vision. Before writing this elegy, Binyon also volunteered, at the age of forty-six, to serve in France as a stretcher-bearer for the Red Cross. Among his many war poems, "Fetching the Wounded" records his experiences with unblinking honesty:

> Now stale odour of blood mingles with keen
> Pure smell of grass and dew. Now lantern-sheen
> Falls on brown faces opening patient eyes
> And lips of gentle answers, where each lies
> Supine upon his stretcher, black of beard
> Or with young cheeks; on caps and tunics smeared
> And stained, white bandages round foot or head
> Or arm, discoloured here and there with red.
>   . . . They fell
> In the trenched forest scarred with reeking shell.
> Now strange the sound comes round them in the night
> Of English voices. By the wavering light
> Quickly we have borne them, one by one, to the air,
> And sweating in the dark lift up with care,
> Tense-sinewed, each to his place.[18]

These lines provide abundantly the kinds of detail purged from the poem on Calderon. There is blood, not only seen but smelled; there are modern caps and tunics, bandages, trenches, shells, and even sweat. Perhaps it was easier for Binyon to confront these stark facts when lifting and praising anonymous French soldiers than when contemplating the death of an English friend whom he considered noble. But the myth of chivalry is complicit in his failure.

In other contexts, Binyon was able to use poetic memory to give weight to feelings of loss and sorrow. His poem "For the Fallen," written in the seventh week of the Great War, has been treasured since 1914 for its solemn and memorable music. Schoolchildren still memorize its finest stanza, which appears on many war memorials:

> They shall grow not old, as we that are left grow old:
> Age shall not weary them, nor the years condemn.
> At the going down of the sun and in the morning
> We will remember them.[19]

Poetic tradition lends power to these famous lines, as Binyon remembers a number of biblical passages evoking the going down of the sun, as well as Shakespeare's praise of Cleopatra: "Age cannot wither her, nor custom stale / Her infinite variety."[20] But in the elegy for Calderon, his memory of chivalric language, which he had practiced in poems written before the war, led him away from achieving either memorable verse or a moral vision worthy of Calderon's memory. Once he had decided to treat Calderon as a chivalric figure, Binyon was powerless to confront his death. Calderon's killer – probably a Turkish artilleryman – fired without knowing who his target was, and Calderon fell without knowing who had struck him down. Unable to describe his friend as a gallant knight defeated by a worthy foe, Binyon, like many other poets, fell back on the tradition equating knighthood with class.

Though Binyon must bear some responsibility for the failure of his elegy for Calderon, the history of chivalric poetry may help to explain why his attempt to write a chivalric elegy was doomed. With each successive phase of chivalric poetry, the distance between military reality and fictional combat increases. As the example from the *Song of Antioch* shows, the writers of the *chansons de geste* exaggerate freely, but still describe the actual weapons and tactics of war in their times. Especially in the *chansons* describing the Crusades, the poets depict large armies and casts of characters including knights, foot soldiers, muleteers, and camp followers. In the fictional chivalric romances of the twelfth and thirteenth centuries, the focus narrows to noble knights and ladies. The battles in Chrétien's poems, for example, are normally single combats. Two knights charge one another on horseback with lances, and if unhorsed, continue the fight on foot with swords. Larger forces, sometimes glimpsed in the background, melt away when their leaders suffer defeat.

Three centuries later, the writers of Renaissance chivalric epics combined plot material based on the *chansons de geste* and the Arthurian romances with amorous themes drawn from the troubadours and an epic grandeur derived from Virgil to create their elaborately literary works. These poems – including Ludovico Ariosto's *Orlando Furioso* (1516–32), Torquato Tasso's *Gerusalemme Liberata* (1576–93), and Edmund Spenser's *The Faerie Queene* (1590–96) – describe heavenly and satanic interventions, miracles and monsters, earthly loves and allegorical visions, yet they still treat war as essentially a series of single combats. Meanwhile, in the real world, the medieval system of knighthood had collapsed in the face of cannon, a faceless weapon that could kill many at once.

Recognizing that death by cannon fire was entirely unheroic, the writers of Renaissance chivalric epics refused to update the forms of combat in their poems.[21] At that point, chivalry became a completely closed system – nostalgic, imaginary, and disconnected from reality. Although monsters have a long and complex history, I suspect that the fire-breathing dragons of Renaissance epic are sometimes a way of representing the threat posed by cannon without actually depicting cannon. In *The Faerie Queene*, for example, the Redcrosse Knight encounters a dragon whose fiery breath hurts him more because of his armor:

> The scorching flame sore swinged all his face,
> And through his armour all his bodie seard,
> That he could not endure so cruell cace,
> But thought his armes to leave, and helmet to unlace.[22]

In this imagined encounter with a dragon, as in real battles involving artillery, the expensive metal armor that defines a man as a knight becomes a liability. Spenser cannot resist turning this disaster into wordplay:

> [Him] fyrie steele now burnt, that earst him arm'd,
> That erst him goodly arm'd, now most of all him harm'd.[23]

Unlike real knights struck down by cannon fire, however, Redcrosse falls backward into a conveniently located holy well, "Full of great vertues, and for med'cine good."

> For unto life the dead it could restore,
> And guilt of sinfull crimes cleane wash away,
> Those that with sicknesse were infected sore,
> It could recure, and aged long decay
> Renew, as one were borne that very day.[24]

As the holy water magically washes away not only sinful crimes and sickness, but also the third-degree burns of the knight seared in his armor, Christian allegory washes away the last vestiges of military realism from the chivalric epic.

Although he knew and drew upon all the Renaissance chivalric poets, especially Spenser, John Milton recognized the fraudulence of their enterprise. Insisting on the difference between his moral purposes and those of chivalric poets, Milton declared that he was

> Not sedulous by Nature to indite
> Wars, hitherto the only Argument
> Heroic deem'd, chief maistry to dissect
> With long and tedious havoc fabl'd Knights
> In Battles feign'd; the better fortitude
> Of Patience and Heroic Martyrdom
> Unsung.[25]

Published in 1667 as a mocking indictment of chivalric epic, these lines may serve as a prophetic critique of such later poems as Aldrich's ode for Shaw or Binyon's elegy for Calderon. By treating their subjects as fabled knights and following in the tradition of chivalric epic, Aldrich and Binyon left crucial aspects of their fortitude, patience, and martyrdom unsung.

In *Paradise Lost*, Milton seizes opportunities to dramatize his disdain for chivalric poetry by depicting exactly those aspects of war that his predecessors avoided. When the angel Raphael tells Adam about the War in Heaven, which pitted the rebellious angels led by Satan against the loyal angels led by the Son of God, he describes the satanic forces inventing gunpowder and cannon. As the loyal angels march forward in their knightly armor, they encounter "deep throated Engins ... disgorging foule / Thir devilish glut."

A hail of iron globes from the cannon reduces the loyal angels to an impersonal heap of tangled metal:

> Whom they hit, none on thir feet might stand,
> Though standing else as Rocks, but down they fell
> By thousands, Angel on Arch-Angel roll'd;
> The sooner for thir Arms; unarm'd they might
> Have easily as Spirits evaded swift
> By quick contraction or remove; but now
> Foul dissipation follow'd and forc'd rout.[26]

These lines satirically enact the threat to traditional ideas of heroism posed by gunpowder technology. Armor, which might have afforded protection against edged weapons, is now a useless encumbrance. Reduced to faceless thousands, the angels lose their heroic individuality, and the hierarchy collapses as angels and archangels roll together in the same humiliating heap. Milton, a radical opponent of monarchy and privilege, served as Latin Secretary to Oliver Cromwell and stoutly defended the beheading of Charles I. His attack on chivalry quite consciously includes an attack on the related notions of rank and privilege.

For a short time, the power of Milton's serious critique of "long and tedious havoc" and the abandonment of chivalric weapons and tactics on real battlefields discouraged poets from invoking the myth of chivalry. From the publication of *Paradise Lost* through the first half of the eighteenth century, most references to knights and chivalry were comic or satiric, and when poets celebrated military victories, they did so in more realistic terms. In *The Campaign* (1704), his poem in praise of the Duke of Marlborough's victories on the Continent, the journalist Joseph Addison is careful to describe actual infantry formations:

> Thick'ning their ranks, and wedg'd in firm array,
> The close compacted *Britons* win their way;
> In vain the cannon, their throng'd war defac'd
> With tracts of death, and laid the battel waste;
> Still pressing forward to the fight, they broke
> Through flames of sulphur, and a night of smoke,
> 'Till slaughter'd legions fill'd the trench below,
> And bore their fierce avengers to the foe.[27]

Despite the formal diction of Addison's prim couplets, he is accurately describing Marlborough's tactics. This passage is the earliest instance I have found of the ominous word *trench* in an English poem on war. In this case the trench was a part of the fortification of the Schellenberg, a fortress guarding access to the Danube near Donauworth in Bavaria. As the English pressed forward, dead bodies filled the trench, allowing those arriving from the rear to cross over and disable the cannon of the enemy. This victory cost Marlborough at least 6,000 men.

Addison clearly recognized that to write about war in this way was to break with the long tradition of chivalric poetry. At the end of the poem, he applauds his hero for needing no "spurious rays," no "borrow'd blaze" of bogus chivalric language – and thus congratulates himself for avoiding poetic fiction:

> *Marlbrô's* exploits appear divinely bright,
> And proudly shine in their own native light;
> Rais'd of themselves, their genuine charms they boast,
> And those who paint 'em truest praise 'em most.[28]

It could not last. In his popular ode for those killed resisting the last Stuart rebellion in 1746, "How sleep the brave," William Collins began the inevitable process by which chivalric myth returned to poetry:

> By Fairy Hands their Knell is rung,
> By Forms unseen their Dirge is sung;
> There *Honour* comes, a Pilgrim grey,
> To bless the Turf that wraps their Clay;
> And *Freedom* shall a-while repair,
> To dwell a weeping Hermit there![29]

Although Collins does not describe the dead as knights, the fairy hands, the dirge, the pilgrim, and the weeping hermit are all Spenserian details. It was a short step from this romanticized medieval coloring to the full-blown chivalric imagery of Sir Walter Scott's poem on Waterloo:

> Now, Island Empress, wave thy crest on high,
> And bid the banner of thy Patron flow,
> Gallant Saint George, the flower of Chivalry,
> For thou hast faced, like him, a dragon foe,

And rescued innocence from overthrow,
And trampled down, like him, tyrannic might,
And to the gazing world mayst proudly show
The chosen emblem of thy sainted Knight,
Who quell'd devouring pride, and vindicated right.[30]

Scott copies Spenser's stanza, with its tricky rhyme scheme and long final line, recovers all the clichés of chivalric diction, and describes Napoleon not as a modern general, but as a dragon. His enthusiastic use of chivalric material, not only in his poems but in his popular novel *Ivanhoe*, was a powerful force in bringing back the myth that Milton had tried so hard to kill. The consequences were not merely poetic, as Mark Twain argued when he blamed Scott for causing the American Civil War:

Then comes Sir Walter Scott with his enchantments, and . . . sets the world in love with dreams and phantoms; with . . . the sham grandeurs, sham gauds, and sham chivalries of a brainless and worthless long-vanished society. . . . It was Sir Walter that made every gentleman in the South a Major or a Colonel, or a General or a Judge, before the war; and it was he, also, that made these gentlemen value these bogus decorations. For it was he that created rank and caste down there, and also reverence for rank and caste, and pride and pleasure in them. . . . Sir Walter had so large a hand in making Southern character, as it existed before the war, that he is in great measure responsible for the war.[31]

Although Twain's rhetoric is comically exaggerated, his larger point is serious. In many periods and cultures, the assumed connection between chivalry and social class has had disastrous results. As machine guns and artillery mowed down vast numbers in the American Civil War, poets on both sides routinely invoked chivalric imagery. As imperial troops extended and solidified Britain's hold on one-fifth of the globe, Alfred, Lord Tennyson devoted fifteen years to composing *The Idylls of the King*, another retelling of Arthurian legend. And in an irony Twain might have appreciated, the constitution of the Ku Klux Klan, adopted in 1886, dedicated its members to "all that is chivalric in conduct."[32] The claiming of a chivalric heritage by racist murderers is a chilling example of the slow debasement of the ideal of gentle knighthood.

As the Great War began, governments recruiting working-class men relied heavily upon the imagery of chivalry, believing (correctly)

Figure 10. "Britain needs you at once."

that uneducated youths might be stirred to enlist by imagining themselves as noble, gentle, courteous knights in armor. In Britain, the legend depicting "Gallant Saint George, the flower of Chivalry" as a slayer of dragons duly appeared on recruiting posters. Scott's "Island Empress," waving her crest on high, served to remind patriotic citizens to purchase war bonds.

Like many poems deploying similar imagery, these illustrations offer ordinary soldiers and citizens a fictional nobility. The implication is that courage and patriotism have replaced rank and caste, so that any brave man may play the part of St. George. But when the war was over, the class system remained in place and even shaped the way

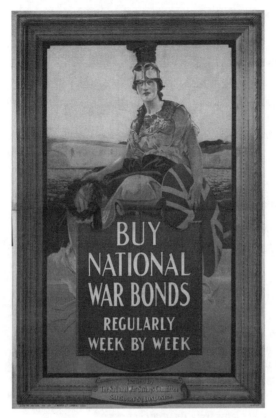

Figure 11. "Buy National War Bonds."

the dead were mourned. As we have seen, C. F. G. Masterman, a Liberal politician with no pretensions to aristocratic status, was nonetheless moved to pen a lament for "the flower of the British aristocracy, 'playing the game' to the last."[33]

As late as World War II, it was possible for a soldier-poet from the middle class to admire the courageous, disinterested stance of a comrade who was an aristocrat by birth. In a poem entitled "Aristocrats," the British tank commander Keith Douglas records the death of one such man, deftly deploying the traditional metaphors of the myth of chivalry:

> The noble horse with courage in his eye,
> clean in the bone, looks up at a shellburst:
> away fly the images of the shires
> but he puts the pipe back in his mouth.[34]

Fighting on horseback was the original marker of knightly nobility, so Douglas, with comic affection, turns his comrade into a noble centaur – part horse, part man – who absurdly displays his courage by smoking his pipe as shells fall nearby. One of them will strike him:

> Peter was unfortunately killed by an 88;
> it took his leg away, he died in the ambulance.
> I saw him crawling on the sand, he said
> It's most unfair, they've shot my foot off.

By describing his mortal wound as "most unfair," the dying man echoes the cherished notion that noblemen fight by fixed and generous rules, playing the game as if it were cricket or polo. Douglas recognizes the folly and obsolescence of such attitudes, but is man enough to admit being moved:

> How can I live among this gentle
> obsolescent breed of heroes, and not weep?
> Unicorns, almost,
> for they are fading into two legends
> in which their stupidity and chivalry
> are celebrated. Each, fool and hero, will be an immortal.
>
> These plains were their cricket pitch
> and in the mountains the tremendous drop fences
> brought down some of the runners. Here then
> under the stones and earth they dispose themselves,
> I think with their famous unconcern.
> It is not gunfire I hear, but a hunting horn.

The horn, of course, is Roland's, and the unicorn a medieval icon. By achieving a delicate, risky balance between the motifs of chivalry and the realities of the North African tank campaign, Douglas finds a solution to the problem Binyon could not solve. He sincerely praises the dead man's heroism and unconcern while honestly recognizing his outdated stance as a form of stupidity. Douglas's own death in the Normandy invasion, at the age of twenty-four, was a great loss for poetry.

Like the idea of nobility, Christian faith is a crucial component of the myth of chivalry, though there is no inherent reason why the two should be linked. The early centuries of Christianity witnessed a lively debate about whether Christians might be soldiers. In the second and third centuries, the influential Church fathers Tertullian and Origen argued strenuously for pacifism. But when the Emperor Constantine's army, carrying Christian symbols on their shields, won a battle against superior forces in 312, his victory looked like proof that a Christian might fight for his faith. St. Augustine (354–430) developed this view more fully in his influential theory of the "just war." After the fall of Rome, many churchmen retreated into monasticism, which was pacifist by nature. Although monasteries and churches were tempting targets for Muslim and Viking raiders, their inhabitants were neither equipped nor inclined to fight back.

The nominally Christian knights of the early Middle Ages had scant regard for the Church, as shown by a gruesome episode from *Raoul de Cambrai*, a *chanson de geste* written about 1180. Angered at an insult to two of his squires, Raoul (c. 900–944) burns a church and convent, killing a number of nuns in the process. When he returns to camp, he summons his cook:

> "Consider food; you'll do me a great boon:
> some roasted peacocks and good peppered swans,
> and lots of fat, rich venison as well,
> so even the least can sit and eat his fill.
> I would not wish for all a city's gold
> that these my barons should make fun of me."
> When the cook heard, he looked him in the eye
> and crossed himself thrice for this blasphemy.
> "In Holy Mary's name, what have you thought?
> You're scorning holy Christianity
> and your baptism and the Lord of Hosts.
> It's Lent, when everyone's supposed to fast –
> the Holy Friday of our Savior's passion
> when sinners should adore the Holy Cross.
> And we offenders in our erring ways
> have burned the nuns and torn the abbey down,
> we never will be reconciled to God
> unless his grace surpass our cruelty."
> When Raoul heard this, he looked at him and said,
> "Son of a whore, for what cause have you spoken?

And why have *they* opposed themselves to me?
Two of my squires they have insulted sorely,
so it's no wonder they must dearly pay;
however, I forgot that it was Lent."[35]

And he goes off grumpily to play chess.

Faced with the real-world versions of such attitudes, the Church first put forward a convention called the Peace of God, which was supposed to prevent armed attacks on clergymen, women, children, and peasants. In 958, Pope John XV proposed a more ambitious Truce of God, which prohibited warfare on Sunday. First put into practice in 1027, the Truce of God eventually extended from Wednesday evening to Monday morning, and included Advent, Lent, and saints' days, so that feudal lords theoretically had only 80 days a year in which to fight each other. Enforced by threats of excommunication, the Truce reduced knightly violence, though it was never a complete success.

Urban's sermon at Clermont in 1095 marks a crucial reversal on the part of the Church. Unable to control the knights, and in need of a military force to regain Jerusalem, the Church now sought to create "knights of Christ," to harness for its own cause the brutality it had been unable to suppress. Once the Church decided to use knights for its own purposes, it was quick to place its mark upon them. An illustration of Urban preaching at Clermont dramatizes the claiming of the sword for the cross. In his right hand, the Pope grasps an Eastern cross; with his left he blesses the sword of a kneeling knight.

As a crude device for a shameful and painful execution, the cross has little in common with the sword, an expensive weapon employed by privileged knights. But the superficial similarity between the shape of a hilted sword and the shape of a cross allowed both visual artists and poets to conflate Christianity with chivalry – not only in the chivalric period, but in much later times. In a striking poster designed to recruit men for the American Navy in 1917, for example, a modern ship is barely visible on the horizon, but the allegorical figure of Liberty brandishes a large sword, and the top frame truncates the blade, encouraging the viewer to see it as a cross.

In a British collection of *More Songs by the Fighting Men*, published in the same year, Collin Brooks sincerely invokes the belief that the sword reveals the cross:

Figure 12. Pope Urban II.

The spoken word holds true: the swords we wield
Upended show the Cross that, potent yet,
Shall prove each wound we suffer on the field
No sacrifice made vainly to abet
A senseless purpose. Wait but for the yield
Of all our toil and – God shall not forget.[36]

As an enlisted man, a sergeant in the Machine Gun Corps, Brooks could not even wear a ceremonial sword as part of a dress uniform. As

Figure 13. Kenyon Cox, "The sword is drawn, the Navy upholds it!"

a machine gunner, he used a terribly efficient, utterly unchivalric weapon. Yet despite ample experience of vain sacrifices for senseless purposes, he imagined wielding a sword and equated that sword with the cross. His poem is a poignant instance of the power added to the myth of chivalry by its Christian content.

For soldiers of the Great War, the link between the sword and the cross was sentimental, symbolic, and patriotic. The highest German military decoration, after all, was the Iron Cross. For medieval Crusaders, however, there was an explicit contractual relation between warfare and religion. After sewing large red crosses onto their tunics, crusading knights took a solemn vow, normally lasting two or three years, to liberate Jerusalem from the infidels. In return, the Church protected them from prosecution in secular courts, forgave them all their normal penances, assured them of salvation if they died during the quest, and awarded them ten percent of its own revenues to support the cost of arms and travel.

Before the Crusades, it was not uncommon for a secular knight to retire to a monastery and live out his last days in orders, hoping to atone for a life of violence. As Guibert de Nogent, the chronicler of the First Crusade, was quick to point out, the opportunity to become a Knight of Christ allowed such men to work out their salvation in armor:

In our own time, God has instituted a Holy War, so that the order of knights and the unstable multitude who used to engage in mutual slaughter in the manner of ancient paganism may find a new way of gaining salvation: so that now they may seek God's grace in their wonted habit, and in the discharge of their own office, and no longer need to be drawn to seek salvation by utterly renouncing the world in the profession of the monk.[37]

As a learned man, Guibert recognized the points of contact between the behavior of early knights and ancient pagans. As a practical man, he recognized the appeal of the new way of gaining salvation. Urban's sermon to the knights makes the same points in a more symbolic and theological mode, referring to the Church as a mother "who poured into your mouths the milk of divine wisdom" and picturing Christ as a general leading his troops toward sure salvation:

Under Jesus Christ, our Leader, may you struggle for your Jerusalem, in Christian battleline, . . . and may you deem it a beautiful thing to die for Christ in that city in which He died for us.[38]

When the Crusaders conquered Jerusalem in 1099, they engaged in wholesale killing and looting, slaughtering most of the inhabitants. Poets, however, piously rewrote that history to show Christian knights embracing the liberation of the city as a holy quest. Tasso's fanciful epic, *Gerusalemme Liberata*, written five hundred years after the events it relates, pictures the Crusaders arriving at the Holy City with "delight," "deep repentance," and "reverend fear and trembling":

> Scantly they durst their feeble eyes dispread
> Upon that town, where Christ was sold and bought,

Where for our sins he faultless, suffer'd pain,
There where he died, and where he liv'd again

Soft words, low speech, deep sobs, sweet sighs, salt tears,
Rose from their breasts, with joy and pleasure mixt;
For thus fares he the Lord aright that fears,
Fear on devotion, joy on faith is fixt.

Tasso goes on to describe the army approaching the city with naked feet, casting aside their colorful scarves, crests, and feathers to become penitent pilgrims rather than soldiers. He even imagines the secret speech by which each man confesses his sins:

Flower of goodness, root of lasting bliss
Thou well of life, whose streams were purple blood
That flowed here, to cleanse the foul amiss
Of sinful man, behold this brinish flood,
That from my melting heart distilled is;
Receive in gree* these tears, O Lord so good,
For never wretch with sin so overgone,
Had fitter time, or greater cause to moan.[39]

Even in this fictional account, however, penance and holy fear quickly give way to arms and warfare. A few stanzas later, those watching from the walls see "sun-bright shields" and "glist'ring helms" as the Christian army approaches. Although Tasso does not mention it, the knights have evidently reclaimed the battle garb they set aside to pray. No longer barefoot, their champion Tancred rides into battle fully armed, and the emotions of confession and devotion give way to the usual feelings of combat: "His heart with rage, his eyes with courage flame."

Thousands of lines later, the Christians win the final battle for Jerusalem and pursue their fleeing foes. Instead of the cleansing blood of Christ or the brinish flood of penitential tears, the poet now emphasizes the rivers of blood that flow from the defeated Muslim army. In place of the earlier vision of bright decorations piously cast aside in penance, he shows us a similar list of the enemy's arms defiled by blood:

* favor, grace.

> The camp was won, and all in blood doth steep,
> The blood in rivers stream'd from tent to tent;
> It soil'd, defil'd, defaced all the prey,
> Shields, helmets, armors, plumes and feathers gay.

In the next stanza, which abruptly concludes the poem, the victorious Godfrey, commander of the Christian army, enters the temple, still clothed in his battle gear, and gives thanks for victory:

> His bloody coat he put not off, but run
> To the high temple with his noble train,
> And there hung up his arms, and there he bows
> His knees, there pray'd, and there perform'd his vows.[40]

By entering the temple in his bloody coat, Godfrey strikingly fulfills Guibert's promise that the Crusaders could seek God's grace in battle clothing, while discharging their duties as soldiers.

Although it concludes a fanciful fiction, this perfunctory moment of piety dramatizes a truth: the Church was willing to bring arms and armed men inside its doors in order to gain control over knighthood. For centuries, there had been rites of initiation welcoming young men to the company of adult warriors. German tribes used a simple ceremony in which an older knight touched the initiate on the shoulder or neck with a sword, "dubbing" him a knight. In the hands of the Church, this pagan practice slowly turned into something like a sacrament. As regularized by a papal edict, the ceremony for the blessing of a new knight required confession, fasting, and a bath of purification. The new knight's sword was placed on the altar, and he took a vow of chivalry on his knees before being dubbed by an older knight serving as a kind of godfather. Even though newly consecrated knights often went forth to fight for territory in wholly secular wars, and even though knights who had taken the vow of chivalry participated in such horrific events as the massacre at Limoges, this ceremony forged a permanent link between knighthood and Christianity. It was a short step from blessing the unused sword of a new knight to allowing a victorious Crusader, still clad in his "bloody coat," to hang his reeking arms in the high temple.

By adapting a pagan rite of initiation, the Church deliberately sought to strengthen the connection between Christianity and chivalry, cross and sword. By adapting pagan myths, especially the story of the quest for the Holy Grail, Christian poets aided that process. Although the details remain obscure, the Grail story began as a pagan fertility myth. In Chrétien's *Perceval,* the oldest poetic version of this story that we have, the hero meets a crippled Fisher King who invites him to a mysterious castle where he witnesses a strange procession. A squire passes through the dining hall carrying a white lance, which appears to be bleeding; a maiden follows him carrying a golden, jewel-encrusted dish, which the poet calls a Grail. They enter another room, and Perceval fails to ask his host the meaning of what he has seen. When he wakes the next morning, everyone has disappeared and all the doors are locked. As he rides across the drawbridge, someone lifts it, so that his horse has to leap to safety. Later in his travels, he meets two different women who scold him for failing to ask questions about the meaning of the lance and the Grail. By asking the correct questions, they tell him, he could have healed the wounds of the Fisher King and restored fertility to his barren kingdom. Ashamed of his failure, Perceval vows to seek the Grail and undo his errors.

Although it originated in a world of magic spells and pagan rituals, the Grail legend was already becoming Christian in Chrétien's hands. In the hands of the imitators who wrote continuations of his unfinished romance, the story became a more obvious allegory. The bleeding lance resembles the lance that pierced Christ's side during the crucifixion, a relic the Crusaders thought they had reclaimed in Antioch. The Grail, as Perceval later learns, contains a single mass wafer, linking it with the chalice of the Last Supper. At least as important as these symbols of the Passion, however, is the theme of education. If Perceval had asked the right questions and learned their answers, he would have taken on the role of a dutiful child learning his catechism. His progress in learning about the Grail parallels his education as a Christian.

After five years pursuing his quest, Perceval encounters a group of barefoot penitents, but he is so unaware of religious convention that he appears before them mounted and in full armor on Good Friday. One of the penitents confronts him with this breach of propriety:

> "It is not good or righteous, then,
> but very wrong," he testified,
> "to bear arms on the day Christ died."
> Since Perceval had in no way

> considered time or hour or day,
> his heart was so dispirited,
> "What day is it today?" he said.
> "What day is it? You don't know then?
> It is Good Friday, when all men
> should hold the cross in reverence,
> weep for their sins in penitence."[41]

Unlike Raoul, Perceval regrets violating Lent. Embarrassed and weeping, he seeks out a holy hermit. Romance conventions allow frequent coincidences, and the hermit turns out to be Perceval's uncle. He gives his nephew the answers to his questions about the Grail and imposes a penance upon him that reveals much about how the Church hoped Christian knights would behave:

> I cajole,
> if you have pity on your soul,
> dear nephew, and you do repent,
> attend church, as a penitent,
> each morning, the first thing you do.
> . . . .
> Respect good women and good men;
> when priests are in your presence stand.
> It is a simple gesture, and
> God greatly loves this courtesy,
> because it shows humility.[42]

In the original pagan myth, the secret knowledge sought by the questing knight had the power to restore fertility to an emasculated king and his arid land. Here the secret knowledge comes accompanied by lessons on good manners: go to church every day; respect women; stand in the presence of priests. Like the emphasis on knighthood as nobility or the pretense that the Crusaders were really pilgrims, Christian quest myths suppress and displace the military vocation of the knight. The wandering, lonely knight on his quest for the Grail, patiently seeking knowledge and wisdom, humbly embracing courtesy and faith, is a figure quite unlike the prideful Roland or the ferocious Raoul. By allegorizing the quest as the Christian's education in proper behavior, later poets effectively censored the angry emotions and violent actions that defined historical knighthood.

Although the Crusaders were eager to recover relics, a quest for a holy object is a much less warlike pursuit than an expedition seeking to reclaim a holy city. Filtered through centuries of fanciful poetry, the myth of the Grail became increasingly abstract. The historical knights who answered Urban's call marched off to conquer a specific city, knowing they would have to slay thousands of infidels along the way. The fictional knights who sought the Grail sometimes had to defeat evil knights or monsters who blocked their way, but these battles were mere episodes in the larger search for the holy knowledge represented by a sacred relic. Eventually the questing figure no longer sought a specific object; he followed a beam of light. In Tennyson's "Merlin and the Gleam," for example, the dying magician urges a sailor to "follow the Gleam" to the ends of the world.

> O young Mariner,
> Down to the haven,
> Call your companions,
> Launch your vessel,
> And crowd your canvas,
> And, ere it vanishes
> Over the margin,
> After it, follow it,
> Follow The Gleam.

The rapid, breathless motion of the short lines brilliantly captures the urgency of the quest, but the gleam remains mysterious and intangible. As the poem develops, the gleam appears to represent both Merlin's magic, taught to him by a mighty wizard, and King Arthur's blameless heroism. As he follows the path of the gleam, Tennyson manages to link Christianity and chivalry without raising the specter of warfare. Merlin tells how the elusive light

> Led me at length
> To the city and palace
> Of Arthur the king;
> Touch'd at the golden
> Cross of the churches,
> Flash'd on the Tournament,
> Flicker'd and bicker'd
> From helmet to helmet,

> And last on the forehead
> Of Arthur the blameless
> Rested The Gleam.[43]

In place of real battle, this vision offers the mock-combat of a tournament. In place of a sword, it offers a helmet as an icon for knighthood. And when the gleam comes to rest on Arthur's forehead, it marks his ethical purity, not his feats in arms.

In this late Victorian fantasy, Tennyson nearly effaces the military aspects of chivalry. His imitators completed the process. In the Sunday Schools of my Southern childhood, we often sang a popular hymn I now realize was plagiarized from Tennyson. Set to a saccharine melody, "Follow the Gleam" invokes chivalric myth without so much as a syllable on warfare:

> To the knights in the days of old,
> Keeping watch on the mountain height,
> Came a vision of Holy Grail
> And a voice through the waiting night:
> Follow, follow, follow the gleam;
> Banners unfurled o'er all the world;
> Follow, follow, follow the gleam
> Of the chalice that is the Grail
>
> And we who would serve the King,
> And loyally Him obey,
> In the consecrate silence know
> That the challenge still holds today,
> Follow, follow, follow the gleam
> Standards of worth o'er all the earth;
> Follow, follow, follow the gleam
> Of the Light that shall bring the dawn.[44]

A few trappings of chivalry remain in this milktoast version. There are banners, a King, and a challenge. But there are no lances, no swords, no horses, and no battles – not even the tournaments and helmets with which Tennyson delicately suggests the origins of chivalry. The mysterious knowledge gained in the consecrated silence of prayer appears to be the need to uphold standards of worth. Written in 1915, this defanged and gelded version of the myth of the Grail won a prize competition at Bryn Mawr College in 1920. Although I doubt that the authors had read Chrétien de Troyes, their reduction of chivalry to high standards is the endpoint of a long process that begins when Perceval's uncle tells him to stand in the presence of priests.

Like nobility and Christianity, the cult of devotion to women served to weaken and distance the violent origins of chivalry. In the intricately rhymed songs of the troubadours, Provençal poets who began to write in the early twelfth century, knights are not only courageous warriors but devoted lovers. In some of these poems, male speakers celebrate their own vigorous sexuality. Guilhem de Peitieu, one of the earliest troubadours, tells how he spent eight days by the fireplace with the wives of two nobles, and counts the number of sexual acts that took place (one hundred and eighty-eight). Ironically, he gains this erotic opportunity by pretending to be mute – an odd pose for a poet. But he begins the poem by insisting that women are obligated to love knights:

> A woman commits a grave and mortal sin
> If she does not love a faithful knight,
> And if she loves a monk or a cleric,
> She acts improperly.[45]

To love a monk, encouraging him to break his vows of celibacy, is merely improper, but to refuse the advances of a knight is mortal sin. Peitieu's comic rhetoric expresses a claim made more seriously in other troubadour poems, the idea that knights had a special right to the love of fine ladies.

In bawdy poems like this one, the knightly poet urges his claim by celebrating his own sexual energies. In the more elevated lyrics that came to define the tradition, he declares chaste devotion to an unattainable lady, usually married, whom he serves without expecting a sexual reward. As Maurice Keen explains, this "ethic of service to a lady . . . was essentially comparable to the ethic of faithful service to a lord: indeed it borrowed not a little of its vocabulary from the legal vocabulary of lordship, fealty, and service."[46] Amorous servitude to a great lady, like military servitude to a count or a duke, was a way of claiming nobility. The knight's self-discipline, his resistance to acting out his desire for the lady, served as proof of his gentle birth. The tension created by his unconsummated desire provided poets with rich opportunities for expressing conflicting emotions.

As some modern medievalists have pointed out, there is no convincing evidence that such a code of "courtly love" ever existed in practice.[47] History records frequent rapes committed by knights, and one common theme in troubadour verse is the seduction of a peasant girl by an armed knight, whose weapons surely lend urgency to his sexual demands. Nonetheless, the celebration of chaste, high-minded, courtly love in poetry became a central component of the myth of chivalry. By imagining handsome knights performing heroic feats for the sole purpose of gaining a smile or a nod from a noble and virtuous lady, poets further obscured the true motives driving medieval warfare. This theme eventually became so dominant that Ariosto, early in the sixteenth century, began his *Orlando Furioso* by pointedly rewriting the Virgilian formula for epic subjects ("arms and the man") to foreground courtly love and give pride of place to the ladies:

> The ladies and the knights, the arms and loves,
> The courtesies, and exploits brave I sing.[48]

Thanks to the cult of the Virgin Mary, pure devotion to noble women also had connections to Christianity. Like the Virgin, these women might be asked to intercede on behalf of their devotees, shielding them from punishment and urging kings and nobles to reward them. As early as the thirteenth century, Wolfram von Eschenbach, the greatest German poet of the Middle Ages, gave one of his heroes an opportunity to link women and religion in a speech to his knights before a great battle. "There are two rewards that await us," declares Willehalm, "heaven and the recognition of noble women."[49] Like the imagined rewards of heaven, the recognition with which noble women will repay the violent efforts of the knights is abstract, metaphysical, otherworldly. As developed by later poets, however, the idea of fighting for the recognition of women became a potent motive for warfare. It redirected erotic desire toward chaste and virtuous ends, but nonetheless urged fighting men to seek those goals in battle.

The troubadours often apply military imagery to love. Numerous poems depict the lady as a castle under siege and the lover as a knight seeking entry, with obvious sexual meaning. In other cases, however, poets stress the weakness of the lover, as in this striking stanza by Giraut de Borneil, which reverses the usual implications of siege imagery:

> Lady, just as the feeble castle
> Is hard beset by strong lords,
> And the perrier breaks the towers,
> And the catapult and the mangonel,*
> And so fierce
> Is the warfare in every part
> that no help comes from cunning or art,
> And the grief and crying is loud and fierce
> From those inside, who have great fear,
> And it looks to you quite certain
> That they will cry for mercy,
> So I cry for your mercy humbly,
> Good lady, noble and virtuous![50]

Giraut compares himself not to the strong besiegers but to the terrified inhabitants of the besieged city, and cries for mercy from his lady, placing her in a position of power. In so doing, he abandons the usual knightly claims to strength, courage, and honor. Although written only a few decades after *The Song of Roland*, this poem represents a major shift. Roland, surrounded by Saracens, is too proud to summon aid, lest his descendants feel shame. Giraut, hard beset by his own desires, is willing to cry humbly for mercy. His feelings for the lady overcome his feelings of shame – so much so that he is willing to apply to himself a metaphor normally used for a woman.

In chivalric romances as in troubadour lyrics, love is more powerful than shame. In Chrétien's story of Lancelot, *The Knight of the Cart*, Sir Lancelot leaps into a cart driven by a dwarf, hoping to gain news of Queen Guinevere, whom he adores. Medieval criminals were ritually shamed by being driven through towns in carts, and no knight would wish to be seen in such a lowly conveyance. Yet Lancelot, who normally appears on a noble steed, is so eager to find the Queen that he mounts the cart. Chrétien stages the scene as a debate between Reason and Love:

> Reason, which holds aloof from Love
> bids him refrain from getting in,
> chastising him and warning him
> to do and undertake no thing

---

* Various kinds of siege weapons. The catapult used twisted ropes; the mangonel used a lever, and the perrier was a primitive cannon. All hurled stones at walls.

that might bring him reproach and shame.
. . . .
But Love, enclosed within his heart,
commands him and exhorts him so
that he must mount the cart at once.
Love wants it, so he jumps right in
with no more fear of feeling shame
for Love commands and wishes it.[51]

In Giraut's lyric and Chrétien's poetic narrative, knightly figures, overcome by their love of women, abandon shame and embrace weakness. The writers of Renaissance chivalric epics took the next logical step by creating female knights who could defeat male knights in combat. Allegorically, such figures represent the moral power of virtue and virginity imagined as martial skill. Their triumphs over male foes represent the defeat of shame, revenge, greed, and violence by politeness, civility, and restraint. When the female warrior, her identity masked by armor and helmet, fights with the man she loves, allegorical combat gains additional layers of meaning. In *The Faerie Queene*, for example, Britomart, who represents the virtue of chastity, fights a violent battle against her true love Arthegall, which ends only when a blow from his sword sheers off her visor:

> With that her angels face, unseene afore,
> Like to the ruddie morne appeard in sight,
> Deawed with silver drops, through sweating sore,
> But somewhat redder than beseem'd aright,
> Through toilsome heate and labour of her weary fight.

As Arthegall lifts his sword, he is paralyzed by her beauty:

> His powerless arme, benumbd with secret feare,
> From his revengefull purpose shronke abacke,
> And cruell sword out of his fingers slacke
> Fell downe to ground, as if the steele had sence,
> And felt some ruth, or sence his hand did lacke,
> Or both of them did thinke, obedience
> To do to so divine a beauties excellence.[52]

By suggesting that the steel of Arthegall's sword has more sense than his fleshly hand, Spenser ingeniously enforces the idea that respect for

female beauty is an integral feature of knighthood, represented here
by the weapon. Britomart's wise companion, Glauce, spells out this
idea more literally, explaining to Arthegall that he should feel no
shame at being conquered by a woman:

> For whylome they have conquerd sea and land,
> And heaven it selfe, that nought may them withstand:
> Ne henceforth be rebellious unto love,
> That is the crowne of knighthood, and the band
> Of noble minds derived from above,
> Which being knit with vertue, never will remove.[53]

The reference to women conquering sea and land is a compliment
to Queen Elizabeth, who had recently defeated the Spanish Armada,
but the larger assertion transcends the particular historical moment.
The true knight, according to Glauce, is submissive to love, recognizing such submission as the crown of knighthood and the band that
links all noble minds. In this version of chivalry, love, not conquest,
defines knighthood. By describing love as "derived from above" and
"knit with vertue," Spenser blurs the distinction between the love of
women and the love of God.

Although this feminized version of chivalry is quite unlike the
chivalry of medieval practice or thought, later poets embraced it as
historical. In 1787, the American poet Joel Barlow published *The
Vision of Columbus; A Poem in Nine Books*, in which he presented an
optimistic account of world history as a progress leading directly to
the infant American republic. Barlow's chronology is often shaky;
Chaucer and Galileo appear in adjacent lines, as if they were contemporaries. But he has enormous faith in the power of commerce
and education. His passage on chivalry describes it as aiding the cause
of Science.

> Bold chivalry romantic aids her cause;
> In honour's name the knight his falchion draws;
> Lured by the charms that grace the guardless fair,
> To suffering virtue bends his generous care,
> Thro' toil and pain in quest of glory roves,
> Braves death and danger for the maid he loves;
> While fired by gallantry, the generous art,
> Improves the manners and amends the heart.[54]

Although introduced between two contrasting adjectives – "Bold" and "romantic" – the chivalry described here tends strongly toward the romantic side. By the end of the passage, it has become a generous art that improves the manners.

Writers like Barlow, more attentive to poetry than to history, continue the process by which the real features of medieval knighthood – "the prickly sense of honour," the "insistence on autonomy," and "the quick recourse to violence" – turn into art, good manners, and self-improvement. Unlike his Renaissance predecessors, Barlow downplays all the other aspects of chivalric myth, including the insistence on nobility and the practice of Christian piety. As a progressive, democratic, secular poet of the Enlightenment, he is most comfortable with that aspect of mythic chivalry concerned with honoring women.

In Barlow's version of history, barbaric cultures are marked by their mistreatment of women:

> When pride and rapine held their vengeful sway,
> And praise pursued where conquest led the way,
> Fair nature's mildest grace, the female mind,
> By rough-brow'd power neglected and confined,
> Unheeded sigh'd, mid empire's rude alarms,
> Unknown its virtues and enslaved its charms.[55]

Thanks to the American Revolution, which Barlow believed would bring greater equality for the sexes, female virtues will improve society:

> A happier morn now brightens in the skies,
> Superior arts, in peaceful glory, rise;
> While softer virtues claim their guardian care,
> And crowns of laurel grace the rising fair.[56]

Because of "states and empires, policies and laws," men will still be needed "To stem the tide of power or guide the war," but women will be at least as important to the new nation:

> With equal honour, as with softer grace,
> The matron virtues guide the rising race.[57]

Barlow's optimism is remarkable, especially in light of the slow progress actually made by American women, who did not gain the right to vote until 1920. In imagining chivalry as a generous art promoting the softer virtues of women, and as a part of the process leading to liberal democracy, he detaches chivalry from its origins in warfare and attempts to harness its power in the service of a democratic vision entirely at odds with the aristocratic conservatism inherent in the tradition.

The female virtues Barlow celebrates in eighteenth-century America are domestic and matronly. But in Victorian Britain, the idea of chivalry became deeply entangled with the ideas of virginity and purity. In *The Idylls of the King*, Tennyson's King Arthur recalls the vows he imposed upon his knights:

> I made them lay their hands in mine and swear
> To reverence the King, as if he were
> Their conscience, and their conscience as their King,
> To break the heathen and uphold the Christ,
> To ride abroad redressing human wrongs,
> To speak no slander, no, nor listen to it,
> To honour his own word as if his God's,
> To lead sweet lives in purest chastity,
> To love one maiden only, cleave to her,
> And worship her by years of noble deeds,
> Until they won her; ...[58]

The sequence is striking. Loyalty to the king is a virtue praised in medieval poems as a way of earning noble status, but the turn by which each knight's conscience becomes a king recasts that medieval idea in the language of a modern guilt culture. "To break the heathen and uphold the Christ" is exactly what Pope Urban hoped his Crusaders would do, but "To ride abroad redressing human wrongs" is a notion of knightly vocation closer to literary romance than historical practice. Then come verbal virtues, avoiding slander and keeping one's word, as if the knights were Boy Scouts devoted to clean speech. Finally, and in a strongly climactic position, comes purest chastity.

The troubadours, at least in poetry, could imagine dedicating years of noble deeds to a woman already married to someone else, but Tennyson redirects this chaste affection toward one maiden only. Arthur goes on to argue that loving such a maiden will promote all the other virtues:

> ... for indeed I knew
> Of no more subtle master under heaven

Than is the maiden passion for a maid,
Not only to keep down the base in man,
But teach high thought, and amiable words
And courtliness, and the desire of fame,
And love of truth, and all that makes a man.[59]

Passion for a maid is a subtle master, disciplining base impulses and teaching courtly virtues. But Tennyson pointedly calls that love a *maiden* passion for a *maid*, pointing to the paradox. By installing male virginity as a central requirement of chivalry, he moves the idea of chivalry as far as possible from its origins in a brutal, rapacious, male world of horses and lances.

Thinking of such passages, Paul Fussell has described the Victorian celebration of chivalry as an attempt to deny the existence of the modern world.[60] His insight parallels my assertion that Tennyson's vision denies the existence of the medieval world. The myth of chivalry celebrates a time that never was. It falsifies the past in order to evade the present, taking refuge from both in a fantasy of genteel propriety. This process continues in our own times. In August of 2001, Terrence Moore, a high school principal described as "a former Marine and history professor," claimed in all seriousness that his students longed for a return to chivalry, imagined in terms not very different from Tennyson's:

Chivalry still retains a significant place in the modern memory. It might surprise us that a generation reared with a bare minimum of discipline should care about a rigorous system of morals and manners. In particular, we may wonder that young men and women would think much of an ethic that encouraged both sexual restraint and the service of men on behalf of women. Yet we must realize that today's youth are hardly enamored with either the sexual revolution or the feminists' struggles to create an androgynous world. Their deeper longings are for a world in which virtuous men both respect and protect modest women.[61]

Moore's bias is apparent in his sneering description of feminism as an attempt to create an androgynous world. But like Tasso, Spenser, Scott, and Tennyson before him, he has found in the artificial system of chivalry, a system created and sustained by poets, a means of pretending that the fundamental motive for military violence is the service of men on behalf of women.

I know of no finer refutation of this murderous falsehood than Virginia Woolf's, written on the eve of World War II and addressed to the men of her class, who were still often fond of chivalric gestures:

If you insist upon fighting to protect me, or "our" country, let it be understood, soberly and rationally between us, that you are fighting to gratify a sex instinct which I cannot share; to procure benefits which I have not shared and probably will not share; but not to gratify my instincts, or to protect myself or my country.[62]

Its capacity to prevent the sober and rational understanding of these truths is among the many sad results of the myth of chivalry.

CHAPTER 5

Comrades in arms

As Woolf doubtless understood, the urgency with which chivalric poets make the claim that men must fight for the sake of women betrays their desire to obscure or suppress the feelings that men in combat have for each other. In wars of all places and times – whether struggles of champions fighting for personal honor or campaigns of armies enforcing the will of nations – men have formed strong bonds. In the phalanx formation favored by ancient Greek hoplites, the hedgehog formation used by Swiss pikemen in the late Renaissance, and the British Square employed by Wellington's riflemen at Waterloo, men lined up with their shoulders touching. More recently, the crowded trenches of World War I, the foxholes of World War II, and the cramped tanks of the two Gulf wars again brought soldiers close enough to smell each other's sweat and stanch each other's blood.

It is easy to understand why men in these circumstances, acutely aware of each other's physical presence, might wish to protect a cherished comrade or avenge his death. But comradeship is no less important in forms of combat that isolate individual warriors. Homeric heroes, medieval knights, and jet fighter pilots exhibit the same affection for their fellows, the same grief when a comrade falls, and the same impulse for revenge. Sometimes more intense than emotions like honor and shame, always more personal than abstractions like empire and chivalry, the love of comrades is a powerful motive for warfare, and a rich and moving subject for poetry.

Until very recently, all combatants were male, so that the strong bonds between war comrades necessarily linked people of the same gender. Soldiers with the gift of poetry have often contrasted these bonds, formed under harrowing stress, with the conventional, heterosexual bonds of domestic life. Some, like Wilfred Owen, have celebrated the love of warriors as not only different from the love of women, but better:

> I have made fellowships –
>   Untold of happy lovers in old song.
>   For love is not the binding of fair lips
>   With the soft silk of eyes that look and long,
>
> By Joy, whose ribbon slips, –
>   But wound with war's hard wire whose stakes are strong;
>   Bound with the bandage of the arm that drips;
>   Knit in the webbing of the rifle-thong.[1]

Multiplying metaphors of binding, Owen chooses the tight and painful bonds of barbed wire, bandages, and rifle slings over the slippery silk ribbons of ordinary love. His word for the fellowships he cherishes – *untold* – has at least three meanings. In one sense it functions as an intensive: the joy of these fellowships is beyond recounting or measuring. In another sense it records suppression: the old songs preserved by the Western tradition, singing the praises of happy conventional lovers, have usually left these other loves untold. Most importantly, it admits to reticence: even those most deeply touched by the fellowships of combat, as Owen clearly was, have been cautious about describing them. Out of that very reticence, however, the greatest poets of wartime comradeship have made high art.

Poems expressing the love of men at war form a special category within the vast tradition of Western love poetry – a body of verse stretching back to the Greek lyricists Theocritus and Sappho, and including the Roman poets Ovid and Catullus, the medieval troubadours of Provence, and the Renaissance sonneteers of Italy and England. Although teachers and textbooks have not always acknowledged this fact, some important poems in every one of those periods and languages praise same-sex love, a feeling experienced and expressed in different ways in different cultures. Poets celebrating wartime comradeship have often drawn upon the broad tradition of earlier love poetry, and have sometimes drawn on particular poems of male affection. But poems on the love of warriors are palpably different from those describing the loves of shepherds or drinking-partners. Comrades in arms are always painfully aware of the mortal danger that circumscribes and intensifies their love. The constant threat of death makes the moments of warmth they try to preserve in verse fragile, temporary, and inexpressibly precious.

Understanding poems in praise of comradeship in arms from other times and other cultures requires some knowledge of how those cultures viewed same-sex relationships. The range is enormous, stretching from the official encouragement of homosexual bonds in the armies of some classical Greek city-states to the repression and suppression of homosexual feelings and acts in modern European and American armies.[2] Even when we gain historical knowledge, our responses inevitably reflect our own culture's guilty and conflicted views. In modern America, assertions of gay pride and political power collide with the stubborn vestiges of Victorian prudery. No one should be surprised that the question of military service has been at issue in that struggle, most recently in the debacle leading to the ludicrous policy described as "don't ask; don't tell." In this climate, modern readers confronting poems of wartime comradeship are probably too interested in speculating about whether the feelings described found physical expression – a question that can rarely be answered decisively, and that is often unimportant to the poem. In this chapter, I am less interested in sexual acts than in the poignancy of loving emotions surrounded and shaped by wartime conditions. For this kind of love, poetry has often been the best means of expression. Poets can convey, often in the same line or stanza, both the intensity of love between men at arms and the power of the forces that constrain the expression of that love: cultural taboos, personal embarrassment, and the looming presence of death.

Reticent about admitting love for a specific man, some poets have expressed their affection for youthful soldiers by celebrating the collective beauty of strong young men facing death and danger. A fine modern example is F. T. Prince's "Soldiers Bathing," in which an officer in World War II admires the naked freedom of his troops:

> The sea at evening moves across the sand.
> Under a reddening sky I watch the freedom of a band
> Of soldiers who belong to me. Stripped bare
> For bathing in the sea, they shout and run in the warm air;
> Their flesh worn by the trade of war, revives
> And my mind towards the meaning of it strives.

> All's pathos now. The body that was gross,
> Rank, ravenous, disgusting in the act or in repose,
> All fever, filth and sweat, its bestial strength
> And bestial decay, by pain and labour grows at length
> Fragile and luminous.[3]

When stripped for bathing, the young men escape the disgusting qualities their flesh has taken on in the trade of war, becoming momentarily "fragile and luminous." A crucial part of what makes them luminous is their vulnerability, heightened here by their nudity. Yet when Prince considers the nakedness of his soldiers, he invents a composite individual:

> 'Poor bare forked animal,'
> Conscious of his desires and needs and flesh that rise and fall,
> Stands in the soft air, tasting after toil
> The sweetness of his nakedness: letting the sea-waves coil
> Their frothy tongues about his feet, forgets
> His hatred of the war.

These lines could have been written in the plural easily enough. But when Prince thinks of someone conscious of desires *and flesh* that rise and fall, he imagines an individual, not a group. Surely part of what the officer-poet feels toward his men is similarly personal and private. The shift to the singular is poignant and revealing.

Drawing on his education, perhaps in an attempt to keep his desires at bay, the poet remembers two works of art featuring naked soldiers. The first is

> ... Michelangelo's cartoon
> Of soldiers bathing, breaking off before they were half done
> At some sortie of the enemy, an episode
> Of the Pisan wars with Florence. I remember how he showed
> Their muscular limbs that clamber from the water,
> And heads that turn across the shoulder, eager for the slaughter,
> Forgetful of their bodies that are bare,
> And hot to buckle on and use the weapons lying there.

For Prince to imagine his fragile Englishmen as muscular Florentines is another displacement. His soldiers face no immediate attack, though their respite from war is temporary. They do not move directly from the water to the slaughter, forgetting to dress in their

Figure 14. Aristotile da Sangallo, *The Battle of Cascina, or The Bathers* after
Michelangelo (1542).

haste. Instead, they quietly dry themselves and dress, and while
combing their hair, "forget the fear and shame of nakedness." The
contrast is striking: Michelangelo's soldiers, urgently buckling on
their weapons, forget that they are naked; Prince's soldiers, clothed
again in their ordinary uniforms, supposedly forget the fear and
shame of nakedness. But the poet has not previously mentioned
fear and shame, which are surely more active in his embarrassed,
conflicted mind than in those of his men.

The other artistic allusion is even more ominous:

> – And I think too of the theme another found
> When, shadowing men's bodies on a sinister red ground
> Another Florentine, Pollaiuolo,
> Painted a naked battle: warriors, straddled, hacked the foe,
> Dug their bare toes into the ground and slew
> The brother-naked man who lay between their feet and drew
> His lips back from his teeth in a grimace.

For Prince, the cruel violence of Pollaiuolo's vision suggests the
central violent action of Christ's passion:

> ... that rage, that bitterness, those blows,
> That hatred of the slain, what could they be

Figure 15. Antonio Pollaiuolo, *Battle of the Ten Naked Men* (1465).

> But indirectly or directly a commentary
> On the Crucifixion?

In these lines, Prince moves from the actual vision of his bathing soldiers through the remembered visions of the Renaissance artists to "the scene / Where Christ hangs murdered, stripped, upon the Cross." What the three quite different scenes have in common is the naked male body – fragile and luminous, ready for sacrifice, and (unavoidably for Prince) erotic.

Contemplating the larger meaning of his vision, Prince contends that "some great love is over all we do," which initially sounds like another religious reference, but eventually reveals itself as the great love for other men that the poet has struggled to avoid expressing directly:

> . . . some great love is over all we do,
> And that is what has driven us to this fury, for so few
> Can suffer all the terror of that love:
>
> . . . .
>
> Because to love is frightening we prefer
> The freedom of our crimes. Yet, as I drink the dusky air,

> I feel a strange delight that fills me full,
> Strange gratitude, as if evil itself were beautiful,
> And kiss the wound in thought, while in the west
> I watch a streak of red that might have issued from Christ's breast.

In these remarkable lines, the frightening love Prince feels for his men, though regarded as a crime or an evil by society, becomes delightful, fulfilling, and beautiful. As the poet kisses the wound in thought, the sunset itself begins to look like the savior's blood.

Throughout this book, I have been praising poets who can bring conflicting forces into equipoise. I have argued, for example, that Virgil's great strength lies in his ability to praise the achievements of the Roman Empire while showing the terrible cost of those achievements. Prince's poem balances two such conflicts. In the visual imagery of the poem, he contrasts the trade of war, the hacking and slaying that makes bodies bestial, with the fragile and luminous beauty displayed by the same bodies in a precious moment of freedom and cleansing. As the speaker's mind strives towards the meaning of the scene he has witnessed, he reluctantly reveals a parallel emotional conflict that deepens and complicates his poem. Prince's sense of propriety – his official responsibility for the soldiers who belong to him, his educated impulse to interpret their bodies in terms of art or religion – is in constant tension with the love he evidently feels for them, a love both great and frightening.

As the poet describes the potential violence of Michelangelo's image and the actual violence of Pollaiuolo's image, he explores the deep and powerful link between the violent and the erotic – a coupling felt in many poems on war, not merely in those about comradeship. Virgil hints at the same dark connection by invoking Erato, the muse of erotic poetry, to help him sing of violence and war. Carefully avoiding the specific, Prince deliberately frames his central conclusion in general terms:

> Because to love is frightening we prefer
> The freedom of our crimes.

These lines admit of many readings, but I think the central one is this: because we are afraid to acknowledge *loving other men*, an emotion forbidden by the ordinary rules of Prince's society, we prefer war, in which we are free to commit acts that would normally be

Figure 16. Walt Whitman (between 1855 and 1865).

crimes, including *killing other men*. As the poem begins, the poet
treats the nakedness of his soldiers as a form of freedom, a sensuous
release allowed to an all-male group as a respite from combat. Here at
the end, he links the potentially erotic freedom of nakedness to the
potentially criminal freedom of military violence. War, he implies,
licenses both. By enacting within the poem the difficulty of facing his
own erotic feelings, Prince transforms the tension between reticent
propriety and passionate desire into art, and links that personal
tension to the larger, more public tension between violence and love.

In the image of kissing the wound, Prince reveals his kinship with
another great poet of wartime comradeship, Walt Whitman, whose
poems display a similar alternation between the collective and the

personal, a similar tension between beauty and destruction. As the American Civil War began, Whitman admired the newly recruited regiments passing through Manhattan:

> (How good they look as they tramp down to the river, sweaty,
>   with their guns on their shoulders!
> How I love them! how I could hug them, with their brown faces
>   and their clothes and knapsacks cover'd with dust!)

Although he was writing eighty years before Prince, Whitman's enthusiasm for the sweaty soldiers is more forthright, less embarrassed than the later poet's. His expressions of affection, however, are not simply aesthetic ("How good they look!"), or even simply erotic ("How I could hug them!"). The love Whitman feels for these soldiers has everything to do with the carnage that lies in their future. As he celebrates "The unpent enthusiasm, the wild cheers of the crowd for their favorites," he notices the modern weaponry that will soon dismember men on both sides:

> The artillery, the silent cannons bright as gold, drawn along, rumble
>   lightly over the stones,
> (Silent cannons, soon to cease your silence,
> Soon unlimber'd to begin the red business.)[4]

Not many years later, Whitman had become all too familiar with the red business of war. In "The Dresser," he describes the ugly task of caring for combat casualties, which was his daily business as a medical orderly in Washington:

> Bearing the bandages, water and sponge,
> Straight and swift to my wounded I go,
> Where they lie on the ground after the battle brought in,
> Where their priceless blood reddens the grass the ground,
> Or to the rows of the hospital tent, or under the roofed hospital,
> To the long rows of cots up and down each side I return,
> To each and all one after another I draw near, not one do I miss,
> An attendant follows holding a tray, he carries a refuse pail,
> Soon to be filled with clotted rags and blood, emptied, and filled
>   again.[5]

Again, the description is collective. The priceless blood that reddens the grass comes from numerous bodies; the long row of cots fills a crowded ward; even the refuse pail will gather clotted rags and blood from many wounded. But the collective inevitably contains the particular. As Whitman describes himself moving through the ward "with hinged knees and steady hand," he encounters a particular soldier:

> One turns to me his appealing eyes – poor boy! I never knew you,
> Yet I think I could not refuse this moment to die for you, if that
>   would save you.

Less explicitly than Prince, but clearly enough, Whitman alludes to the atonement: he would die for this young soldier if the sacrifice would save him. But the love he feels for the wounded, though expressed here in Christian terms, is also personal and erotic. After a catalogue of specific cases – "The crushed head," "the stump of the arm," "the perforated shoulder," the "gnawing and putrid gangrene" – Whitman directly admits that even these disgusting, broken bodies still attract his desire:

> These and more I dress with impassive hand, (yet deep in my
> breast a fire, a burning flame.)
> . . . .
> The hurt and wounded I pacify with soothing hand,
> I sit by the restless all the dark night, some are so young,
> Some suffer so much, I recall the experience sweet and sad,
> (Many a soldier's loving arms about this neck have crossed and
>   rested,
> Many a soldier's kiss dwells on these bearded lips.)

As in some poems with civilian settings, Whitman takes the risk of acknowledging the burning flame of homoerotic love. Less cautious than Prince, he is also far less subtle. The parenthesis around the confession is a perfunctory gesture toward reticence, as if mere punctuation could restrain the intensity of feeling. The formula of the closing lines ("Many a soldier's loving arms . . . Many a soldier's kiss") turns the plural into the singular, as if mere grammar could solve the fundamental problem of the homoerotic poem in praise of a group of soldiers. When the poet's feelings become tender, protective, or explicitly erotic, the collective always collapses into the personal. And in the face of death, that collapse is inevitable.

War poets who begin where Whitman ends, with the love between two individuals, must also confront the close connection between male comradeship and death. In a poem to his fellow-officer and fellow-poet Siegfried Sassoon, written at the end of World War I,

Robert Graves captures that connection with striking honesty. The poem opens informally, with a gesture of disbelief and rough rejoicing at having survived:

> And have we done with War at last?
> Well, we've been lucky devils both,
> And there's no need of pledge or oath
> To bind our lovely friendship fast,
> By firmer stuff
> Close bound enough.[6]

The casualty rate for officers on the Western Front was appalling, and both Sassoon and Graves had been wounded, Graves badly enough to be reported dead. Under these circumstances, the mere fact of their joint survival makes their friendship more lovely, and constitutes a firmer bond than any formal pledge or oath.

The second stanza makes it clear that the bond goes beyond the simple fact of shared survival to specific shared memories of places in France where the misery and loud sound of combat shattered many a spring day:

> By wire and wood and stake we're bound,
> By Fricourt and by Festubert,
> By whipping rain, by the sun's glare,
> By all the misery and loud sound,
> By a Spring day,
> By Picard clay.

Graves probably borrowed the metaphor of a friendship bound by wire, wood, and stake, the strongest image in this stanza, from Wilfred Owen, who had written of fellowships "wound with war's hard wire whose stakes are strong." He later remembered that the news of Owen's death reached him at the same time as the news of the Armistice, sending him out to walk "alone along the dyke above the marshes . . . cursing and sobbing and thinking of the dead."[7]

In the powerful final stanza, already quoted in the Introduction (p. 3 above), the jaunty colloquialism of the first stanza and the geographic detail of the second give way to something far deeper:

> Show me the two so closely bound
> As we, by the wet bond of blood,

> By friendship blossoming from mud,
> By Death: we faced him, and we found
> Beauty in Death,
> In dead men, breath.

In its formal intensity and compression, this fine stanza mirrors the emotional intensity and compression of wartime friendships, formed quickly under heavy stress and often ended suddenly by death. The first gesture is a challenge: "Show me the two so closely bound / As we." It is a peculiarly male and even military gesture to praise a friendship by asserting its victory in an imagined competition, a contest with points awarded for the closest bonds. So the next line, where the force that binds the two men becomes a wet bond of blood, is a surprise, especially after the earlier reference to their being bound by wire and wood and stake. Borrowing that language from Owen, a comrade pointlessly machine-gunned in the last days of the war, may have triggered in Graves a deeper meditation on what the living owed the dead, and may also have enabled in him the bravery that saw the bond as wet and acknowledged the beauty in death.

The feelings Graves expresses here in a modern lyric mode are as old as warfare. Homer's Achilles, reluctantly agreeing to allow his friend Patroclus to enter the battle, expresses his love for Patroclus by wishing that everyone else on both sides were dead, leaving the two of them free to demolish Troy by themselves:

> "Oh would to god – Father Zeus, Athena and lord Apollo –
> not one of all these Trojans could flee his death, not one,
> no Argive either, but we could stride from the slaughter
> so we could bring Troy's hallowed crown of towers
> toppling down around us – you and I alone!"[8]

Achilles' wish is murderous, genocidal, extreme. Yet his heartless prayer for thousands of deaths is the only way he has to express his intense feelings for Patroclus and his desire for a moment when they might be left alone. By wishing that he and Patroclus could be the sole survivors on both sides, claiming all the glory of victory for themselves, Achilles shows just how much he cherishes his friend.

Achilles fondly imagines himself and Patroclus, like Graves and Sassoon, finding "Beauty in Death, / In dead men, breath." In actual war, however, surviving unscathed with a beloved comrade is a wish that often goes unfulfilled. Despite Achilles' fantasy of a shared private victory, Patroclus is fated to die in the armor of Achilles, trying to conquer Troy by himself. The terrible revenge Achilles then takes on Hector sets in motion a chain of events that leads to his own death. Many narrative poems of comradeship follow this tragic pattern, with the bereaved partner channeling his grief into suicidal violence. One of the striking features of such poems is the way that the surviving partner takes on the identity of the dead partner. Even before the second man dies, the two have become one. In the *Iliad*, this process begins when Patroclus dresses himself in Achilles' armor and ends when his ghost, appearing to Achilles in a dream, asks that their bones be put into the same two-handled urn, a burial custom normally reserved for married couples.

When the news of his comrade's death comes to Achilles, Homer writes the scene as if it were the death of Achilles himself. First comes physical action, as Achilles enacts a version of self-burial:

> A black cloud of grief came shrouding over Achilles.
> Both hands clawing the ground for soot and filth,
> he poured it over his head, fouled his handsome face
> and black ashes settled onto his fresh clean war-shirt.
> Overpowered in all his power, sprawled in the dust,
> Achilles lay there, fallen . . .[9]

Two of the formulas from which Homer constructs these lines – "Overpowered in all his power" and "sprawled in the dust" – occur repeatedly in the *Iliad*, but in every other instance they refer to a dead man. By using those phrases to depict Achilles' grief, Homer is telling us that he is already doomed.

Two groups of women join the mourning. First the captive women from the tents of Achilles gather around him, beating their breasts with their fists. It is entirely natural that these women, who have served both Achilles and Patroclus, should mourn the loss of Patroclus, just as the Trojan women will later mourn for Hector. But Homer doubles the impact by adding a second circle of immortal women. Achilles' mother Thetis, deep in the sea, hears his terrible, wrenching cry, and cries out in turn, summoning the Nereids, her attendant sea-nymphs. Homer devotes a dozen lines to the colorful names of the Nereids, which include Greek equivalents of "Glory" and "Healer of Men" and "one who rescues kings." In oral poetry, such an expansive, cataloguing gesture marks a moment as especially important, but the Nereids are not gathering to mourn for Patroclus. Instructed by Thetis, they are already weeping for Achilles:

> The silver cave was shimmering full of sea-nymphs,
> all in one mounting chorus beating their breasts
> as Thetis launched the dirge: "Hear me, sisters,
> . . . .
> Yes, I gave birth to a flawless, mighty son . . .
> he splendor of heroes, and he shot up like a young branch,
> like a fine tree I reared him – the orchard's crowning glory –
> but only to send him off in the beaked ships to Troy
> to battle Trojans! Never again will I embrace him
> striding home through the doors of Peleus' house."[10]

Thetis brings the Nereids across the sea, where they join the mortal women, "clustered closely round the great runner Achilles." Surrounded by two female circles – one mortal, one immortal – the hero vows revenge:

> "My spirit rebels – I've lost the will to live,
> to take my stand in the world of men – unless,
> before all else, Hector is battered down by my spear
> and gasps away his life, the blood-price for Patroclus,
> Menoetius' gallant son he's killed and stripped!"[11]

When Thetis reminds him that his own death will follow hard upon Hector's, Achilles embraces his fate:

> "Then let me die at once"–
> Achilles burst out, despairing – "since it was not my fate
> to save my dearest comrade from his death! Look,
> a world away from his fatherland he's perished,
> lacking me, my fighting strength, to defend him."[12]

With a fury redoubled by grief, he goes on to slaughter scores of Trojans, making the river Simois run red with blood and fighting his way to the city walls, where he avenges Patroclus by killing Hector – all in the certain knowledge that his own doom is sealed. Just as Homer does not need to tell the story of the fall of Troy, which he compresses into a simile at the moment of Hector's death, so he does not need to tell the story of Achilles' death, which he has already told by proxy in the death of Patroclus.

Although his taking up arms again requires Achilles to set aside his anger at Agamemnon, he is really trading one kind of anger for another. His original anger at Agamemnon led him to withdraw from battle and take satisfaction in Trojan gains, but now he remembers promising to bring Patroclus home safe to his father and berates himself for failing to keep that promise. Describing himself as "a useless, dead weight," he at last abandons his anger at Agamemnon and directs his rage at Hector, "who destroyed the dearest life I know." Grief for his comrade accomplishes what gifts and embassies could not, and as he goes forth to avenge Patroclus, Achilles appears to embrace his own death: "I'll meet it freely," he declares, "whenever Zeus and the other deathless gods would like to bring it on!"[13] Because Hector, who has slain Patroclus, is fighting in armor that once belonged to Achilles, we might even envision Achilles as symbolically slaying himself when he kills Hector.

Despite huge cultural differences, the close friendship at the heart of the *Song of Roland* offers an intriguing parallel. By insisting on fighting off a much larger force with his friend Oliver and a few others, Roland enacts something like Achilles' dream of being left alone with Patroclus to claim all the glory. When Roland finally sounds his horn, Oliver upbraids him for waiting too long, with the result that few in their party are left alive, and those few certain to die. He dramatizes his anger by promising to withhold from his friend the favors of his sister, to whom Roland is engaged:

> Oliver said: "Now by this beard of mine,
> If I can see my noble sister, Aude,
> once more, you will never lie in her arms."[14]

This threat is surely Oliver's way of expressing the damage done to his own love for Roland by the hero's foolhardy need to monopolize the glory. But the bond between the two men does not break, despite Oliver's justified anger. Now fighting against impossible odds, Oliver is run through from behind by an enemy's spear. He uses his waning strength to kill his assailant and as many more as he can while making his way to Roland for a last farewell. When Roland sees Oliver's pale, drained face, and his blood spattering on the earth, he swoons on his horse. His emotional response to the loss of his comrade mirrors his comrade's physical fainting from loss of blood.

By now, Oliver is so far gone that he feebly attacks Roland, mistaking him for an enemy:

> He has lost so much blood, his eyes are darkened –
> he cannot see, near or far, well enough
> to recognize a friend or enemy:
> and when he came upon his companion,
> he struck his helm, adorned with gems in gold,
> cut down straight through, from the point to the nasal,*
> but never harmed him, he never touched his head.
> Under this blow, Count Roland looked at him;
> and gently, softly now, he asks of him:
> "Lord, Companion, do you mean to do this?
> It is Roland who always loved you greatly.
> You never declared that we were enemies."
> Said Oliver: "Now I hear it is you –
> I don't see you, may the Lord God see you.
> Was it you I struck? Forgive me then."
> Roland replies: "I am not harmed, not harmed,
> I forgive you, Friend, here and before God."
>
> And with that word, each bowed to the other
> And this is the love, lords, in which they parted.[15]

As in the case of Patroclus and Achilles, the death of the beloved companion guarantees the death of the hero. The medieval poet dramatizes that truth by having Oliver physically attack Roland. Although the blow is ineffective and the pardon touching, there is a deep sense in which the blow Oliver strikes represents the reproach Roland knows he deserves from himself. As his own death approaches, he makes his way back through the mountains of dead bodies and carries the corpse of Oliver to the side of his ally Archbishop Turpin, who has also received his death-wound, so that the holy man may give Oliver a final blessing.

The *Iliad* and the *Song of Roland* are separated by something like 1800 years, and the cultures that produced them were very different in religion, politics, and military tactics. The deep similarities in the way

---

* The nose-piece of the helmet.

these epics dramatize comradeship are therefore all the more striking. By encircling Achilles as he weeps for Patroclus, mortal and immortal women amplify his grief. By threatening to deny Roland his sister's embraces, Oliver dramatizes his disappointment at his friend. In both cases, women express by proxy those untold emotions that men cannot directly or fully acknowledge. Furious at his failure to protect Patroclus, Achilles attacks himself in the figure of Hector, the immediate cause of Patroclus' death, who is conveniently wearing armor that once belonged to Achilles. Swooning from loss of blood, Oliver mistakenly attacks the man he most loves, but that attack makes possible their final reconciliation. In both cases, these older epic poems present in narrative form the link between the erotic and the violent that Prince, Whitman, and Graves explore more lyrically, personally, and psychologically.

In the first throes of his grief, Achilles calls Patroclus "the man I loved beyond all others, loved as my own life." The events that follow do nothing to lessen the intensity of his grief. Even after slaying Hector, even after presiding over splendid funeral games in honor of Patroclus, even after staging an elaborate cremation including the ritual killing of twelve young Trojans, even after days and days of dishonoring Hector's corpse, Achilles still cannot sleep:

> ... he turned and twisted, side to side,
> he longed for Patroclus' manhood, his gallant heart –
> What rough campaigns they'd fought to an end together,
> what hardships they had suffered, cleaving their way
> through wars of men and pounding waves at sea.
> The memories flooded over him, live tears flowing,
> and now he'd lie on his side, now flat on his back,
> now facedown again.[16]

Although the love Achilles feels for Patroclus is evidently intense, Homer gives no sign that this love has a sexual dimension. As he longs for Patroclus, Achilles remembers campaigns, hardships, and pounding waves, not moments of physical intimacy. Later Greeks, however, living in societies that accepted and encouraged homosexual relations between adult males and adolescent boys, imposed their own expectations on Homer's heroes. In fragments surviving from a lost play by Aeschylus, Achilles speaks of kisses and alludes to sexual intimacies with Patroclus.[17] For those who now imagined the love of these ancient heroes as fleshly passion, Achilles' drive to avenge his comrade's death took on additional intensity. To the grief, shame, and anger dramatized by Homer, this later reading added an erotic dimension, with feelings of sexual frustration channeled into suicidal revenge.

Conscious of the power of such affection in warfare, some city-states in classical Greece encouraged homosexual relations in their armies. The Sacred Band of Thebes, the most striking example, was a force made up of 150 homosexual couples, each consisting of an older man and a younger man; its success allowed Thebes to dominate its region for forty years. At the battle of Khaironeia in 338 BC, the forces of Philip of Macedon, father of Alexander the Great, destroyed the Sacred Band. All of the soldier-lovers died together; there were no survivors. Perhaps because no poet celebrated their deaths, the story of the Sacred Band did not pass into the mainstream of Western literature on war. All of its key elements, however, appear in Virgil's poignant account of Nisus and Euryalus, a "fortunate pair" of Trojan warriors, one much older than the other, who die together in battle. Although sometimes described as a mere friendship, their relationship clearly follows the Greek model of love between an adult and an adolescent. If Virgil's language about Nisus and Euryalus is not as overtly sexual as his language in the explicitly homoerotic *Second Eclogue*, where the shepherd Corydon *burns* for the beautiful Alexis,[18] he gives sufficient indications that the love these comrades feel for each other is deep and complete. Yet despite its homoerotic nature, the story of Nisus and Euryalus has long been a favorite episode in the *Aeneid*, invoked in hundreds of later poems.

Nisus and Euryalus make their first appearance as runners in a footrace, one event in the funeral games Aeneas holds in honor of his father Anchises. Euryalus is "marked out by his blooming form and youth; Nisus, by his pious love for the boy."[19] Two words in that short description, however, echo a phrase used for Aeneas himself at the very beginning of the epic, where he is called "a man marked out by piety." By quietly applying to the soldier-lovers words already used for his hero, Virgil is endorsing their relationship as not only acceptable but honorable, dignified, and connected to central Roman values.

The footrace is a comic episode, but it has both erotic and violent overtones. Nisus is well ahead, with a runner named Salius in second place, and Euryalus in third, but with the finish line in sight, he slips on the blood and dung left on the grass by some sacrificed cattle. Though disappointed, he remembers Euryalus, and manages to trip Salius so that his loved one can win. Salius complains loudly, but the audience favors Euryalus, whose decorous tears and beautiful body, stripped bare for the race, make him an object of sympathy. Aeneas judiciously resolves the quarrel by awarding prizes to everyone.

Like any pratfall into a dungheap, Nisus's accident is funny at a basic, childish level. When requesting a prize for himself, he garners a laugh by displaying his soiled face. But Virgil, who based this episode on a similar race in the *Iliad*, made a significant alteration in adding the blood. Not only filthy but bloody, Nisus is now marked for death. In addition to the generally dark symbolism of the blood, there is a specific echo of an earlier scene recounted in Aeneas' narrative of the fall of Troy. In the fire and confusion of Troy's last night, Pyrrhus, a sadistic son of Achilles, breaks into the palace and kills one of King Priam's youngest sons before the very eyes of his parents. Although Priam protests and hurls a futile spear at him, Pyrrhus brutally slaughters the trembling old man: "he drags him to the altar, sliding on the flowing blood of his son."[20] Priam, sliding to the altar on the blood of his son, is a grisly sacrifice. Nisus, sliding into the dungheap on the blood of the oxen, is a comic sacrifice, but the comedy is ominous.

His fall is temporary. Virgil even says that he *rises* from his fallen position to trip his rival and assure his comrade's victory. But the next time one of the lovers falls, the loss will be permanent. In the night-raid undertaken by the loving pair during the war in Italy, the improvised teamwork that works so well in the footrace breaks down, leaving both men dead. As this fatal episode begins, Italian forces under Turnus have laid siege to the Trojan camp. Aeneas is away gathering allies, so the Trojans are confined within their stockade. The elders ask for a messenger to get word to Aeneas, and Nisus decides to volunteer, hoping to slaughter some enemy soldiers while passing through their camp. As he presents his plan to Euryalus, Nisus speaks of his longing for glory:

"Do the gods implant this ardor in our minds,
Euryalus, or does each man's dire desire
become a god for him? My mind has urged me
a long time now to undertake a fight
or something else as great, and cannot rest
content with placid quiet."[21]

He points to the besieging forces, "dissolved in sleep and wine," and
proposes to undertake the mission on one condition:

... if they will give to you what I demand
(since fame for the action is enough for me).[22]

Euryalus refuses to be left behind and insists on joining the
mission. He is also willing to die for the sake of honor:

Here, here is a spirit scornful of the light,
who believes the honor you seek is well worth a life.[23]

The Latin word *honor,* which we have taken into English, occurs forty-
five times in the *Aeneid.* Twenty of those passages refer to the gods,
who demand, often petulantly, that mortals pay them honor through
sacrifice. In passages involving mortals, *honor* most often means
respect, as when Aeneas inaugurates the funeral games in honor of
his father Anchises. In only a few passages does *honor* resemble Greek
timê, and this, significantly, is one of them. Where we might have
expected a simple appeal to comradeship and love, Virgil gives us glory
and honor, with the implication that Nisus and Euryalus, like the
couples in the Sacred Band, represent the highest form of honor. But
he also acknowledges that a man's desire, whether for glorious fame or
erotic pleasure, can become a god, demanding obedience.

As Virgil shows his warrior-lovers volunteering for the mission, he
deliberately imitates the old gift code of the *Iliad.* Aeneas' son
Ascanius, left in charge during his father's absence, weeps for joy at
their courage and promises rich rewards: silver bowls, tripods, male
and female slaves. Euryalus reminds Ascanius that his aged mother
remains in the Trojan camp and secures a promise that she will
receive his share of the prizes if the mission fails. Like the earlier
dialogue on honor, these displays of lavish gift-giving and filial
devotion serve to connect Nisus and Euryalus to the most ancient
and respected traditions of Trojan and Roman piety. But again there

are troubling elements: Euryalus' bargaining on behalf of his mother reveals a keen interest in booty that will soon have disastrous results.

At first, the mission goes well. In the Rutulian camp, Nisus slaughters ten men, including a king, and Euryalus kills another four. Although these triumphs over sleeping victims are hardly heroic, the exultant companions seize rich spoils from their victims. One gleaming helmet happens to fit Euryalus, who proudly puts it on. But as they seek to escape, the moonlight reflected from that helmet catches the attention of a cavalry troop just arriving from Latium. Nisus avoids being captured by moving through the dark woods, but Euryalus is not so lucky. When Nisus turns back in search of his loved one, he sees the boy in the hands of a multitude. Realizing that he will now have to watch the death of his loved one, he tries to imagine his own violent death, now certain, as a thing of beauty:

> What should he do? By what force or what arms
> dares he rescue the youth? Or should he fling
> his own self, dying, into the midst of swords
> and hasten on a beautiful death by wounds?[24]

Nisus starts by striking from afar, and kills two men with spear-casts from his place of concealment. Then the Latin commander, Volcens, decides that Euryalus "can pay the fines of both men with warm blood," and Nisus reveals himself, begging to be made the sole victim:

> "Me, me, here I am who did it, on me turn your steel
> Rutulians! Mine was the whole fraud, and he has dared nothing,
> he couldn't; witness this sky and these all-seeing stars
> he did nothing more than delight his unfortunate friend."[25]

The plea, of course, is in vain. Euryalus falls "like a purple flower cut off by a plow" and Nisus, ramming his sword into the mouth of Volcens, "throws himself, mangled, onto his lifeless friend, at peace at last in death."[26]

No Trojan is present to mourn for the lovers, so Virgil himself steps forward, in lines that have been treasured now for twenty centuries:

> Oh fortunate pair! If my songs hold any power,
> no day will blot you from the remembrance of ages,

so long as the house of Aeneas dwells beside
the enduring rock of the Capitol and so long
as a Roman father holds imperial sway.[27]

There is no comparable moment of praise anywhere in the poem. By speaking directly to the fictional lovers, and by linking their deaths to the endurance of the Empire under its "Roman father" (a name for the emperor Augustus), Virgil was placing the love of comrades at the honored center of Roman life. He was even upstaging his hero, whose friendship with his own faithful comrade Achates remains inert and unfocused, and whose relations with women remain unfulfilled. Aeneas' first wife Creüsa vanishes when Troy falls; his great love Dido commits suicide when he abandons her; and his future wife Lavinia is only a promise as the poem ends. But Nisus and Euryalus, locked in the bloody embrace of death, gain a glory intensified by their love.

Virgil's first Roman readers were far less squeamish about same-sex love than readers in many later periods. Horace and Catullus, like Virgil, wrote poems expressing homosexual desire. Surviving Roman fictions in prose – the *Satyricon* of Petronius and the *Golden Ass* of Apuleius – also have homosexual content. But Virgil's discreet caution in telling the story of Nisus and Euryalus suggests his awareness that not all his readers were ready to accept a sympathetic account of a pair of warrior-lovers. When the historian Suetonius suggested that Julius Caesar himself had had homosexual affairs, he did so with a sneering satirical edge.[28] By surrounding his fortunate pair with the imagery of Trojan piety and Roman power, I believe Virgil was taking pains to protect, elevate, and dignify the love of men engaged in warfare, to mark such love as especially high, pure, and noble.

The afterlife of this part of the poem confirms his success. In many different periods, the martial heroism of this episode appears to have made it acceptable to cultures that strongly criticized other signs of same-sex affection. Let me offer snapshots from four different centuries. In the twelfth century, as Europe began to emerge from the long night of ignorance, an anonymous French poet recast the *Aeneid* as the *Roman d'Eneas*, a rhyming chivalric romance. The poetic effect of the clipped short lines of this Old French poem is utterly unlike the majesty of the sonorous, long lines of Virgil's original, and the cultural context is also quite different. When Aeneas comes courting Lavinia, the French poet invents a comic exchange for which there is no basis in the *Aeneid*. Queen Amata, Lavinia's mother, tells her daughter that Aeneas, like other Trojans, prefers boys to women, a message she delivers in bawdy and satiric terms:

> What have you said, you brainless fool?
> Do you know to whom you've turned yourself?
> . . . .
> He'd much prefer to hug a boy
> Than you or any other girl.
> . . . .
> He loves the tripes of little boys;
> That's how the Trojans get their food.[29]

Amata's nasty gibes sound the familiar tones of homophobia, which evidently existed in medieval culture. This poem often dramatizes what the medievalist Christopher Baswell calls "the threat of homo-eroticism," perhaps because the nobles for whom it was written were passionately interested in preserving their lines of descent through marriage. Despite these attitudes, however, the French poet places the episode of Nisus and Euryalus at the exact center of his poem, laying heavy emphasis on a story Baswell accurately calls "entirely male, military, and amatory."[30] His version of the story, which follows Virgil's fairly closely, enhances the touching, sentimental qualities of the love between the warriors. Virgil's Nisus, at the point of realizing that Euryalus is lost, imaginatively addresses his companion:

> In what place have I lost you, luckless Euryalus?
> And where can I find you now?[31]

At the same point in the story, the Nisus of the *Roman d'Eneas* utters a lyric lament:

> Euryalus, my sweetest friend,
> For your love I shall lose my life
> And after you I'll live no more.
> Your youth was so unfortunate:
> On you I had placed all desire,
> I've lost you in a grain of time. . . .[32]

And so on for twenty more lines. By picturing an explicitly suicidal Nisus, who cannot imagine living on after the loss of his loved one, the French poet increases the pathos of this moment. He must have done so in the confidence that his knightly readers, though clearly capable of homophobia, would exempt the love of soldiers from their scorn.

From the Middle Ages forward, European homophobia was so severe that many unfortunate homosexuals suffered at the hands of the law. Hundreds died during the Spanish Inquisition, and there were executions for the next several centuries in France, Italy, Germany, Holland, and England, which made sodomy a capital offense in 1553.[33] Yet John Dryden, the English Poet Laureate during the later seventeenth century, quoted Virgil's lines in praise of Nisus and Euryalus as the Latin epigraph to his serious ode on the death of Charles II, linking the King with his brother and successor James II and suggesting that their affection and loyalty resembled the noble sentiments of the Trojan warriors. He appears to have had no fear that he would be sullying the memory of the dead king or undercutting the reputation of the new one by comparing them to a pair of ancient male lovers. In one of his most personal poems, a lament for the young poet John Oldham, who died of the smallpox in his thirties, Dryden even compared himself and Oldham to Nisus and Euryalus, evoking the image of the footrace:

> To the same goal did both our studies strive,
> The last set out the soonest did arrive,
> Thus Nisus fell upon the slippery place,
> While his young friend perform'd and won the race.[34]

There is no reason to think that Dryden was any more sympathetic to homosexual desires and practices than other men of his time. In the 1690s, he gleefully satirized King William's fondness for beautiful Dutch boys. But for him as for other poets, the tragic fate of Nisus and Euryalus made them exempt from such scorn and available as heroic models.

In 1762, George Cockings published a poem called simply *War*, which recounts the Battle of Quebec in rhyming couplets. As one brave Briton, Ochterlony, is attacked by two Indian scalpers, he calls to a wounded comrade for help:

> He call'd to wounded Peyton, deeply pain'd;
> And of the outrage, to his friend complain'd
> As rush'd the Trojan hero from the shade,

And dealt destruction, with his mortal blade;
Soon as he saw, (the fatal,) yawning wound!
And a brave dying friend, upon the ground;
Like him, fierce Peyton, straightway, boldly rear'd;
Defiance frown'd; and both the Indians dar'd;
Rouz'd, tho' in pain! 'twixt bravery, and hate!
He groan'd in flame; and sent the leaden fate;
Which gain'd th' event, the gallant Peyton hop'd,
By death arrested, down an Indian dropp'd;
On Ochterlony fell, (design'd his prey;)
And grinning, groan'd his savage soul away![35]

Cockings produces a curious, almost comic variant: instead of Nisus falling upon Euryalus in a gory embrace of death, the Indian, shot by Peyton, falls grinning on Ochterlony. Perhaps this departure from the original model reflects some eighteenth-century British anxiety about male embraces, even among military men. In 1772, just ten years after the publication of these lines, there was a near-riot when Captain Robert Jones, convicted of sodomy and scheduled to hang at Tyburn, was pardoned.[36] Despite such attitudes, Cockings evidently felt there was some poetic power remaining in the myth of the Trojan hero Nisus.

In most of Europe, executions for sodomy peaked in the sixteenth and seventeenth centuries, falling off rapidly thereafter. The French completely decriminalized homosexual practices in 1791. In England, however, judges hanged at least sixty men for sodomy during the first three decades of the nineteenth century.[37] Although fully aware of that frightening danger, Lord Byron published in 1807 a poetic translation of the story of Nisus and Euryalus, in which he heightened and increased the language of love at every opportunity. Here, for example, is his version of the death of Nisus:

> Thus Nisus all his fond affection proved –
> Dying, revenged the fate of him he loved;
> Then on his bosom sought his wonted place,
> And death was heavenly in his friend's embrace![38]

The assertion that Euryalus' bosom was Nisus' accustomed place makes explicit what Virgil so carefully leaves unsaid, and the notion that Nisus' death was heavenly, with its overtones of pleasure, even orgasm, is a far cry from Virgil's version, in which Nisus simply finds peace in death. Despite these revealing changes, Byron must have hoped that the traditional and honorable nature of the story would keep literary reviewers or public authorities from concluding (correctly) that he had been drawn to the story by his own homosexual feelings.

Historians of sexuality have often argued that our modern definitions of "homosexuality" stem from the Victorian period, notable for its anxiety about all forms of sexuality. In Latin classes, Victorian schoolmasters often skipped Virgil's second *Eclogue*, embarrassed by its frank acknowledgment of emotions that were common enough in all-male schools. As Paul Fussell has pointed out, the omission of that poem from the list of set texts probably made some boys more eager to read it.[39] But the same schoolmasters taught the story of Nisus and Euryalus as a central example of the comradeship necessary to sustain the Empire, and historians now recognize that many of the military heroes who created and defended the British Empire were homosexual in orientation or practice. Niall Ferguson, who believes that a "remarkably high proportion" of the British officer class were homosexuals, has argued that conditions at home made service abroad attractive to such men: "As late Victorian Britain grew ever more prudish – and laws against sodomy were ever more strictly enforced – the Empire offered homosexuals ... boundless erotic opportunities."[40] Ferguson may well be correct about the reasons some of these men chose military careers abroad, but I also believe the tolerance with which they were treated within the British Army owed something to the continuing power of Virgil's lines linking Nisus and Euryalus with the sustaining of Empire. The acceptance of officers entirely oriented toward other males, like the remarkable frankness of many poems of male affection from World War I, reflects the message delivered by British schools in the late nineteenth century. Unlike the love of male couples at bars in Soho or pastoral picnics in the countryside, the love of males at war could be construed as noble.

For Nisus and Euryalus, as for many other pairs of comrades in narrative poems, comradeship ends in nearly simultaneous death. As the poetic fervor of Virgil's account suggests, there is something fitting, even beautiful about such a shared death: it unites in one fate, and sometimes in one grave, men whose strongest emotion was love for each other; it preserves in our memories the beauty of youth and youthful affection. When only one of a pair of comrades survives, however, a part of the poetic expression of unbearable loss is often the survivor's ambivalence about being left alive. Edmund Blunden's "1916 Seen from 1921," a fine example, explores the plight of the survivor and captures the sense of uselessness we have seen more recently among Vietnam veterans.

> Tired with dull grief, grown old before my day,
> I sit in solitude and only hear
> Long silent laughters, murmurings of dismay,
> The lost intensities of hope and fear;
> In those old marshes yet the rifles lie,
> On the thin breastwork flutter the grey rags,
> The very books I read are there – and I
> Dead as the men I loved, wait while life drags
> Its wounded length from those sad streets of war
> Into green places here, that were my own; . . .[41]

The essential contrast here is between the marshes where the war was fought – places where rifles, rags, and forgotten books still lie – and the green places here in England, pastoral landscapes that once were comforting, but now seem dull when measured against the lost intensities of wartime.

Blunden reveals something important by remembering that he left some books behind in the trenches. This is a self-consciously literary poem, and capturing its meaning requires tracking the allusions. The opening phrase – "Tired with dull grief" – echoes the opening of a Shakespeare sonnet, "Tired with all these for restful death I cry."[42] Though Blunden stops short of crying for death in his poem, he has pointed toward that temptation through the allusion. Shakespeare's poem consists mainly of a list of annoying injustices, such as "captive good attending captain ill," which make the speaker wish for death. At the very end, however, the speaker refutes the whole list with one powerful, personal reason to stay alive:

> Tired with all these, from these would I be gone,
> Save that to die, I leave my love alone.

Blunden lacks even that reason to live. His love is already gone; he is the one left alone; and now he feels as dead as the men he loved in the trenches. When he speaks of how "life drags / Its wounded length from those sad streets of war / Into green places here," the language comes from Virgil by way of Pope. Blunden evidently remembers Pope's *Essay on Criticism*, specifically a passage on versification criticizing the use of a six-foot "Alexandrine" line to signal a conclusion:

> A needless Alexandrine ends the song,
> That, like a wounded snake, drags its slow length along.[43]

Pope in turn remembered a striking simile from the *Aeneid*, in which Virgil compares a disabled sailing vessel to a snake crushed on the highway by a metal wheel, using his remaining strength to drag his maimed and useless sections behind him. Like Virgil's snake, Blunden will find no real comfort in moving from sad streets to green places. Those pastoral settings were once his own, but are his no longer.

> But now what once was mine is mine no more,
> I seek such neighbours here and I find none.
> With such strong gentleness and tireless will
> Those ruined houses seared themselves in me,
> Passionate I look for their dumb story still,
> And the charred stub outspeaks the living tree.

Blunden's punctuation connects strong gentleness and tireless will to the ruined houses of France, but these human qualities are surely displaced descriptions of his dead comrades. As the lost men were superior to his current civilian neighbors, so a charred stub remembered from No Man's Land now means more than a living tree. At the end, however, Blunden describes a pastoral interlude stolen amid orchard plots in France. In this lush landscape, the general and plural lament for "the men I loved" narrows to a specific memory of a particular comrade:

> Sweet Mary's shrine between the sycamores!
> There we would go, my friend of friends and I,
> And snatch long moments from the grudging wars,
> Whose dark made light intense to see them by.
> Shrewd bit the morning fog, the whining shots
> Spun from the wrangling wire: then in warm swoon
> The sun hushed all but the cool orchard plots,
> We crept in the tall grass and slept till noon.

The permanent pastoral of England does nothing to assuage Blunden's dull grief, but the memory of long moments of warm swoon snatched from the grudging wars is intense and sensual. Although it begins as a meditation on survivor guilt, this poem ultimately reveals itself as a poem of homoerotic nostalgia. The movement from the general reference to the dead men the poet loved to the specific memory of his particular friend is like Prince's movement from the group of naked soldiers to the one man imagined as conscious of his desires, or Whitman's movement from the collective wounded to the one poor boy with appealing eyes. Like Prince, Blunden is cautious and reticent, leaving us to infer that the friend of friends is among the dead, and leaving us to guess at the closeness of their bond. But he has left hints, even in his bookish allusions. Shakespeare's sonnet ends by mentioning a loved one who is almost certainly male. Virgil's simile of the snake comes only twenty lines before the first appearance of Nisus and Euryalus.

The poet and composer Ivor Gurney, who spent most of his postwar years in a mental hospital, wrote his finest poem on the loss of a single cherished comrade. Happily for Gurney, the man he thought dead turned out to have been taken prisoner; happily for poetry, he kept and published the poem, changing his original title. "On a Dead Poet" became "To his Love" – a title that appears to recall such familiar love poems as Marvell's "To his Coy Mistress" or Marlowe's "The Passionate Shepherd to his Love." Like Blunden, Gurney describes an English pastoral landscape, but he uses it very differently. For Blunden, the green landscape of England is no longer consoling; he actually misses the charred stubs and ruined houses of the War. For Gurney, the Cotswold plains and the river Severn are memories of a time before the War, places to which he cannot return because his companion is gone.

> He's gone, and all our plans
> Are useless indeed.
> We'll walk no more on Cotswold
> Where the sheep feed
> Quietly and take no heed.[44]

The memory of the friends walking in the Cotswolds invokes an especially nostalgic piece of English countryside, but the detail of the sheep points toward the whole pastoral tradition, including Virgil's *Second Eclogue*. Something not yet named, but obvious to any reader in 1919, has intervened to make it impossible for the friends to recover their pastoral idyll.

Gurney's language here is deliberately stripped-down and laconic. Of the twenty-four words in this stanza, twenty are monosyllables, yet the poet seems determined to show how much emotion he can produce with simple materials. Despite the title ("*To* his Love"), the speaker does not actually address his comrade, but speaks of him in the third person ("*He's* gone"). Gurney will not even allow himself the conventional poetic comfort of addressing the lost friend as if he were still alive. He invokes *our* plans, now useless, and ruefully admits that "*We'll* walk no more."

The second stanza, equally simple in diction, appears to introduce a third person, an unnamed *you* to whom the poet describes his lost love:

> His body that was so quick
> Is not as you
> Knew it, on Severn river
> Under the blue
> Driving our small boat through.

The editor of Gurney's letters has made the ingenious suggestion that the poem is addressed to the fiancée of the lost man, which solves the ambiguity of the pronouns and allows us to parse the title differently.[45] But I believe the poet is also talking to himself here, as if one part of him were patiently reminding another of difficult facts, quietly insisting that the lost man's body "Is *not* as you / *Knew* it" under those happier circumstances. The poem is about to pivot on the tense of that verb:

> You would not know him now ...
> But still he died
> Nobly, so cover him over
> With violets of pride
> Purple from Severn side.

Like the sheep, the flowers are a pastoral detail. In Virgil's *Second Eclogue*, Corydon warns Alexis against trusting too much to the beautiful color of his skin, and reminds him that "white cypress blossoms fall, and dark hyacinths are gathered."[46] This reminder of the fragility of life colors a later exuberant passage describing nymphs bringing baskets overflowing with lilies, violets, and poppies for the beautiful boy. Gurney also imagines "thick-set / Masses" of flowers, but his are the flowers of a funeral, hiding something unspeakable:

> Cover him, cover him soon!
> And with thick-set
> Masses of memoried flowers –
> Hide that red wet
> Thing I must somehow forget.

Thing, the most shocking word in the poem, gains added emphasis from the line-break, and from *red* and *wet*, adjectives that might apply to flowers, but take on far more painful meanings when applied to a body. A loved one remembered as a quick and agile companion has died nobly, but the supposed nobility of his death does not change the fact that he is now a red wet thing. Also delayed until the final line is the one occurrence of the first-person pronoun. The poet and his friend, once happy companions, are now a *Thing* and an isolated *I*.

When an enemy is no longer a menacing threat but a red wet thing, the victor often feels sorrow, pity, or affection for his victim. In the American Civil War, the enemy was often a man of similar class, faith, and background, and might even be a kinsman. As Herman Melville suggests in his requiem for the dead at Shiloh, imminent death made men more conscious of their kinship than of the differences that had made them enemies. The poet describes a church pressed into service as a field hospital,

> That echoed to many a parting groan
>   And natural prayer
> Of dying foemen mingled there –
> Foemen at morn, but friends at eve –
> Fame or country least their care:
>   (What like a bullet can undeceive!)
>   But now they lie low,
> While over them the swallows skim,
> And all is hushed at Shiloh.[47]

Death is the great leveler. As the groaning wounded lie in the pews, the fame, honor, or reputation that induced them to enlist no longer seems important. Even *country*, a concept tested by the Civil War, no longer matters as much as the prayers both sides are now offering to the same God. Unfortunately, this shifting of priorities happens only in the face of death. "What like a bullet can undeceive!" exclaims the poet. But then, as if unnerved by his own suggestion that the ideology driving both sides might seem pointless to men about to die, he encloses that insight in parentheses. Melville's perception that foe-men might be friends was as brief and temporary as the fellowship of the doomed men in Shiloh Church. A few months later, in a wholly conventional poem, he was celebrating General McClellan's victory at Antietam and describing the Confederate foe as a "rebel and maligner."[48]

Thanks to its plurals ("foemen," "friends"), the Shiloh requiem is general and detached. The poem does not single out individuals or develop a focused vision of comradeship. Thomas Hardy, in "The Man He Killed," gives similar ideas more bite by focusing on one soldier, a rifleman from the Napoleonic Wars who imagines his dead enemy as a man much like himself:

> "Had he and I but met
> By some old ancient inn,
> We should have sat us down to wet
> Right many a nipperkin!
>
> "But ranged as infantry,
> And staring face to face,
> I shot at him and he at me,
> And killed him in his place.[49]

Guessing that his enemy was a man from his own class, the survivor surmises that in peaceful circumstances, they might have had a drink or two together. On the battlefield, however, neither man has a choice. Both fire; one falls.

As the survivor struggles to make sense of what has happened, Hardy uses hesitation and repetition to dramatize his uncertainty:

> "I shot him dead because –
> Because he was my foe,
> Just so: my foe of course he was;
> That's clear enough; although . . .

There is no reason to imagine that the speaker of the poem is unusually intelligent, but his mind rebels against the conventional reasons the Army has given him for killing others, and leaps to an imaginative account of the reasons why the other man might have enlisted:

> "He thought he'd 'list, perhaps,
> Off-hand like – just as I –
> Was out of work – had sold his traps –
> No other reason why.

The fragmentary grammar produces deliberate ambiguities: it is not quite clear whether *he* or *I* was out of work. Of course, that is Hardy's point. Both men probably enlisted offhandedly, without compelling personal or political reasons for fighting, yet in a confrontation of infantry staring face to face, one of them must die. In a rough gesture of affection, the speaker returns to the idea of sharing a drink with his foe, and now imagines himself paying the bill and lending the dead man money:

> "Yes; quaint and curious war is!
> You shoot a fellow down
> You'd treat if met where any bar is,
> Or help to half-a-crown."

Everything here depends upon the perception of fundamental similarities between British and French soldiers. Yet some surprisingly similar ideas surface in poems from the imperial campaigns of the nineteenth century, in which the enemy could be stigmatized as inferior in race and culture. Kipling's soldier-narrators, despite their thoroughly racist vocabulary, respect the courage of their foes and sometimes express affection for men from very different cultures. In "Fuzzy-Wuzzy," for example, the narrator calls his Sudanese foe an "injia-rubber idiot" and a "big black boundin' beggar." At the same time, however, he is honest enough to certify the skill shown by his enemy "In usin' of 'is long two-'anded swords." Fuzzy-Wuzzy may be "a pore benighted 'eathen," but he is also "a first-class fightin' man." Recognizing the unfairness of attacking such enemies with modern armaments, the Cockney soldier salutes the courage that allowed the Sudanese to break a British Square:

Then 'ere's to you, Fuzzy-Wuzzy, an' the missis and the kid;
Our orders was to break you, an' of course we went an' did.
We sloshed you with Martinis,* an' it wasn't 'ardly fair;
But for all the odds agin' you, Fuzzy-Wuz, you broke the square.[50]

By imagining even the exotic, alien Fuzzy-Wuzzy as a man with a
wife and a child, and therefore a man like himself, the soldier
expresses an affection that breaks through the ingrained prejudices
of his culture. As the courage of Nisus and Euryalus made it possible
for readers in many later periods to admire them, despite the homo-
phobic intolerance of their times, so the courage of Fuzzy-Wuzzy
makes it possible for Kipling's soldier to admire him, despite the
racist assumptions of the Empire.

Neither Fuzzy-Wuzzy nor the man Hardy's soldier killed can be heard
in his poem. For the speakers in both cases, respect shades into comradely
affection without anything like an erotic charge. But in "Strange
Meeting," Wilfred Owen's poem about confronting a dead German,
the bulk of the poem is a speech by the dead man, and his speech, though
deliberately vague and dreamlike, points toward a more complex relationship between enemies – a mystic comradeship shading toward eroticism.
Owen dreams of descending into an underground landscape – part
sapper tunnel, part granite quarry, part cathedral, part Hell:

It seemed that out of battle I escaped
Down some profound dull tunnel, long since scooped
Through granites which titanic wars had groined.[51]

Among the "encumbered sleepers" in the tunnel, one springs up
and stares at Owen "With piteous recognition in fixed eyes." The
dead man, it develops, recognizes Owen as the man who bayoneted
him to death on the previous day, but I suspect there is another
dimension to the recognition. Though the language is dreamlike
and deliberately vague, I believe the German also recognizes Owen
as a man susceptible to the love of other men, a man with whom he
shares a secret.

Owen realizes that the dream landscape is Hell, but attempts to
comfort his strange friend by pointing out that both of them have
escaped from the intolerable noise of battle.

---

* Martini-Henry rifles.

With a thousand pains that vision's face was grained;
Yet no blood reached there from the upper ground,
And no guns thumped, or down the flues made moan.
'Strange friend,' I said, 'here is no cause to mourn.'

The German's reply, which fills the rest of the poem, is a catalogue of losses:

'None,' said that other, 'save the undone years,
The hopelessness. Whatever hope is yours,
Was my life also; I went hunting wild
After the wildest beauty in the world,
Which lies not calm in eyes, or braided hair, . . .'

The ghost's language becomes more and more difficult to parse in the course of this reply. His mourning for the years he has lost and the hope now denied him is clear enough, but his gesture of brotherhood with Owen ("Whatever *hope* is yours, / Was my *life* also") appears to conflate his lost life with the future life for which Owen hopes. Like Achilles and Patroclus or Roland and Oliver, the two men are merging into one. The German may even be hinting that Owen's unspoken *hope* for a fulfilling relationship with another man was already a feature of his own *life*. When he says that he has hunted for "the wildest beauty in the world, / Which lies not calm in eyes, or braided hair," he is rejecting the domestic and the feminine. Owen makes a similar gesture in the poem quoted in the opening pages of this chapter, where he prefers the "fellowships Untold" of men in the trenches to "the binding of fair lips / With the soft silk of eyes that look and long."

When the German speaks of what the world has lost in his death, he speaks of the joy, sorrow, and pity he might have given to many men.

For by my glee might many men have laughed,
And of my weeping something had been left,
Which must die now. I mean the truth untold,
The pity of war, the pity war distilled.

These lines deliberately echo Owen's draft preface, where the British poet had declared that his subject was "War, and the pity of War."

The German, in short, is a "secret sharer," a *Doppelgänger*, another version of the Englishman who has killed him. His warning of a dire future might just as easily be spoken by Owen himself:

> Now men will go content with what we spoiled,
> Or, discontent, boil bloody, and be spilled.
> They will be swift with swiftness of the tigress.
> None will break ranks, though nations trek from progress.

Chillingly accurate as a prediction of how the Treaty of Versailles created the discontent that boiled into another bloody World War, these lines also capture the power of war to impede or reverse progress in all periods. As the nations "trek *from* progress," time runs backwards. The German describes "the march of this retreating world / Into vain citadels that are not walled" – a scene that sounds vaguely medieval. He speaks of chariots driven over corpses, their wheels clogged with blood – a detail straight from the *Iliad*. In this grotesque landscape, a composite of past wars, he imagines becoming a healer, perhaps a wound-dresser like Whitman:

> Then, when much blood had clogged their chariot-wheels,
> I would go up and wash them from sweet wells,
> Even with truths that lie too deep for taint.

When the charioteers are filthy from driving over the red wet bodies of their foes, rank and bestial and desperate for cleansing like Prince's bathing soldiers, the dead German will wash them – not merely with water from sweet wells, but with "truths that lie too deep for taint."

Owen adapts the last line here from the final stanza of Wordsworth's "Ode: Intimations of Immortality":

> And O, ye Fountains, Meadows, Hills, and Groves,
> Forebode not any severing of our loves!
> . . . .
> Thanks to the human heart by which we live,
> Thanks to its tenderness, its joys, and fears,
> To me the meanest flower that blows can give
> Thoughts that do often lie too deep for tears.[52]

In Owen's version of this Romantic hymn to Nature, thoughts become truths, and tears become taint. Both changes are worth pondering in the context of the issues raised in this chapter. The act of washing a fellow-soldier whose body is stained with blood is an act of love. To wash him with truths is to acknowledge and respect the loves that may blossom in the hellish tunnels of war. Although society, even in our times, may speak of "the taint of homosexuality,"

Owen's language beautifully expresses his belief that the untold fellowships of men in combat are free from any taint – heroic as the love of Nisus for Euryalus, legitimate expressions of the human heart, its tenderness, its joys, and fears. As the poem ends, the dead man invites his slayer to lie down with him in eternal comradeship:

> 'I am the enemy you killed, my friend.
> I knew you in this dark: for so you frowned
> Yesterday through me as you jabbed and killed
> I parried; but my hands were loath and cold.
> Let us sleep now. . . .'

CHAPTER 6

The cause of liberty

"Strange Meeting" may be Owen's greatest poem. It is certainly his most radical. As the speaker discovers his kinship with his German foe, he gives a poetic voice to emotions felt during the Christmas truce of 1914, when soldiers who had been firing at each other for months swapped cigarettes and played soccer in No Man's Land. Conditioned by propaganda vilifying the Germans as sub-human monsters, the Allied soldiers who came out of the trenches during this brief truce were amazed to find their enemies so much like them. For men on both sides, meeting the enemy face to face raised troubling questions about the reasons for the war. Alert to the danger, commanders moved quickly to forbid "fraternization," and within a few days, the war returned to its "normal" state.[1]

Considered in this context, "Strange Meeting" is a deeply subversive poem. By presenting the dead man as a sensitive and appealing figure, Owen questions the personal morality of killing other men for any cause. By using the German to speak almost the entire poem, he erases the differences that propagandists on both sides were insistently exaggerating. And by claiming that war makes nations move away from progress, he reaches a whole new level of skepticism. He dares to question the cherished belief that "good wars" advance the inevitable progress of mankind toward freedom, democracy, and brotherhood.

These liberal ideals, developed and celebrated during the Enlightenment, have had a powerful appeal ever since. The English radical Joseph Priestley, rejoicing in the American and French Revolutions, announced in 1791 that the world was moving "from darkness to light, from superstition to sound knowledge, and from a most debasing servitude to a state of the most exalted freedom."[2]

Over a century later, the same ideas were still appealing – not only to the French and the Americans, whose national myths were shaped by revolutions, but also to the English. Owen's contemporaries, many of whom rejected such traditional motives as honor, shame, empire, or chivalry, responded eagerly to the call to take up arms in defense of enlightenment, knowledge, and freedom – causes still honored in our own times.

The continuing power of Enlightenment ideals as motives for warfare reflects not only the philosophical and political appeal of liberal principles, but the eloquence of eighteenth-century poets, who honored Liberty as a goddess and gave her stirring words to speak. Although many of them were privileged, these poets invoked the dignity of the common man, muting the elements of class inherent in the myths of honor and chivalry. Enthralled by their own noble sentiments, they imagined the powerful bonds of male sympathy and companionship extending to other races and nations, making possible a brotherhood of mankind.[3] Some of them fervently opposed slavery and criticized the racism inherent in the building of empires. Yet even while looking forward to the peace and prosperity that these progressive ideas were supposed to bring to the world, most Enlightenment poets still assumed that warfare would be necessary in order to achieve their liberal goals. As admirers and imitators of ancient epic, they were also reluctant to abandon war as a thrilling and powerful subject for poetry.

Though few today remember his poems, Joseph Addison played a central role in shaping sentimental liberalism. His poetic drama *Cato* (1713) celebrates the principles of a Roman republican who committed suicide rather than yield to the monarchical ambitions of Julius Caesar. It was the most influential English play of the eighteenth century, and its language lived in the hearts of the patriots who began and sustained the American Revolution. Speaking to his African ally Juba, Cato urges resistance:

> The hand of fate is over us, and heav'n
> Exacts severity from all our thoughts:
> It is not now a time to talk of aught
> But chains or conquest; liberty or death.[4]

Patrick Henry, imploring his fellow Virginians to join in the Revolution, echoed those lines:

Is life so dear or peace so sweet, as to be purchased at the price of chains and
slavery? Forbid it, almighty God! I know not what course others may take,
but as for me, give me liberty, or give me death![5]

Later in the play, Cato celebrates the sacrifice of his son, who has
fallen defending Roman freedom:

> How beautiful is death, when earn'd by virtue!
> Who would not be that youth? what pity is it
> That we can die but once to serve our country![6]

There proved to be great power in the idea that a death suffered in the
defense of democratic ideals was beautiful. In real-life struggles,
political actors drew courage from poems expressing democratic
enthusiasm in aesthetic terms. Nathan Hale, with the noose around
his neck, supposedly reworked Cato's lines as his dying speech: "I
only regret that I have but one life to give for my country."[7] In fact,
there is no eyewitness report to verify what Hale said, and his words
appeared in a variety of versions in newspapers and memoirs before
being set in stone some seventy years after his death. But it makes
little difference whether Hale himself or one of his admirers drew on
Cato. Attached to the familiar stories of Henry and Hale, Addison's
fine phrases decisively shaped American beliefs about liberty and
warfare – including the idea that both were beautiful.

Beginning with Addison and his contemporaries, poets and
painters have frequently linked democratic values to military
might. Many images of Liberty show her in the company of
armed men in uniform; she takes on masculine and heroic qualities
when she takes up arms. In the World War I poster shown here, a
kneeling Boy Scout offers a gigantic Liberty a sword far too large
for his own hands, but well-suited to her muscular arms and
grasping fingers. The wholesale carnage of twentieth-century wars
should have discredited such images, but the idea of fighting for
freedom has proved hard to kill. Even today, no Fourth of July
parade is complete without a display of military hardware. The
modern tank or ancient cannon that rolls along behind the high-
school band enforces the traditional claim that freedom must be
gained and defended by armed force.

The song we sing so badly on such occasions, "The Star Spangled
Banner," is a lyrical version of the same theme. Francis Scott Key

Figure 17. J. C. Leyendecker, "Weapons for Liberty."

created it in 1814 by fitting new words to a drinking song, carefully placing the word *free* on the highest note of the melody and the word *brave* on the final cadence. His imagery also associates freedom with warfare. By lighting up the sky, the rockets and bombs Key saw while writing his poem revealed that the American flag was still flying over the beleaguered Fort McHenry. At a larger level, however, the national anthem celebrates the rockets' red glare and the bombs bursting in air as beautiful, moving evidence of Americans' determination to defend their liberty and independence.

Most of us know only the opening stanza of Key's poem, which is embarrassing enough. The others are appalling. In the fourth stanza,

Key describes the War of 1812 as a defensive action and credits God with preserving the United States:

> O thus be it ever, when freemen shall stand
>> Between their loved homes and the war's desolation;
> Blest with victory and peace, may the heav'n-rescued land
>> Praise the Power that hath made and preserved us a nation![8]

The touching picture of freemen protecting their homes implies that Americans have taken up arms reluctantly. Yet Key's belief in the justice of self-defense did not prevent him from exulting at enemy losses. In the third stanza, he mocks the "vaunting band" of British invaders as "hirelings and slaves," whose "blood has washed out their foul footsteps' pollution." This shocking language is a poignant instance of the inevitable contradictions built into the Enlightenment's linking of freedom and warfare. When they embrace warfare as necessary to advance or defend the cause of liberty, even liberal, sentimental poets will be tempted to celebrate battle as beautiful. And once they see battle as beautiful, they risk becoming bloodthirsty.

Politicians have not hesitated to justify foreign adventures by appropriating poetic language originally crafted to celebrate freedom. As America belatedly entered World War I, Woodrow Wilson drew upon the tradition in listing his reasons for fighting "the war to end all wars." "The world," he insisted, "must be made safe for democracy. Its peace must be planted upon the tested foundations of political liberty."[9] Poems recited in the Presbyterian parsonage of Wilson's childhood flowed into this speech. In the imagery of planting, I hear echoes of John Greenleaf Whittier's "Worship" (1848), a vision of a future shaped by Christian love:

> Then shall all shackles fall; the stormy clangor
>> Of wild war music o'er the earth shall cease;
> Love shall tread out the baleful fire of anger,
>> And in its ashes plant the tree of peace![10]

Though steeped in the poetry of liberalism, progress, and piety, Wilson's words lay open to obvious moral objections even before events proved them false. Why should a war be the only way to end the horrors of war? Why should warfare, as opposed to diplomacy and persuasion, make possible a future world in which liberal and progressive values might prevail? Yet few if any voices raised these questions at the time. In his radical critique of the mystique of liberty, his bleak prediction that war would actually reverse progress, Wilfred Owen stood apart from most of his poetic contemporaries. For poets, though not for politicians, his stance has proved prophetic. Recent wars, though horrific in the scale of their destruction, have produced no expansive poetic narratives, no grand hymns to freedom. Instead, poets have written compressed accounts of small episodes or meditations on particular moments, often highlighting the modern soldier's *lack* of freedom. By their choice of subjects, thoughtful poets have implicitly questioned the controlling myths that wed liberal democracy to military force.

In politics, however, the old ideas are still alive. President Bush has repeatedly described the invasion of Iraq as a mission to liberate a nation from a tyrant, bringing freedom, democracy, and justice to people who should be grateful for those gifts. Although I am sure the President is not drawing directly on eighteenth-century poetry, his claim that liberty is an adequate motive for war owes an unacknowledged debt to arguments made more eloquently three hundred years ago. As early as 1695, Addison praised the European expeditions of King William in terms remarkably similar to those invoked by supporters of the war in Iraq:

> His Toils for no Ignoble ends design'd,
> Promote the common welfare of mankind;
> No wild Ambition moves, but Europe's Fears,
> The Cries of Orphans, and the Widow's Tears;
> Opprest Religion gives the first alarms,
> And injur'd Justice sets him in his Arms;
> His Conquests Freedom to the world afford,
> And nations bless the Labours of his sword.[11]

In the Nine Years' War as in the Second Gulf War, the toils of the invaders are supposed to quiet the cries of orphans, dry the widow's tears, free religion from oppression, restore a justice injured by tyranny, and promote the common welfare of mankind. Assuming that their own values are universal, apologists for wars fought in the cause of liberty, whether in 1695 or in 2003, confidently expect the grateful nations liberated in these wars to bless the labors of the conquering sword. There is something very odd, however, about the line in which Addison claims that William's "Conquests Freedom to the world afford." The awkward word order places the subject of the sentence ("Conquests") right next to its object ("Freedom"). Although such shifts in word order are common enough when couplet poets look for rhymes, this one – perhaps unwittingly – exposes the political and moral awkwardness of the claim that conquest brings freedom.

While praising William's wars, Addison insists that his king has no selfish motives. William's toils, he pointedly argues, have no ignoble ends; no wild ambition moves him. Over two hundred years later, President Wilson used similar language to deny that he was declaring war with any motive other than the rights of mankind:

We have no selfish ends to serve. We desire no conquest, no dominion. We seek no indemnities for ourselves, no material compensation for the sacrifices we shall freely make. We are but one of the champions of the rights of mankind.

When poets and presidents urge such claims, they invite skeptics to consider the ignoble ends for which the rhetoric of freedom and self-denial might be a cover. By pursuing his annual campaigns in Flanders, William hoped to thwart French ambitions and cling to his shaky throne. By entering World War I, Wilson hoped to give America a decisive role in shaping the political structures of the post-war world. By invading Iraq, Bush hoped to alter the balance of power in the Middle East and secure his reelection. Yet the fact that all of these rulers invoked the idea of liberty does not prove that they or their supporters were entirely cynical. Liberty is a powerful seductress. She often works her magic by persuading us that the wars we are pursuing for political or economic ends are noble campaigns to defend or extend the cause of freedom.

In creating the myth of Liberty as we now know it, eighteenth-century poets gave her an ancient genealogy, even though doing so often meant rewriting history. The ancient Romans recognized Libertas as a goddess, but because she was a belated invention, an abstraction turned into a deity, Libertas lacked a mythic narrative of the kind that gave Venus or Juno a definite personality. Her most prominent marker was a symbolic costume, a red "Phrygian cap" that slaves freed in Rome received as a sign of their new status.[12] When Julius Caesar was assassinated, one of his assailants came out of the

Figure 18. Denarius of Brutus (circa 43–42 B. C.)

Senate building waving a red cap on a spear. The crowd understood this symbolic display as a claim that the conspirators had killed the dictator to restore republican freedoms. The coin their leader Brutus had struck to commemorate the event displays a cap and two daggers, driving home the same point.

During the American and French Revolutions, actual revolutionaries and symbolic figures wore similar caps. When Eugène Delacroix painted "Liberty Leading the People" (1830), an allegorical celebration of a popular uprising against the last Bourbon king, he was careful to give Liberty her Phrygian bonnet, which she wears on American coins

Figure 19. Eugène Delacroix, *Le 28 juillet 1830: La Liberté guidant le peuple* (detail).

of many periods. As late as World War I, depictions of Liberty, including those shown in Figures 13 and 17, still included the traditional cap.

Although visual artists marked Liberty for centuries by repeating the humble motif of the freedman's cap, poets often changed her image by giving her the attributes of other mythic figures. The Scottish poet James Thomson, for example, deliberately reshaped the tradition in his long Miltonic poem titled *Liberty* (1736). As the poet meditates amid the ruins of Rome, "the fair majestic POWER / Of LIBERTY" appears before him in a carefully altered costume:

> ... Not, as of old,
> Extended in her hand the Cap, and Rod,
> Whose slave-inlarging touch gave double life:
> But her bright Temples bound with *British* Oak,
> And Naval Honours nodded on her Brow.
> Sublime of Port: loose o'er her Shoulder flow'd
> Her sea-green Robe, with Constellations gay.
> An island-Goddess now; and her high Care
> The Queen of Isles, the Mistress of the Main.[13]

By removing Liberty's cap, crowning her with British oak, and dressing her in a flowing robe, Thomson replaces a costume designed to emphasize Liberty's sympathy for the lowly with one designed to insist on her power and might. The visual allegory expresses his belief that Britain is the last, best home of liberty. By transforming Liberty into an island-goddess, the poet claims for one small country a figure usually presented as universal, effectively turning Liberty into Britannia. By speaking of British oak and naval honors, he links the blessings of liberty to the supremacy of the British Navy, the same message expressed more compactly in his most famous song:

> Rule, Britannia, rule the waves;
> Britons never will be slaves.[14]

In the song as in the historical poem, military might guarantees freedom from slavery. In his enthusiasm about British liberty, Thomson shows no concern for those Britannia will conquer to assure her own freedom.

Liberty is a "progress piece," a poem tracing the development of an idea from prehistory to the present. Eighteenth-century titles of this sort include *The Progress of Genius, The Progress of Rhyme, The Progress of Error, The Progress of Patriotism, The Progress of Pedantry*, and *The Progress of Fancy*. In Thomson's poem, Liberty traces her own progress from the world of primitive hunters through Greece and Rome to Britain. As she tells her story, Thomson reshapes ancient history to fit eighteenth-century ideas. The Greeks appear as philosophers, preferring persuasion to arms:

> Since Virtue was their Aim,
> Each by sure Practice tried to prove his Way
> The best. Then stood untouch'd the solid Base
> Of *Liberty*, the *Liberty* of *Mind*:
> For Systems yet, and Soul-enslaving Creeds,
> Slept with the Monsters of succeeding Times.
> From priestly Darkness sprung th' enlightening Arts
> Of Fire, and Sword, and Rage, and horrid Names.[15]

Although Thomson uses the word *enlightening* sarcastically, this passage perfectly illustrates the way Enlightenment poets rewrote the past. Thomson had surely read the *Iliad*, that great poem of rage, and probably remembered Plato's description of the constant warfare between Greek city-states, but his Whig politics compelled him to treat liberty of mind as the essence of ancient Greek thought. Suppressing ancient violence, he assigned fire, sword, and rage to the priestly darkness of the Middle Ages, from which he hoped a progressive and democratic Europe was now emerging.

When Liberty describes the Roman republic, Thomson cannot conceal the fact that the Romans were a warrior nation, so he deliberately revises their motives. The goddess praises Roman soldiers as selfless idealists fighting for freedom:

> "HER *Tribes*, her *Census*, see; her Generous Troops,
> Whose Pay was Glory, and their best Reward
> Free for their Country and for ME to die;
> Ere Mercenary Murder grew a Trade."[16]

I wonder whether the poet was aware of all the ironies these lines attach to the word *free*. Roman soldiers were conscripted for long periods of service, so the implication that they were free to choose their glorious deaths is dubious. Even during the days of the Republic, the Roman army served to capture slaves and extend Rome's sway over more territory, so Liberty's claim that these men died for her is fanciful. And in light of the way Roman armies systematically plundered the cities they conquered, the contrast Liberty urges between generous soldiers fighting for free and the mercenary murderers of later ages is also unconvincing. Despite

Thomson's efforts to downplay the importance of Greek warfare and redefine the aims of Roman warfare, he could not imagine how the cause of liberty might advance without armed conflict.

Even the most progressive of eighteenth-century poets shared this view, and for those who were also eager to achieve the sublime, to stimulate terror and awe in their readers, war remained an attractive subject for aesthetic reasons. Joel Barlow is a telling example of both these contradictions. After publishing *The Vision of Columbus*, Barlow spent time in France among Revolutionary circles and embraced their radical ideas. He then rewrote his poem as *The Columbiad*, a visionary progress piece. The aged Columbus, languishing in prison, receives a visit from Hesper, the allegorical spirit of the progressive West, who shows him the rational, democratic, peaceful future that the reign of Freedom will bring to the lands he discovered. Among the additions in this version is a preface criticizing Homer and Virgil as war-mongers. Barlow begins by praising Homer's "wonderful judgment," which makes it possible for the *Iliad* to "elevate the mind of the reader, and excite not only a veneration for the creative powers of the poet, but an ardent emulation of his heroes."[17] These phrases signal the presence of the sublime, which was supposed to produce elevation, excitement, and emulation. But in the same breath, Barlow frets about Homer's tendency "to inflame the minds of young readers with an enthusiastic ardor for military fame" and "to inculcate the pernicious doctrine of the divine right of kings."

Virgil comes in for equally harsh criticism. If he had written "one or two centuries earlier," during the supposedly admirable Republic, his countrymen "must have glowed with enthusiasm in reciting the fabulous labors of their ancestors, and adored the songster who could have thus elevated so endearing a subject." But Virgil wrote for Augustus, and "the real design of his poem," according to Barlow, "was to increase the veneration of the people for a master, whoever he might be, and to encourage like Homer the great system of military depredation."[18] The Roman poet Lucan, whose *Pharsalia* tells the story of the Roman Civil Wars, gains Barlow's sympathy as "the only republican among the ancient epic poets." Although "rambling" and "badly arranged," his poem "abounds in the most exalted sentiments and original views of manners, highly favorable to the love of justice and the detestation of war."[19]

In light of the pacifism that appears to drive Barlow's literary judgments of past poets, we might expect his own poem to express the hatred for war he so admired in Lucan. Quite the contrary. Not only does he describe war as sublime, for example in the account of the Battle of Saratoga quoted in the Introduction (see p. 5 above); he actually endorses war as a means of achieving progress. When Hesper celebrates the future, his tone is ecstatic and hopeful:

> Yes! righteous Freedom, heaven and earth and sea
> Yield or withhold their various gifts for thee;
> Protected Industry beneath thy reign
> Leads all the virtues in her filial train; . . .[20]

Freedom, addressed here as a goddess, receives the gifts of heaven, earth, and sea. She has become a secular, democratic version of the royal mistress shown in Figure 8, a symbolic recipient of the world's bounty. But she does not merely *receive* the natural resources of a newly discovered continent; she shares them with a newly invented sister goddess, Industry. This little allegory demonstrates the early origins of the now-conventional belief that democracy and capitalism go hand in hand. Flourishing in a free nation and protected by Liberty, Industry in turn spawns a train of virtuous daughters, including Probity, Contentment, Moderation, Labor, and Art. She promotes domestic and international peace and harmony. Yet instead of making war unnecessary by peaceful means, Industry ends it by force:

> Protected Industry, careering far,
> Detects the cause and cures the rage of war
> And sweeps with forceful arm to their last graves
> Kings from the earth and pirates from the waves.

The sequence of verbs is telling. Like a shrewd Enlightenment intellectual, Industry *detects* the cause of war. Like a scientific physician, she *cures* its rage. But the cure does not come from rational argument or effective medicine. With the forceful arm of a warrior, Industry *sweeps* kings and pirates to their graves. Barlow is specifically thinking of the American Revolution, a successful war against a king, and of the less successful American campaigns against the Barbary pirates during the first decade of the nineteenth century. His lines exemplify a basic contradiction that Enlightenment poets seem not to have noticed – a contradiction that politicians continue to ignore today. By arguing that a forceful arm was the way to cure the rage of war, Barlow and his contemporaries were already making the claim that President Wilson would make a century later by calling World War I "the war to end all wars." We have heard the same claim once more in President Bush's assertion that the United States, by invading Iraq in a campaign marked by "shock and awe," was seeking to advance liberty and peace.

The history of American war poetry in the years that separate Barlow from Bush records a slow loss of faith in the constellation of values that the Enlightenment brought together: liberty, progress, beauty, and the military sublime. For Barlow and other poets of the Revolution, the cause of liberty was a way to justify treating carnage as magnificent. In their battle poems, they transferred to whole armies Addison's claim that a death earned by virtue was beautiful. In Barlow's eyes, the virtuous motive that justified the Revolution was securing liberty from Britain and its kings. In Francis Scott Key's eyes, the virtuous motive that justified the War of 1812 was preserving that precious liberty. And in the eyes of Northern abolitionists, the virtuous motive that made the Civil War sacred was extending liberty to Southern slaves. The most familiar poem expressing those sentiments, Julia Ward Howe's "Battle Hymn of the Republic," begins by invoking the sublime:

> Mine eyes have seen the glory of the coming of the Lord:
> He is trampling out the vintage where the grapes of wrath are stored;
> He hath loosed the fateful lightning of His terrible swift sword:
> His truth is marching on.[21]

As many of her contemporaries would immediately have realized, Howe drew these images from Isaiah 63, where God treads upon his rebellious people like a man treading grapes in a winepress, and from the expansion of that prophetic imagery in the book of Revelation:

And I saw heaven opened, and behold a white horse; and he that sat upon him was called Faithful and True, and in righteousness he doth judge and make war. . . . And out of his mouth goeth a sharp sword, that with it he should smite the nations: and he shall rule them with a rod of iron: and he treadeth the winepress of the fierceness and wrath of Almighty God.[22]

Even a reader not steeped in the Bible can recognize Howe's celebration of violence. The juice that God will trample out of the grapes of wrath is blood, and his lightning is not only fateful but fatal. Not content to picture God striking down the wicked with lightning bolts, which leave the dead body intact, Howe imagines his vengeance as a terrible swift sword, an edged weapon that will cut apart the foes of freedom.

In the third stanza, God's sword turns into the fixed bayonets of the Union troops:

> I have read a fiery gospel writ in burnished rows of steel:
> "As ye deal with my contemners, so with you my grace shall deal;
> Let the Hero, born of woman, crush the serpent with his heel,
> > Since God is marching on."

The bayonets are both weapons and pens, inscribing their fiery gospel in blood on the enemy's body. This gospel, however, involves a massive distortion of orthodox Christianity. God's grace, normally meaning his mercy, turns into violence, with the soldiers playing the part of a heroic, vengeful Jesus. Howe drew the image of Christ crushing the serpent Satan from a traditional allegory, but she was surely aware that the historical Jesus was not an advocate of armed violence. In order to make Christianity an inspiration for warfare, she needed to invoke the Old Testament principle of vengeance and the violent imagery of Revelation.

It is difficult to reconcile these terrifying images with the gospel imagery of Christ as a suffering servant, atoning for the sins of the world by making himself a sacrifice. In her final stanza, Howe develops the idea of atonement, but her attempt at soft lyricism rings hollow:

> In the beauty of the lilies Christ was born across the sea,
> With a glory in his bosom that transfigures you and me:
> As he died to make men holy, let us die to make men free,
> > While God is marching on.

As they die to free the slaves, the Union troops will imitate Jesus, who died to atone for the sins of all mankind. By invoking the lilies, a traditional icon for the annunciation of the savior's miraculous birth, and by alluding to the transfiguration, a visual sign of his glory, Howe suggests that the dead soldiers will also take on the Godlike aspects of Christ's being. The refrain offers the same idea from another angle by describing God as a marching soldier.

When the poem appeared in *The Atlantic Monthly*, this was the fifth and final stanza, but in an earlier draft, Howe included a sixth:

> He is coming like the glory of the morning on the wave,
> He is wisdom to the mighty, he is honor to the brave,
> So the world shall be his footstool, and the soul of wrong his slave,
> Our God is marching on.[23]

In this stanza, God appears in many forms. The language praising his glory and his wisdom is familiar from the Psalms, as is the image of the earth as his footstool. The idea that God is *honor* to the brave, however, equates a potent deity with a human construct Howe must have known was suspect. Even worse is the allegory of the third line, in which God himself becomes a slaveholder. This line is an extreme case of the contradictions I have been exploring throughout this chapter. Addison argues that conquest brings freedom; Joel Barlow imagines Industry curing the rage of war by sweeping kings to their graves; and Howe pictures God ending slavery by making the soul of wrong his *slave*. In light of her later career as an advocate of peace, I suspect Howe was aware of the dissonance produced by this language, and perhaps aware of the clash between the violent, apocalyptic grapes of wrath and the hopeful, transcendent beauty of the lilies. She knew what she was doing when she deleted this stanza, but the larger problem she could not solve haunts her poem and others like it.

Union poets continued to employ a rhetoric of liberation throughout the Civil War, but Southern poets were also eager to claim some traditional aspects of the myth of liberty. Writing just after the War, Abram J. Ryan remembered the enthusiasm of the first days of secession, the thrill of unfurling a new flag:

> Once ten thousands hailed it gladly,
> And ten thousands wildly, madly,
> Swore it should forever wave;
> Swore that foeman's sword should never
> Hearts like theirs entwined dissever,
> Till that flag should float forever
> O'er their freedom or their grave![24]

The last line, posing a choice between freedom and the grave, recalls Patrick Henry's choice between liberty and death, itself an echo of Addison's *Cato*. By claiming a place in that succession of allusions, Ryan was casting the South as the Roman republic, preserver of traditional liberties, and the North as an invading Empire.

Southern poets also emphasized the need to defend one's home against an invader, the theme of "The Star Spangled Banner." A week after the first shots were fired at Fort Sumter, Northern troops passing through Baltimore were surrounded by a secessionist mob, and a few panicky men fired. James Ryder Randall, a Maryland native living in Louisiana, immediately wrote a poem urging his home state to secede. His language turns the Union troops into agents of tyranny and destruction:

> The despot's heel is on thy shore,
> Maryland!
> His torch is at thy temple door,
> Maryland!
> Avenge the patriotic gore
> That flecked the streets of Baltimore,
> And be the battle queen of yore,
> Maryland, my Maryland![25]

The image of the despot's heel marring the shore of Maryland recalls Francis Scott Key's claim that the foul footsteps of British invaders in 1812 were a form of pollution. Key's grandson, a supporter of the South, was among those arrested in Baltimore. The notion that the invaders will burn the temples of the South casts doubt upon the religious motives embraced by many on the Northern side. In Randall's eyes, the Union troops were not agents of God's will, as Howe had claimed, but iconoclasts, destroying the sacred institutions of their neighbors. He refrained, however, from specifying slavery as one of those institutions.

While eagerly embracing themes that equated the Confederacy with the brave revolutionaries of 1776 or the defenders of freedom in 1812, Southern poets were uniformly silent on the subject of slavery. While celebrating the themes of emancipation and union, Northern poets suppressed the fact that their side achieved its victory by turning the war against the civilian population of the

South. "The stars in our banner shone brighter," wrote Samuel Byers in a popular song, "When Sherman marched down to the sea."[26] Although Byers mentions Atlanta and Savannah, he pretends that Sherman's march was a series of military engagements, ignoring the systematic destruction of homes, farms, and cities along his path. For both sides, the scale of the slaughter made it difficult to sustain high-minded paeans to liberty and patriotism. On one horrible day at Antietam, 3,650 men died in battle; in the absence of anything like proper medical care, many more died within days from their wounds. In three days at Gettysburg, 51,112 were killed, mortally wounded, or listed as missing. The official statistics list 558,052 men killed in the war, far more than in any other war of our history. They do not count many who died years later from their wounds, including my great-grandfather.

The Union was saved; the slaves were freed; the cost was appalling. And if poets on both sides had been guilty of fond distortion and willful blindness, some now rose to the challenge of assessing the damage. No longer could serious poets naïvely invoke the Enlightenment's optimistic cluster of images: liberty, progress, beauty, and the military sublime. Gaining liberty for the slaves required denying the Southern states the liberty to secede. Progress toward racial equality, for which abolitionists hoped and freedmen longed, was painfully slow. Addison's notion of a beautiful death earned by virtue faded in the presence of Matthew Brady's stark photographs of bloated corpses. Only the sublime remained, and in the best poems of the period just after the war, the sublime strain turned from the supposedly magnificent and sonorous spectacle of battle toward the dark and terrifying gloom of a charnel house. In a short poem of great power, Whitman hailed Liberty as a "Victress on the peaks," but offered her a disturbing gift:

Lo! Victress on the peaks!
Where thou, with mighty brow, regarding the world,
(The world, O Libertad, that vainly conspired against thee;)
Out of its countless, beleaguering toils, after thwarting them all;
Dominant, with the dazzling sun around thee,
Flauntest now unharm'd, in immortal soundness and bloom – lo! in these
   hours supreme,

No poem proud, I, chanting, bring to thee – nor mastery's rapturous verse;
But a book, containing night's darkness, and blood-dripping wounds,
And psalms of the dead.[27]

The moral and sexual identity of the personified Liberty had long
been fluid. When James Thomson, writing some forty years before
the American Revolution, pictured Liberty as a sublime island goddess, crowned with naval honors, he made her not only less universal,
but notably less feminine. When Joel Barlow, writing just after the
American Revolution, pictured Freedom receiving the gifts of the
globe, he drew on earlier female figures representing peace, plenty,
and empire, but by pairing Freedom with Industry and promising
death to tyrants, he also invoked the forceful arm of might and
power. Advocates of the French Revolution, as the modern historian
Lynn Hunt has argued, used the "tranquil visage and statuesque
pose" of Liberty to efface the violence they had used to overthrow
the old monarchy.[28] By replacing the male figure of monarchy
with the female figure of Liberty, they sought to emphasize the
nurturing, maternal qualities of Liberty, who appears in revolutionary prints and poems as a secular Virgin Mary, an object of adoration.
Delacroix took the next step by depicting his Liberty bare-breasted
(Figure 19), adding a more explicitly erotic dimension to her maternal character.

Whitman's Libertad is neither nurturing nor erotic. She is dominant, unharmed, and supreme, flaunting her triumph as if she had
magically merged with Nike, the goddess of Victory. A goddess of
such stature demands tribute, but Whitman refuses to write a conventional celebration of a victory whose bloody cost he knew first-
hand from tending the wounded. In rejecting the rapturous verse of
mastery, he rejects the idea that the North should celebrate the end of
master-slave relations by flaunting its mastery over the defeated
South – the very idea Howe had expressed by hoping that God
would make the soul of wrong his slave. Despite Liberty's place on
the peaks, lit by the dazzling sun, Whitman offers her a gift more
fitting for the goddess Persephone, queen of the underworld, "a
book, containing night's darkness, and blood-dripping wounds."

In the same period, poets far less talented than Whitman also drew
Liberty into the orbit of darker myths. George Frederick Cameron,

writing to celebrate "Our Hero Dead" in 1877, describes Northern volunteers coming "from cottage and from hall ... To answer Union's trumpet-call."

> From every vale, from every hill
> These heroes came, and with a will, –
> For still the Syren Freedom sang.[29]

Everything here is conventional until Freedom becomes a Siren. In Homer's *Odyssey*, the Sirens sing a high, thrilling song that no sailor can resist. Their music represents their seductive power, and the rocks on which they sit are littered with the bones of shipwrecked men. Perhaps Cameron had not fully considered the implications of his image, but they were at work somewhere in his mind, and in the minds of his contemporaries. Already unnerving as a female figure linked with armed might, Liberty after the Civil War came trailing the odor of death.

This aspect of her character grew stronger in the twentieth century, as poets found it difficult to reconcile Enlightenment values with the mechanized slaughter of the World Wars. Lamenting the death of a "Soldier-Poet," the American writer Hervey Allen, later the author of *Anthony Adverse*, made a compelling allegory out of the process by which some soldiers in World War I shifted their emotional allegiance from romance, France, and chivalry to the larger ideal of Liberty:

> I think at first like us he did not see
> The goal to which the screaming eagles flew;
> For romance lured him, France, and chivalry;
> But Oh! Before the end he knew, he knew!
> And gave his first full love to Liberty,
> And met her face to face one lurid night
> While the guns boomed their shuddering minstrelsy
> And all the Argonne glowed with demon light.
> And Liberty herself came through the wood,
> And with her dear, boy lover kept the tryst;
> Clasped in her grand, Greek arms he understood
> Whose were the fatal lips that he had kissed –
> Lips that the soul of Youth has loved from old –
> Hot lips of Liberty that kiss men cold.[30]

This is a brave and unusual poem. Allen uses an old-fashioned form, the Shakespearean sonnet, and deliberately old-fashioned words like *minstrelsy* and *tryst* to capture the alluring appeal that romance, France, and chivalry held for many young Americans. By pointing out that the dead man was "like us," he avoids any hint of condescension. For the soldier-poet as for his comrades, a day in the trenches was probably long enough to dispel naïve romantic and chivalric notions about war. France, first imagined as a land of wine and women, turned out to be a nightmare landscape, glowing with demon light. Repeatedly insisting that his friend knew the truth before the end, Allen describes an incomplete process of maturation. The soldier-poet discards the fantasies of chivalric romance in favor of a higher, more abstract devotion to Liberty, but he never becomes an adult. Even in death, he is the dear, *boy* lover of Liberty, a huge and powerful goddess who clasps him in her grand, Greek arms. The imagery bears an uncanny resemblance to the pairing of the Boy Scout and Lady Liberty in Figure 17.

In picturing the seduction, Allen draws on Shakespeare's *Venus and Adonis*, in which a demanding Venus pulls the boy Adonis off his horse and imprisons him in her embrace. In the final, frightening lines, however, he also remembers *Dr. Faustus*, by Shakespeare's contemporary Christopher Marlowe. At the end of Marlowe's tragedy, Faustus embraces Helen of Troy, whose image he has conjured up by magic. He asks her to make him "immortal with a kiss," then recoils in horror as she sucks forth his soul.[31] By applying these myths of fatal seduction to Liberty, Allen bravely imagines Liberty, whose lips "the soul of Youth has loved from old," as a demonic killer.

In serious poems from World War II, the figure of Liberty all but disappears. Some of the dark female qualities that Allen found in her, however, shape one of the greatest short lyrics of that conflict, Randall Jarrell's "The Death of the Ball Turret Gunner."

> From my mother's sleep I fell into the State,
> And I hunched in its belly till my wet fur froze.
> Six miles from earth, loosed from its dream of life,
> I woke to black flak and the nightmare fighters.
> When I died they washed me out of the turret with a hose.[32]

Allen's soldier-poet, cast forever as a boy lover, cannot achieve maturity, but Jarrell's ball turret gunner cannot even achieve birth. Unborn, unchristened, he has no name. From his mother's sleep he falls into another womb, the airplane turret to which the State consigns him. He hunches like a fetus in the belly of the State, here imagined as the airplane, and his death looks like an abortion. In Jarrell's chilling picture of the State as a cruel surrogate mother, I see a twisted, grotesque distortion of the once-hopeful image of Liberty.

These increasingly negative images of Liberty dramatize a loss of faith in the Enlightenment values she once symbolized. That loss of faith did not come about simply because believing in liberty or progress began to look naïve or old-fashioned, though the earnest optimism of Joel Barlow's generation must have looked dated to Whitman, born just seven years after Barlow died. Nor was it merely a matter of the sheer numbers killed in the Civil War, though death on that scale dramatically underscored the cost of liberty. A third crucial element was the discovery that a government founded on Enlightenment values could pursue policies at odds with those values while cynically invoking the rhetoric of freedom. For many Americans, this sobering discovery came with the annexation of the Philippines in 1898. In this imperialistic campaign, the United States betrayed the native insurgents it had earlier backed against Spain. The most important native leader, Emilio Aguinaldo, was called "the George Washington of the Philippines," but President McKinley refused to recognize his revolutionary government and claimed the islands for the United States. The resulting war, in which American troops killed 20,000 Filipino soldiers and 200,000 civilians, lasted until 1902. A vigorous protest movement, for which Mark Twain, William James, and Andrew Carnegie were active spokesmen, opposed the war on the grounds that America now appeared to be fighting to *deny* the Filipinos their liberty.

In criticizing President McKinley for betraying the cause of liberty, poetic opponents of the war often invoked the heroes of past conflicts, imagining how displeased brave men who had died for liberty would be to see their descendants pursuing lesser goals. References to the Minutemen were frequent, as were comparisons between the noble cause of the Union in the Civil War and the crass greed for empire that appeared to be driving the Philippine campaign. For me, the most poignant poems of this period are those invoking Robert Gould Shaw and the Massachusetts Fifty-Fourth. For a pure example of the high calling of liberty, it would be hard to improve upon a regiment of men born slaves, fighting to liberate their captive brethren, led by a privileged white man driven by his faith in their worth. Unveiled in 1897, St. Gaudens's monument (Figure 9) was a fresh and compelling image for those opposed to the war in the Philippines, which began just one year later.

In William Vaughn Moody's "Ode in Time of Hesitation," written in 1900, the speaker stands in front of the monument, his mind moving gradually from the past to the present:

> Before the solemn bronze Saint Gaudens made
> To thrill the heedless passer's heart with awe,
> And set here in the city's talk and trade
> To the good memory of Robert Shaw,
> This bright March morn I stand,
> And hear the distant spring come up the land;
> Knowing that what I hear is not unheard
> Of this boy soldier and his negro band,
> For all their gaze is fixed so stern ahead,
> For all the fatal rhythm of their tread.
> The land they died to save from death and shame
> Trembles and waits, hearing the spring's great name,
> And by her pangs these resolute ghosts are stirred.[33]

When the speaker credits the Fifty-Fourth with dying to save America from death and shame, he implies that Shaw's men fought to save their nation from the death of being pulled apart by secession and the shame of tolerating slavery. Though he has not yet revealed his purpose, Moody is preparing to argue that the ignoble war in the Philippines will make the dead ashamed of the land they died to save. He is deploying the tired trope of shame in a new and powerful way. In the cases explored in Chapter Two, from Homeric times to Vietnam, "men killed, and died, because they were embarrassed not to." Moody, by contrast, is working to persuade his reader that men should now be embarrassed to kill and die for the wrong reasons. A nation that truly honored the principles of freedom for which Shaw and his men laid down their lives would be ashamed to engage in warfare for the purpose of *denying* freedom to others.

Moody uses the time of year, a bright morning in March, to describe the coming of spring across the whole North American continent, offering a catalogue of place-names – Virginia, Cape Ann, Oswego, Dakota, and the white Sierras – calculated to remind his reader of the vast tracts of land already controlled by the United States. Enjoying not only freedom but a continent rich in resources and natural beauty, Americans should be rejoicing in their good fortune and honoring the sacrifice of Shaw and his men. But the ominous sounds coming from the Pacific, heard not only by the living but by the ghosts of the dead, prevent rejoicing and humble patriotic pride:

> Alas! what sounds are these that come
> Sullenly over the Pacific seas, –
> Sounds of ignoble battle, striking dumb
> The season's half-awakened ecstasies?
> Must I be humble, then,
> Now when my heart hath need of pride?
> Wild love falls on me from these sculptured men;
> By loving much the land for which they died
> I would be justified.

As Yeats, not many years later, would imagine his Irish patriots dying from "excess of love," Moody imagines the sacrifice of Shaw's soldiers as an act of "wild love" directed toward future Americans, including himself. Inspired by their acts of love and courage, Moody wants to remember his country's "goodliness, make sweet her name." But an accusing shade "of sorrow or of blame" confronts him, lifting "the lyric leafage" from the brow of the nation and pointing "a slow finger at her shame." This forced change of costume reverses the action of Thomson's poem, in which Liberty gains a wreath of "British oak." Here the female figure of America *loses* her lyric laurels, which I read as her capacity to make or deserve poetry.

In a shrill, urgent stanza, the speaker tries to defend his country, insisting that "The wars we wage / Are noble," but his hysteria betrays his inability to sustain the claim.

> Lies! lies! It cannot be! The wars we wage
> Are noble, and our battles still are won
> By justice for us, ere we lift the gage.
> We have not sold our loftiest heritage.
> The proud republic hath not stooped to cheat
> And scramble in the market-place of war;
> Her forehead weareth yet its solemn star.

The irony here is effective. By dramatizing his speaker's intense need to deny the ugly motives driving the war in the Philippines, Moody forces the reader to acknowledge those motives. Too young to have fought in the Civil War himself, he invokes the example of Shaw, who led "despisèd men, with just-unshackled feet." If America continues on her imperialistic path, Moody argues, the men who died with Shaw will be stripped of the wreaths of praise they earned. They will curse those who have now betrayed the cause of freedom.

> For save we let the island men go free,
> Those baffled and dislaureled ghosts
> Will curse us from the lamentable coasts
> Where walk the frustrate dead.

Imagining the anger of the ghostly dead enables Moody to rise to his conclusion, in which he finally attacks the nation's leaders, turning the "intolerable self-disdain" he now feels into righteous indignation:

> Then on your guiltier head
> Shall our intolerable self-disdain
> Wreak suddenly its anger and its pain;
> For manifest in that disastrous light
> We shall discern the right
> And do it, tardily. – O ye who lead,
> Take heed!
> Blindness we may forgive, but baseness we will smite.

In these fine lines, Moody approaches the fervor of the Hebrew prophets, who were similarly courageous in confronting sinful rulers, similarly violent in their poetic language. In a world where American soldiers humiliate prisoners, forcing them into sexually degrading postures, we need a poet with a similarly acute sense of national shame and a similarly prophetic stance toward the leaders who have condoned such gross betrayals of the cause of liberty.

Sadly, there is at least one moment of blindness in Moody's ode, a phrase that those of us who admire it may find hard to forgive. In praising Shaw's leadership, Moody pictures him "Crouched in the sea fog" on the night before the battle,

> . . . speaking some simple word
> From hour to hour to the slow minds that heard,
> Holding each poor life gently in his hand

And breathing on the base rejected clay
Till each dark face shone mystical and grand
Against the breaking day;
And lo, the shard the potter cast away
Was grown a fiery chalice crystal-fine
Fulfilled of the divine
Great wine of battle wrath by God's ring-finger stirred.

Although the poet can imagine the black freedmen transformed into fiery crystal by Shaw's leadership and God's power, entering battle filled with the sublime wine of wrath, he cannot escape the unexamined, paternalistic racism of his era, as the embarrassing references to slow minds and poor lives reveal.

In the same year, an African-American poet, Paul Laurence Dunbar, wrote his own poem in praise of Colonel Shaw, in which he bitterly suggested that the studious Shaw should have remained in the "classic groves" of college life, since his courage had not changed the world:

Far better the slow blaze of Learning's light,
The cool and quiet of her dearer fane,
Than this hot terror of a hopeless fight,
This cold endurance of the final pain, –
Since thou and those who with thee died for right
Have died, the Present teaches, but in vain![34]

Some of Dunbar's first readers may have read the last line as simply another instance of the rhetoric Moody employed, using the bravery of the past to shame the imperialism of the present. But I believe Dunbar was also referring, with quiet dignity, to a domestic failure. The racial equality for which Shaw's soldiers had fought was (and is) far from complete – a complaint exemplified by Moody's unfortunate language.

Racism was a factor in the decision to annex the Philippines. McKinley himself spoke of the Filipinos as our "little brown brothers," and Kipling, in "The White Man's Burden," called them "Your new-caught, sullen peoples, / Half-devil and half-child." So it is especially satisfying to balance these dismissive remarks by recounting the decisive role played by a dead Filipino poet in persuading American legislators that his people deserved their freedom. José Rizal, a novelist and poet executed by the Spanish in 1896, had gained the world's attention through his writings about his native country. For the Filipinos who had first fought the Spanish and then fought the Americans, he was a sacred martyr. As the war drew to a close in 1902, some members of the US House of Representatives opposed a bill setting up a Philippine legislature, believing that the native peoples were too primitive to engage in self-government. Congressman Henry Cooper of Wisconsin turned the tide in favor of the bill by reading on the House floor "Mi Ultimo Adios" ("My Last Farewell"), a poem Rizal had written on the eve of his execution. His conclusion offers one fine poet as proof of the worth of a despised race:

I say to all those who denounce the Filipinos indiscriminately as barbarians and savages, without the possibility of a civilized future, that this despised race proved itself entitled to the respect of mankind when it furnished to the world the character of José Rizal.[35]

For many Americans, the dirty little war in the Philippines called into question the authority of traditional poetic language about liberty. But American losses were modest (4,200), and the war was pursued without a draft. American losses in World War I were much larger (116,708), though small in comparison to those suffered by England, France, and Germany. Thanks to conscription, however, the World War touched a broad range of American families. Although advertised as "the war to end all wars," it was grim, destructive, and unheroic; worse yet, it failed to produce a lasting peace. After the war, some poets felt free to treat the conventional language of patriotic songs and slogans with open mockery. In one such poem, e. e. cummings, a pacifist who had served as an ambulance driver, produced a vivid parody of a political orator piling up the standard clichés:

> "next to of course god america i
> love you land of the pilgrims' and so forth oh
> say can you see by the dawn's early my
> country 'tis of centuries come and go
> and are no more what of it we should worry
> in every languagE. E.ven deafanddumb
> thy sons acclaim your glorious name by gorry
> by jingo by gee by gosh by gum
> why talk of beauty what could be more beaut-
> iful than these heroic happy dead

> who rushed like lions to the roaring slaughter
> they did not stop to think they died instead
> then shall the voice of liberty be mute?"

He spoke.   And drank rapidly a glass of water[36]

Speaking as rapidly as he drinks, cummings's blowhard orator does not bother to finish any of the scraps of patriotic verse he quotes. Fragmented and disjointed, the phrases from national hymns that he slaps together have no more meaning than the bywords that end the recitation: "by gorry / by jingo by gee by gosh by gum." Speakers like this one may keep the voice of liberty from becoming mute, but silence would surely be preferable to this rushed recitation of empty formulas. Although cummings has cunningly shaped the speaker's regurgitated fragments into a perfectly rhymed Petrarchan sonnet, most of the rhyming words come in the middle of phrases. The formal order clashes with the urgent but pointless rhetorical order of the speech. When the speaker shifts from quotation to rhetorical question, asking "what could be more beaut- / iful than these heroic happy dead," the breaking of the word *beautiful* by the line-end enacts the final destruction of the Enlightenment notion of a beautiful death earned by virtue. By treating words as if they were only sounds, cummings expresses his contempt for conventional patriotism, his belief that its formulas are now empty of meaning.

Like a soldier scrawling "Kilroy was here" on a building, however, he is still concerned to leave his mark on the poem. Continually experimenting with typography, cummings always signed his name in lower-case letters ("e. e. cummings"), but in this poem, he capitalizes his initials as part of a typographical joke:

in every languagE. E.ven deafanddumb

There is a touching message in this odd-looking line. Politicians and orators may destroy the meaning of language, but poets, even as they record and mock that destruction of meaning, may still contrive to carve their initials into the otherwise meaningless surface. To do so is an assertion of freedom – not the grand, collective Liberty celebrated by the Enlightenment and its heirs, but the simple, personal freedom to be, to speak, to make a mark.

In this poem, cummings works by impersonation, representing and mocking the debasement of language by war. In a poem written at the height of the war in Vietnam, Denise Levertov takes that debasement as her subject. Like cummings, she employs ventriloquism, recording what sounds like a news bulletin:

> "'It became necessary
> to destroy the town to save it,'
> a United States major said today.
> He was talking about the decision
> by allied commanders to bomb and shell the town
> regardless of civilian casualties,
> to rout the Vietcong."[37]

But then her tone becomes elegiac. She addresses language as the "mother of thought" and laments its erosion by war.

> O language, mother of thought,
> are you rejecting us as we reject you?

> Language, coral island
> accrued from human comprehensions,
> human dreams,

> you are eroded as war erodes us.

The danger Levertov fears is real. The disinformation, propaganda, and empty slogans of war can erode the coral island of language. Fortunately, her own poem, even as it sounds the alarm about the erosion of language, constitutes a stand against that erosion. In a world where the optimistic formulas of Enlightenment and liberty have lost their meaning, prophecy and elegy become imperative for poets. Thanks to its capacity for irony, poetry is one of the most expressive media for showing how traditional symbols have lost their meaning while simultaneously lamenting that loss.

I know no finer instance of this process than Robert Lowell's great poem "For the Union Dead" (1960). Lowell's title suggests a conventional ode in memory of fallen heroes, but his poem deplores the corruption and meaninglessness of modern life. From a wry, angular perspective, the poet describes the "old white churches" of New England, where "frayed flags / quilt the graveyards of the Grand Army of the Republic." But the master image of the poem is a huge excavation for a parking garage under Boston Common:

> Behind their cage,
> yellow dinosaur steamshovels were grunting

> as they cropped up tons of mush and grass
> to gouge their underworld garage.[38]

The violence of the digging threatens sacred monuments, including St. Gaudens' relief of the Massachusetts Fifty-fourth, now "propped by a plank splint against the garage's earthquake." As he muses on the strange landscape, the poet remembers the story of Colonel Shaw's burial in 1863. The Confederates, who normally separated officers and men when burying enemy dead, were so outraged at finding a white man in command of a black regiment that they threw Shaw's body into a mass grave with his men. Shaw's father, with remarkable dignity, treated the intended insult as an honor. In a letter to Brigadier General Quincy A. Gillmore, the Union officer in command, the elder Shaw expressed his belief that "a soldier's most appropriate burial place is on the field where he has fallen," and asked the General to "prevent the disturbance of his remains or those buried with him."[39] Lowell was personally close to this history because one of his ancestors, Charles Russell Lowell, married Shaw's sister. His poem draws on a letter Charles Lowell wrote about Shaw before his own death in combat: "I am thankful that they buried him with his 'niggers.' They were brave men and they were his men."[40]

The contrast between the ditch where Shaw lies and the ditch being dug for the garage is the pivot on which Lowell's poem turns:

> Shaw's father wanted no monument
> except the ditch,
> where his son's body was thrown
> and lost with his "niggers."
> The ditch is nearer.
> There are no statues for the last war here;
> on Boylston Street, a commercial photograph
> shows Hiroshima boiling
>
> over a Mosler Safe, the "Rock of Ages"
> that survived the blast.

When a picture recording the deaths of some 200,000 civilians in Hiroshima becomes a commercial photograph to advertise a safe, the ditch of meaninglessness is indeed nearer. Shaw's ditch, the burial site his family accepted with pride, is a sacred shrine to freedom, where the colonel and his men enact in death a brotherhood living

Americans still find elusive. The ditch beneath the Common, turning historic ground into lucrative parking, is a symbol of crass greed. And the ditch that was once Hiroshima, a site of civilian death on an unprecedented scale, explains why there are no statues for the last war here.

Although writing in 1960, Lowell evidently thought of World War II as "the last war." His observation about the absence of statues has become even truer in the last forty years. There are very few traditional statues commemorating the wars in Korea, Vietnam, and the Persian Gulf. Although he did not live to see it, I like to think that Lowell would have admired Maya Lin's stark, minimalist Vietnam Memorial. Concealed from its surroundings in a geometric ditch, Lin's polished wall of names bears witness not only to our losses, but to our unease about traditional ways of commemorating loss. When opened in 1982, the memorial sparked passionate debate, and those who objected to it, primarily veterans of earlier wars, succeeded in having a more conventional monument with human figures added to the site. Since that time, however, Vietnam veterans have come to cherish Lin's work. For the vast majority of the survivors, the wall, with its 58,220 names, entered in the chronological order of their deaths, has come to seem the best kind of monument, gaining much of its power from what it omits. The names appear without ranks, so that each death is of equal significance. There is no officer on horseback, marked as more important than the men he leads. And there is no poetic inscription, Latin or English, rehearsing old lies about beautiful deaths in the cause of liberty.

The same unease that has made us reluctant to erect traditional statues commemorating recent wars has had a crippling effect on poets. A visual artist like Maya Lin can express our modern distrust of the grandiose by a deliberate minimalism, but it is hard to imagine a poet commemorating war losses by constructing a poem entirely from the names of the dead. For many poets, silence has seemed the only option. World War II produced far fewer poems than World War I, for reasons succinctly expressed by the British poet C. Day Lewis. "Where are the War Poets?" an editorial writer asked in 1943. Taking that question as his title, Lewis answered in eight crisp lines:

> They who in folly or mere greed
> Enslaved religion, markets, laws,
> Borrow our language now and bid
> Us to speak up in freedom's cause.
>
> It is the logic of our times,
> No subject for immortal verse –
> That we who lived by honest dreams
> Defend the bad against the worse.[41]

Although he took part in the war effort by joining the Home Guard and working in the Ministry of Information, Lewis was a severe critic of his own government. To treat the war as a subject for immortal verse or pretend that it was really being fought in freedom's cause seemed to him acts of bad faith, betrayals of the honest dreams of true poetry. In the face of the Nazi threat, it may have been logical, even imperative, to defend the bad against the worse, but it was not a subject for poetry.

The editorial writer was presumably asking poets to sound a stirring call to take up arms in freedom's cause. For all the reasons explained in this chapter, poets from Lewis's time to ours have been unable to write such poems with the confidence of an Addison or a Barlow. But that loss of faith in Enlightenment mythology need not mean that poets should keep silent in the face of modern warfare. The rich harvest of poems and songs from the war in Vietnam provides many examples of authentic poetry, though few in that war even believed they were defending the bad against the worse. Refusing to retreat into silence or minimalism, the best of the Vietnam poets use a full range of poetic effects to express the shame and helplessness felt by participants in a pointless, wasteful war.

In "Waiting for the Fire," Philip Appleman begins with a list of beautiful things destroyed by the fighting:

> Not just the temples, lifting
> lotuses out of the tangled trees,
> not the moon on cool canals,
> the profound smell of the paddies,
> evening fires in open doorways,
> fish and rice the perfect end of wisdom;
> but the small bones, the grace, the voices like
> clay bells in the wind, all wasted.[42]

In the slang of the time, *wasted* was a common term for *killed*. American soldiers wasted the enemy in firefights or got wasted by stepping on land mines. Applying this ugly word more broadly and thoughtfully, Appleman deplores the wasting of physical structures ("the temples"), peaceful nature ("the moon on cool canals"), and age-old customs ("fish and rice the perfect end of wisdom"). He realizes that the invaders have wasted a whole culture, as well as a people whose small bones, grace, and musical voices he cherishes.

As a poem of shame, "Waiting for the Fire" has elements in common with Moody's "Ode in Time of Hesitation." Like Moody, Appleman expresses self-disdain in a prophetic mode. The difference, a profound one, lies in the poet's willingness to accept responsibility for the policies he deplores. Moody ultimately blames President McKinley for the baseness of the war in the Philippines, separating himself from his nation's acts, but Appleman identifies fully and deeply with the *we* who wasted another culture and betrayed our own.

> If we ever thought of the wreckage
> of our unnatural acts,
> we would never sleep again
> without dreaming a rain of fire:
> somewhere God is bargaining for Sodom,
> a few good men could save the city; but
> in that dirty corner of the mind
> we call the soul
> the only wash that purifies is tears,
> and after all our body counts,
> our rape, our mutilations,
> nobody here is crying; people who would weep
> at the death of a dog
> stroll these unburned streets dry-eyed.

Our unnatural acts, including rape and mutilation, deserve a punishment like the rain of fire God used to destroy the sinful city of Sodom. Appleman trusts his reader to remember not only the fire of God's wrath in the Old Testament, but the widespread use of napalm to rain down fire on Vietnam. He remembers how Abraham bargained with God for the fate of Sodom, begging him to spare the city for the sake of the few remaining righteous men, and slyly works in a phrase from a modern recruiting campaign: "The Marines are looking for a few good men." Both parallels are bitterly ironic. By showering fire on the straw huts of innocent rice farmers, American helicopters performed a grotesque parody of God's punishment of the wicked in Sodom. When looking for a few good men, the Marines sought strong men willing to kill, not righteous men for whose sake God might spare others.

After such shame, what forgiveness? Tears might serve to purify, but the conflict has so damaged Vietnamese culture that people who would weep at the death of a dog are no longer able to cry. The atrocities have numbed their senses. Realizing that American soldiers might wish to regain their innocence by simply forgetting their acts, Appleman insists that we need the wisdom of losses to prevent us from repeating our evil deeds:

> But forgetfulness will never walk
> with innocence; we save our faces
> at the risk of our lives, needing
> the wisdom of losses, the gift of despair,
> or we could kill again.

These simple yet trenchant lines may stand as an answer to the long, sordid history of shame as a motive for combat. When we kill because we are embarrassed not to, as men have done for centuries, we save our faces at the risk of our lives. Moral wisdom requires losses; despair may be a gift.

In the closing lines, the moon that shines on the water, one of the peaceful elements wasted by the war, merges with the rain of fire we deserve for our unnatural acts. Cunningly shifting his pronouns, Appleman finally addresses the reader as *you*, reminding us that we are all complicit in the acts of our nation:

> Where are those volunteers
> to hold back the fire? Look:
> when the moon rises over the sea,
> no matter where you stand
> the path of the light comes to you.

When Appleman wrote this poem, he imagined the path of the light coming over the sea to shine its accusing beam on those responsible for the war in Vietnam. From today's perspective, his poem has increased its prophetic power. We have not gained wisdom from our losses, and the accusing light now falls on those responsible for the atrocities in Iraq. But as Appleman's brave use of the little word *you* makes clear, the light we may like to imagine falling on Lyndon Johnson or Donald Rumsfeld comes to each of us as well.

The accusing light shines on Americans with special intensity because we have enjoyed the privilege of freedom, a point made with considerable power by Oscar Fay Adams in a poem deploring the war in the Philippines, published in 1906:

> Alas for us! the sons of patriot sires,
>   Breathing the air of freedom from our birth,
> Who might have kindled in far lands the fires
>   Of liberty, transfigurer of earth;
> Who might have raised a grateful people up
> To drain deep draughts from freedom's brimming cup;
> Who might have shown them the sure way to peace –
> Alas for us! who did no deeds like these.[43]

Like many of the poets quoted in this chapter, Adams appears to have had the gift of prophecy. His words apply to recent wars as well as to the wars of his own time. Instead of kindling the fires of liberty, we have rained down the fire of napalm. Instead of raising a grateful people up, we have thrown them down to cower, naked, in degrading poses. It is time to ask once more the question of what it means for poets to speak up in freedom's cause. Those truest to that cause, I believe, must now take up the mantle of the prophets, teaching our rulers – and all the rest of us – how to bear the wisdom of losses, how to gain the gift of despair.

Adams insists that those of us who have grown up breathing the air of freedom from our birth incur a special responsibility to spread and protect the blessings of liberty. Educated and privileged like virtually all the poets quoted in this book, he does not imagine how hollow the rhetoric of freedom must seem to an enlisted man ordered into a war supposedly fought for the cause of liberty. Trained to obey, often by brutal methods, the soldiers we send to fight our wars have very little freedom. A powerful recent expression of that painful irony is Bruce Springsteen's rock anthem, "Born in the U. S. A."

In tough, simple lines, Springsteen's speaker describes a childhood of suffering that clashes violently with the myth of America as a land of freedom and progress:

> Born down in a dead man's town
> The first kick I took was when I hit the ground
> You end up like a dog that's been beat too much
> Till you spend half your life just covering up.
> Born in the U. S. A.
>
> I was born in the U.S.A
> I was born in the U. S. A.
> Born in the U. S. A.[44]

Springsteen helps us sense the contrast between reality and myth by creating a strong musical contrast between the verse and the chorus. The verse is nearly a chant; the chorus, a lyrical outcry. The intensity of the repeated chorus expresses the speaker's outrage: a child born in the U. S. A. is not supposed to end up like a dog.

Things only get worse when the speaker joins the Army:

> Got in a little hometown jam
> So they put a rifle in my hand
> Sent me off to a foreign land
> To go and kill the yellow man.

Although the speaker does not give details of the little hometown jam, I suspect his story was like that of several young men in my Basic Training company at Fort Knox in 1968. In the cases I knew, a judge about to convict a teenager of car theft or marijuana possession offered him a choice between jail and the Army. Most, like Springsteen's character, took the Army.

The speaker says nothing about his own experiences in the war, complaining instead about his ill treatment as a veteran:

> Come back home to the refinery
> Hiring man says "Son if it was up to me"
> Went down to see my V. A. man
> He said "Son, don't you understand"

Perhaps because his life as a survivor is so hollow, the speaker immediately remembers a brother who did not return:

> I had a brother at Khe Sahn fighting off the Viet Cong
> They're still there, he's all gone
> He had a woman he loved in Saigon
> I got a picture of him in her arms now

There is a terrible eloquence in the description of the lost brother as *all gone*. Nothing remains but a tattered photograph of the dead man in the arms of the woman in Saigon.

With no brother and no woman of his own to love, the speaker remains in the shadow of the penitentiary, the fate he tried to avoid by going to war, and hangs out near the refinery that refused to hire him.

> Down in the shadow of the penitentiary
> Out by the gas fires of the refinery
> I'm ten years burning down the road
> Nowhere to run ain't got nowhere to go
>
> Born in the U. S. A.
> I was born in the U. S. A.
> Born in the U. S. A.
> I'm a long gone Daddy in the U. S. A.
> Born in the U. S. A.
> Born in the U. S. A.
> Born in the U. S. A.
> I'm a cool rocking Daddy in the U. S. A.

The variations in the final chorus are telling. The speaker may want to believe that he is a cool rocking Daddy, but after ten years of burning down the road, he is surely a long gone Daddy, as finished in his own way as the brother who is all gone.

During the 1984 campaign, President Reagan misread this savage indictment of conscription, pointless violence, and the hard lot of the veteran as a patriotic hymn expressing pride in America. Claiming to be a Springsteen fan, he asked to use the song in his campaign. Springsteen politely refused. The President may have been influenced by the columnist George Will, who reviewed a Springsteen concert in patriotic terms:

I have not got a clue about Springsteen's politics, if any, but flags get waved at his concerts while he sings songs about hard times. He is no whiner, and the recitation of closed factories and other problems always seems punctuated by a grand, cheerful, affirmation: "Born in the U. S. A.!"[45]

When we want to feel good about ourselves and our nation, especially in times of war, we may hear in a poem or song only the message we wish to hear. Because of the power of the long tradition of poems in praise of liberty, we may respond to any invocation of that tradition with an automatic, unthinking pride in our democratic beliefs and institutions. Like Addison or Barlow, we may persuade ourselves that death in the cause of liberty is beautiful, even sublime. Like Will and Reagan, we may hear the bitter lament of the battered veteran as a grand, cheerful, affirmation. Many of the poems considered in this chapter, however, are valuable precisely because they tell darker stories. Through parody and satire, they expose the emptiness of patriotic slogans. Through elegy and mourning, they remind us of the fate of dear, boy lovers and ball turret gunners. And through prophecy and outrage, they express the intolerable self-disdain we should feel when our nation betrays its heritage.

As I have tried to show throughout this book, poets as a group have no special claim to the moral high ground. Some have misused their gifts to sustain false versions of honor and chivalry, or to celebrate the creation of empires. They have eaten the bread of kings and generals, and falsely sung their praises. But the poets I mean to honor, the ones most true to their high calling, have grasped and made real the rich, contradictory emotions that war calls forth in all of us. They are my heroes.

Notes

INTRODUCTION: TERRIBLE BEAUTY

1. John Keegan, *A History of Warfare* (New York: Alfred Knopf, 1993), xvi.
2. See Keegan, 40–45.
3. *Iliad* 4.139–142.
4. Bertran de Born, "Be●m plai lo gais temps de pascor," in *The Poems of the Troubadour Bertran de Born*, ed. William D. Paden *et al.* (Berkeley: University of California Press, 1986), 342–343.
5. William Butler Yeats, "Easter 1916," in *The Collected Works of W. B. Yeats*, vol. I, *The Poems*, ed. Richard J. Finneran (New York: Scribner, 1997), 182–184.
6. Robert Graves, "Two Fusiliers," in *Complete Poems* (Manchester: Carcanet, 1999), I, 37.
7. Joel Barlow, *The Columbiad* (Washington: Joseph Milligan, 1825), Book VI, p. 240.
8. *Columbiad*, Preface, xvi–xvii.
9. See *Columbiad*, IV, 138.
10. Walter Benjamin, "The Work of Art in the Age of Mechanical Reproduction" (1936), in *Illuminations*, ed. Hannah Arendt, trans. Harry Zohn (New York: Harcourt, Brace, 1968), 219–244.
11. Tim O'Brien, *The Things They Carried* (Boston: Houghton Mifflin, 1990), 80–81.
12. See Eric Havelock, *Preface to Plato* (Cambridge: Belknap Press of Harvard University Press, 1964), *passim*.
13. Stephen Vincent Benét, *John Brown's Body* (Garden City: Doubleday Doran, 1928), 329.
14. This is the version inscribed on the equestrian statue of Jackson at the Manassas National Battlefield Park.
15. "Dr. Hunter McGuire's Account of [Jackson's] Last Hours," printed as an appendix to John Eston Cooke, *Stonewall Jackson: A Military Biography* (New York: Appleton, 1876), 477–485.

16. See Charles A. Fenton, *Stephen Vincent Benét: The Life and Times of an American Man of Letters* (New Haven: Yale University Press, 1958), 72–75.

17. *John Brown's Body*, 329.

18. *John Brown's Body*, 331.

1: HONOR AND MEMORY

1. Douglas MacArthur, "Duty, Honor, Country," in *Reminiscences* (New York: McGraw-Hill, 1964), 423–426.

2. *Oxford English Dictionary*, s.v. *honour*.

3. Paul Fussell, *The Great War and Modern Memory* (Oxford: Oxford University Press, 1975), 21–22.

4. See *Friends and Apostles: The Correspondence of Rupert Brooke and James Strachey, 1905–1914*, ed. Keith Hale (New Haven: Yale University Press, 1998), 13, and Paul Delany, *The Neo-pagans: Rupert Brooke and the Ordeal of Youth* (New York: Free Press, 1987), 132.

5. The Reverend W. R. Inge quoted "The Soldier" in his Easter sermon at St. Paul's on 4 April 1915. A notebook containing the autograph manuscript of the sermon is among the Brooke papers at King's College, Cambridge, shelfmark Xb/2.

6. Rupert Brooke, "The Soldier," in *The Poetical Works*, ed. Geoffrey Keynes (London: Faber and Faber, 1970), 24.

7. "Death of Rupert Brooke" by "W. S. C.," *The Times* (London), 26 April 1915. My thanks to Professor Cedric Reverand II, who drew my attention to this passage.

8. "The Dead," *Poetical Works*, 22.

9. William Shakespeare, *Henry V*, IV, iii, 61–63. This and all quotations from Shakespeare follow *The Arden Shakespeare Complete Works*, ed. Richard Proudfoot, Ann Thompson and David Scott Kastan (Walton-on-Thames: Thomas Nelson, 1998).

10. Siegfried Sassoon, "The Poet as Hero," in *Collected Poems: 1908–1956* (London: Faber and Faber, 1961), 320.

11. Wilfred Owen, *The Complete Poems and Fragments*, ed. Jon Stallworthy (London: Chatto & Windus, 1983), 192.

12. Jean Moorcraft Wilson, *Siegfried Sassoon: The Making of a War Poet* (New York: Routledge, 1999), 400.

13. Richard Hovey, "The Call of the Bugles," in *An American Anthology, 1787–1900*, ed. Edmund Clarence Stedman (Boston: Houghton Mifflin, 1900), 703–704.

14. Donald Kagan, *On the Origins of War and the Preservation of Peace* (New York: Doubleday, 1995), 8.

15. Richard Lovelace, "Song. To Lucasta, Going to the Wars," in *The Cavalier Poets: An Anthology*, ed. Thomas Crofts (New York: Dover, 1995), 70.
16. Thomason Tracts 669.f.10 (47), 8 April 1646.
17. Katharine Tynan, "A Lament (For Holy Cross Day, 1914)," in *Flower of Youth: Poems in War Time* (London: Sidgwick & Jackson, 1915), 35–36.
18. See C. J. Wortham, "Richard Lovelace's 'To Lucasta, Going to the Wars': Which wars?" *Notes and Queries* 26 (1979): 430–431.
19. Anne Finch, "All is Vanity," in *Miscellany Poems, On Several Occasions* (1713), 9–10.
20. Herbert Asquith, "The Volunteer," in *Georgian Poetry, 1916–1917*, comp. Edward Marsh (New York: G. P. Putnam's Sons, 1918), 181.
21. Ernest Hemingway, *A Farewell to Arms* (New York: Scribner Classics, 1997), 169.
22. Rudyard Kipling, "The Bridegroom," in *Selected Poetry*, ed. Craig Raine (London: Penguin, 1992), 168.
23. "To Lucasta, On Going to the Wars – For the Fourth Time," in *Complete Poems*, I, 36–37.
24. *Complete Poems and Fragments*, 99.
25. Thomas Gray, "Elegy Written in a Country Church Yard," in *The Complete Poems of Thomas Gray*, ed. J. R. Hendrickson and H. W. Starr (Oxford: Clarendon Press, 1966), 37–43.
26. Francis Parkman, *The Conspiracy of Pontiac*, vol. I (Lincoln: University of Nebraska Press, 1994), 131–132.

2: SHAME AND SLAUGHTER

1. Arthur Waugh, "War Poetry (1914–18)," in *Quarterly Review* 230 (October 1918), 381. Quoted in Samuel Hynes, *A War Imagined* (New York: Atheneum, 1991), 258–59.
2. Homer, *Iliad* 16.345–50. This and all quotations from the *Iliad* follow the translation by Robert Fagles (New York: Viking, 1990), here quoting pp. 423–424.
3. Tim O'Brien, *The Things They Carried*, 20–21.
4. For a recent account, see W. Donlan, "Duelling with Gifts in the *Iliad*: As the Audience Saw It," in *Colby Quarterly* 29 (1993) 155–172.
5. *Iliad* 1.163–168; Fagles, 83.
6. *Iliad* 1.178–179; 184–186; Fagles, 83.
7. *Iliad* 1. 276–281; Fagles, 86.
8. *Iliad* 1.231; Fagles, 85.
9. *Iliad* 1.116–120; Fagles, 81.

10. E. R. Dodds, *The Greeks and the Irrational* (Berkeley: University of California Press, 1951), 17.

11. Hans van Wees, *Status Warriors* (Amsterdam: J. C. Gieben, 1992), 156.

12. Alexander Pope, *Iliad*, ed. Maynard Mack *et al.* (London: Methuen, 1967), I, 145–154.

13. R. C. Jebb, *Homer: An Introduction to the Iliad and the Odyssey* (Boston: Ginn and Company, 1894), 55.

14. A. E. Housman, "XXXVI," in *Collected Poems and Selected Prose*, ed. Christopher Ricks (London: Penguin, 1988), 182.

15. Epitaph attributed to Simonides, as quoted in Herodotus, *History*, VII.228; translation mine.

16. *Letters and Diary of Alan Seeger* (New York: Charles Scribner's Sons, 1918), 86.

17. Alan Seeger, "Champagne, 1914–15," in *Poems by Alan Seeger* (New York: Charles Scribner's Sons, 1917), 135.

18. *Iliad* 22.411; Fagles, 555.

19. Adam Parry, "The Language of Achilles," in *The Language of Achilles and Other Papers* (Oxford: Clarendon Press, 1989), 7.

20. *Iliad* 9.149; Fagles, 256.

21. See Donald Lateiner, "The *Iliad*: an unpredictable classic," in *The Cambridge Companion to Homer*, ed. Robert Fowler (Cambridge: Cambridge University Press, 2004), 11–30, here quoting p. 25.

22. *Iliad* 9.378–379; Fagles, 264.

23. *Iliad* 9.405–409; Fagles, 265.

24. *Iliad* 19.147–150; Fagles, 493.

25. *Iliad* 19.204–208; Fagles, 495.

26. *Iliad* 22.114–117; Fagles, 545.

27. *Iliad* 22.122–125; Fagles, 545.

28. *Iliad* 22.345–354; Fagles, 553.

29. *Letters and Diary*, 211.

30. Julian Grenfell, "Into Battle," in Nicholas Mosley, *Julian Grenfell, His Life and the Times of his Death, 1888–1915* (New York: Holt, Rinehart and Winston, 1976), 256–57.

31. Viola Meynell, *Julian Grenfell: A Memoir* (London: Burns and Oates, 1917), 17–18.

32. *Iliad* 6.407–410; Fagles, 209.

33. *Iliad* 6.442–443; Fagles, 210.

34. *Iliad* 6.476–481; Fagles, 211.

35. Pope, *Iliad*, VI, 611, 615.

36. George H. Boker, "Upon the Hill before Centreville" in *Poems of the War* (Boston: Ticknor and Fields, 1864), 30–47.

37. *The Times* (London, 18 September 1914), quoted in Hynes, *A War Imagined*, 27.

38. "S. I. W.," in *Complete Poems and Fragments*, 161–162.

39. *Iliad* 12.317–321; Fagles, 335.

40. Pope, *Iliad*, XII, 377–386.

41. George Lyttelton, *History of the Life of Henry II* (3 vols., London, 1767), III, 178.

42. Ezra Pound, "Hugh Selwyn Mauberley," in *Collected Shorter Poems* (New York: New Directions, 1949), 188.

43. In the Brooke papers at King's, volume Pr/88, described as "Homer, *Iliad* (Oxford, 1904). Signature Hood Battalion R. N. D. Feb. 1915."

44. "Other fragments," in Brooke, *Poetical Works*, 205.

45. *Iliad*, 16.679–683; Fagles, 434.

46. C. F. G. Masterman, *England After War* (London, 1922), 31–32, quoted in Hynes, *A War Imagined*, 316.

47. Horace, *Odes*, III.ii.13.

48. *Iliad*, 16.486; Fagles, 428.

3: THE COST OF EMPIRE

1. Sebastian Mallaby, "The Reluctant Imperialist: Terrorism, Failed States, and the Case for American Empire," in *Foreign Affairs* (March/April, 2002), 2.

2. Robert Kaplan, *Warrior Politics* (New York: Random House, 2002), 148, emphases mine.

3. Alfred Lord Tennyson, "The Defence of Lucknow," in *The Poems of Tennyson*, ed. Christopher Ricks (3 vols., Berkeley: University of California Press, 1987), III, 37.

4. Samuel Taylor Coleridge, "Fears in Solitude," 42–54, in *Coleridge's Poetry and Prose*, ed. Nicholas Halmi, Paul Magnuson, and Ramindao Modiano (New York: W. W. Norton, 2004), 111.

5. Cicero, *De Republica*, III, xxiv.

6. Joseph Schumpeter, *Imperialism [and] Social Classes: Two Essays*, trans. Heinz Norden (New York: Meridian Books, 1955), 5.

7. See *Iliad* 13.130–135, 16.212–218.

8. Victor Davis Hanson, *The Western Way of War* (New York: Alfred Knopf, 1989), 4.

9. Plato, *Laws* 626a.

10. Michael Grant, *History of Rome* (New York: Scribner's, 1978), 65.

11. See Charlton T. Lewis and Charles Short, *A Latin Dictionary* (Oxford: Clarendon Press, 1980), s.v. "*pietas.*"

12. See Schumpeter, *Imperialism*, 52–53.

13. Polybius, *The Histories*, 10.15.4–6, trans. W. R. Paton (London, W. Heinemann, 1922–27), iv, 137.

14. William V. Harris, *War and Imperialism in Republican Rome, 327–70 B. C.* (Oxford: Clarendon Press, 1979), 53.

15. W. B. Yeats, "The Circus Animals' Desertion," l. 40, in *The Poems*, 348.

16. Harris, 53.

17. Virgil, *Aeneid* 1.1–7. This and all citations from Virgil follow the Latin text given in *Virgil* (Cambridge: Harvard University Press, 1999–2000); all translations are mine.

18. *Aeneid* 1.10.

19. *Aeneid* 1.378.

20. *Aeneid* 7.41–45.

21. "The Two Voices of Virgil's *Aeneid*," in *The Language of Achilles and Other Papers*, 93.

22. Robinson Jeffers, "Shine, Empire," in *The Collected Poetry of Robinson Jeffers*, ed. Tim Hunt (3 vols., Palo Alto: Stanford University Press, 1991), III, 17.

23. *Aeneid* 1.148–153.

24. *Aeneid* 1.278–279.

25. *Aeneid* 1.263–264.

26. *Aeneid* 1.286–290.

27. Plutarch, *Life of Caesar*, xv; *Oxford Classical Dictionary* (Oxford: Clarendon Press, 2003), s.v. "Iulius Caesar."

28. *Aeneid* 1.291–296.

29. See *A Latin Dictionary*, s.v. "*impius.*"

30. *Aeneid* 6.795.

31. *Aeneid* 6.846–853.

32. See Grant, *History of Rome*, 143.

33. W. Y. Sellar, *The Roman Poets of the Augustan Age: Virgil* (Oxford: Oxford University Press, 1897), 328.

34. Claudian, *De Consulatu Stilichonis*, III, 136.

35. John Dryden, *Annus Mirabilis*, stanza 297. This and all citations of Dryden from *The Works of John Dryden*, ed. Edward Niles Hooker, H. T. Swedenberg, *et al.* (Berkeley: University of California Press, 1955–).

36. Sir Edwin Arnold, "The British Empire. From Claudian," in *Potiphar's Wife and Other Poems* (London: Longmans, Green and Co., 1892), 99.

37. *De Consulatu Stilichonis*, III, 150–153.

38. Matthew 23.37, KJV.

39. John Milton, *Paradise Lost*, I, 19–22. This and all citations of Milton from *Milton: Complete Poems and Major Prose*, ed. Merritt Y. Hughes (Indianapolis: Bobbs-Merrill, 1957).

40. Niall Ferguson, *Empire* (London: Allen Lane, 2003), 151.

41. G. Essex Evans, "The Crown of Empire," in *The Collected Verse of G. Essex Evans: Memorial Edition* (Sydney: Angus & Robertson, 1928), 28.

42. *Aeneid* 4.229.

43. *Aeneid* 4.393–396.
44. "The White Man's Burden," *in Selected Poetry*, 127–129.
45. *The Indian Emperour*, V, ii, 135–136.
46. Alexander Pope, *Windsor-Forest*, 355–362. This and all citations of Pope from *The Twickenham Edition of the Works of Alexander Pope*, ed. John Butt *et al.* (Methuen, 1950–1967).
47. *Windsor-Forest*, 413–421.
48. See David Morris, "Virgilian Attitudes in Pope's *Windsor-Forest*," *Texas Studies in Literature and Language* 15 (1973): 231–250.
49. *Windsor-Forest*, 369–374.
50. *Windsor-Forest*, 385–396.
51. *Windsor-Forest*, 397–406.
52. *Aeneid* 8.722–725.
53. *Windsor-Forest*, 407–410.
54. *An Essay on Man*, I, 105–108.
55. *Windsor-Forest*, 325–326.
56. *Aeneid* 6.826–831.
57. *Aeneid* 6.832–835.
58. *Aeneid* 12.952.
59. Philip Appleman, "Peace with Honor," in *Carrying the Darkness: The Poetry of the Vietnam War*, ed. W. D. Ehrhart (Lubbock, TX: Texas Tech University Press, 1989), 3–5.
60. Robert Williams Buchanan, "To a Poet of the Empire," in *Complete Poetical Works* (2 vols., London: Chatto & Windus, 1901), II, 387.

4: THE MYTH OF CHIVALRY

1. William James, "Robert Gould Shaw," reprinted in *Memories and Studies* (New York: Longmans, Green, and Co., 1911), 43–44.
2. Thomas Bailey Aldrich, "An Ode on the Unveiling of the Shaw Memorial on Boston Common," in *The Poems of Thomas Bailey Aldrich* (Boston: Houghton, Mifflin and Company, 1907), 411.
3. Michael Foss, *People of the First Crusade* (New York: Arcade Publishing, 1997), 5–6.
4. Michael Foss, *Chivalry* (London: Michael Joseph, 1975), 16–17.
5. This is the version of Urban's sermon recorded by Balderic, Archbishop of Dol, as translated in August C. Krey, *The First Crusade: The Accounts of Eyewitnesses and Participants* (Princeton: Princeton University Press, 1921), 33–36.
6. See Foss, *People of the First Crusade*, 57–62.
7. Richard Kaeuper, *Chivalry and Violence in Medieval Europe* (Oxford: Oxford University Press, 1999), 7–8.

8. *La Chanson d'Antioche*, ed. Suzanne Duparc-Quioc (Paris: P. Geuthner, 1976), cclxi.6333–6342. Translation mine.

9. *La Chanson d'Antioche*, cclxi.6343–6345; 6352–6356.

10. *The Song of Roland*, trans. Frederick Goldin (New York: W. W. Norton, 1978), 82.

11. Jean Froissart, *Chronicles of England, France, Spain and the Adjoining Countries, From the Latter Part of the Reign of Edward II to the Coronation of Henry IV*, trans. Thomas Johnes (2 vols., London: Henry G. Bohn, 1849), Book I, ch. 290.

12. Maurice Keen, *Chivalry* (Oxford: Oxford University Press, 1986), 16.

13. See Constance Brittain Bouchard, *"Strong of Body, Brave and Noble": Chivalry and Society in Medieval France* (Ithaca: Cornell University Press, 1998), 13.

14. Chrétien de Troyes, *Perceval or, The Story of the Grail*, trans. Ruth Harwood Cline (New York: Pergamom, 1983), 1090–1098.

15. Geoffrey Chaucer, *The Canterbury Tales*, "General Prologue," l. 72, following the text given in *The Works of Geoffrey Chaucer*, ed. F. N. Robinson (Boston: Houghton Mifflin, 1957).

16. Edmund Spenser, *The Faerie Queene*, Book I, canto i, stanza 1. This and all citations of Spenser follow the text given in *Spenser: Poetical Works*, ed. J. C. Smith and E. De Selincourt (London: Oxford University Press, 1970).

17. Laurence Binyon, "In Memory of George Calderon," *Collected Poems of Laurence Binyon: Lyrical Poems* (London: Macmillan, 1931), 252–254.

18. "Fetching the Wounded," *Collected Poems*, 220–221.

19. "For the Fallen," *Collected Poems*, 210.

20. *Antony and Cleopatra*, II, ii, 245–246.

21. See Michael Murrin, *History and Warfare in Renaissance Epic* (Chicago: University of Chicago Press, 1994), 83–84.

22. *The Faerie Queene*, I, xi, 26.

23. *The Faerie Queene*, I, xi, 27.

24. *The Faerie Queene*, I, xi, 30.

25. *Paradise Lost*, IX, 27–33.

26. *Paradise Lost*, V, 586–598.

27. Addison, *The Campaign*, 146–153, in *Miscellaneous Works of Joseph Addison*, ed. A. C. Guthkelch (London: G. Bell and Sons, 1914), 161.

28. *The Campaign*, 477–480.

29. William Collins, "Ode, Written in the Beginning of the Year 1746," 7–12, in *The Works of William Collins*, ed. Richard Wendorf and Charles Ryskamp (Oxford: Clarendon Press, 1979), 34.

30. Sir Walter Scott, *The Field of Waterloo*, "Conclusion," 37–45, in *The Poetical Works of Sir Walter Scott* (Edinburgh: Robert Cadell, 1841), 506–507.

31. Mark Twain, *Life on the Mississippi* (1883) (Oxford: Oxford University Press, 1996), 467–469.

32. "This is an institution of Chivalry, Humanity, Mercy, and Patriotism; embodying in its genius and its principles all that is chivalric in conduct, noble in sentiment, generous in manhood, and patriotic in purpose." The Ku Klux Klan, *Organization and Principles*, 1886.

33. See above, p. 58.

34. Keith Douglas, "Aristocrats," in *The Collected Poems of Keith Douglas*, ed. John Waller and G. S. Fraser (London: Editions Poetry, 1951), 38. An earlier draft, titled "Sportsmen," has often been reprinted, but it is clear that "Aristocrats" represents the author's final preferences.

35. *Raoul de Cambrai*, ed. Sarah Kay (Paris: Livre de Poche, 1966), lxxiv, 1381–1404, translation mine.

36. Collin Brooks, "To Another Poor Poet," in *More Songs by the Fighting Men* (London, 1917), 18. My thanks to Professor Samuel Hynes of Princeton for his gift to me of this rare volume.

37. Quoted in Keen, *Chivalry*, 48–49.

38. Krey, *The First Crusade*, 35.

39. Torquato Tasso, *Gerusalemme Liberata*, III, v–vi, viii, in the translation of Edward Fairfax (1600).

40. *Gerusalemme Liberata*, XX, cxliii–cxliv.

41. *Perceval*, 6258–6268.

42. *Perceval*, 6439–6443; 6460–6464.

43. Tennyson, "Merlin and the Gleam," 123–131, 64–74, in *The Poems of Tennyson*, III, 206–210.

44. "Follow the Gleam," words by Helen Hill Miller, music by Sallie Hume Douglas. http://www.cyberhymnal.org.

45. Peitieu, "Farai un vers, pos mi sonelh," trans. Frede Jensen in *Troubadour Lyrics: A Bilingual Anthology* (New York: Peter Lang, 1998), 70–75.

46. Keen, *Chivalry*, 30.

47. See D. W. Robertson, *A Preface to Chaucer* (Princeton: Princeton University Press, 1962), especially ch. 5.

48. "Le donne, i cavallier, l'arme, gli amori, / le cortesie, l'audaci imprese io canto." *Orlando Furioso*, ed. Emilio Bigi (Milan: Rusconi, 1982), I, i, 1–2, translation mine.

49. "zwei lôn uns sint bereit, / der himel und werder wîbe gruoz." Wolfram von Eschenbach, *Willehalm*, 299, 26–27, as translated in Joachim Bumke, *The Concept of Knighthood in the Middle Ages*, trans. W. T. H. and Erika Jackson (New York: AMS Press, 1982), 93.

50. Giraut de Borneil, "Can lo glatz," 40–52, in *Anthology of the Provençal Troubadours*, ed. Thomas G. Bergin (2 vols., New Haven: Yale University Press, 1973), I, 69, translation mine.

51. *Lancelot, ou le Chevalier de la Charrette*, 365–369, 372–375, in Chrétien de Troyes, *Oeuvres complètes*, ed. Daniel Poirion *et al.* (Paris: Gallimard, 1994), 516, translation mine.
52. *The Faerie Queene*, IV, vi, 19, 21.
53. *The Faerie Queene*, IV, vi, 31.
54. Joel Barlow, *The Vision of Columbus* (Hartford, 1787), VII, 185–192.
55. *The Vision of Columbus*, VII, 193–198.
56. *The Vision of Columbus*, VII, 215–218.
57. *The Vision of Columbus*, VII, 225–230.
58. *Idylls of the King*, Book XI, *Guinevere*, 464–474, in *The Poems of Tennyson*, III, 542.
59. *Idylls of the King*, Book XI, 474–480.
60. Paul Fussell, "The Fate of Chivalry and the Assault upon Mother," in *Thank God for the Atom Bomb and Other Essays* (New York: Summit, 1988), 222.
61. Terrence Moore, "A Return to Chivalry?" *On Principle* (August 2001).
62. Virginia Woolf, *Three Guineas* (New York: Harcourt, Brace and World: 1966), 108.

5: COMRADES IN ARMS

1. "Apologia pro Poemate Meo," *Complete Poems and Fragments*, 124.
2. See, generally, Eve Kosofsky Sedgwick, *Between Men: English Literature and Male Homosocial Desire* (New York: Columbia University Press, 1985).
3. F. T. Prince, "Soldiers Bathing," in *Collected Poems: 1935–1992* (Manchester: Carcanet, 1993), 55–57.
4. Walt Whitman, "Drum-Taps," in *Leaves of Grass* (Washington, 1872), 263.
5. Whitman, "The Dresser," in *Leaves of Grass*, 286–287.
6. Graves, "Two Fusiliers," in *Complete Poems*, I, 37.
7. Robert Graves, *Good-bye to All That*, ed. Richard Perceval Graves (Oxford: Berghahn Books, 1995), 248.
8. *Iliad* 16.97–100; Fagles, 415.
9. *Iliad* 18.23–27; Fagles, 468.
10. *Iliad* 18.50–60; Fagles, 469.
11. *Iliad* 18.90–94; Fagles, 470.
12. *Iliad* 18.98–100; Fagles, 470.
13. *Iliad* 18.104, 114–116; Fagles, 471.
14. *Song of Roland*, trans. Goldin, 101.
15. *Song of Roland*, 109.
16. *Iliad* 24.3–11; Fagles, 588.
17. See Kenneth J. Dover, *Greek Homosexuality* (Cambridge: Harvard University Press, 1989), 197.

18. "Formosum pastor Corydon ardebat Alexin." Virgil, *Eclogue* II, 1.

19. *Aeneid* 5.294–296.

20. *Aeneid* 2.550–551.

21. *Aeneid* 9.184–187.

22. *Aeneid* 9.194–195.

23. *Aeneid* 9.205–206.

24. *Aeneid* 9.399–401.

25. *Aeneid* 9.427–430.

26. *Aeneid* 9.435; 9.444–445.

27. *Aeneid* 9.447–449.

28. Suetonius, *Lives of the Caesars*, trans. J. C. Rolfe, Loeb Classical Library (Cambridge: Harvard University Press, 1913), I, i, ii: "He dawdled so long at the court of Nicomedes that it was suspected that his chastity was prostituted to the king."

29. *Le Roman d'Eneas*, ed. Aimé Petit (Paris: Livre de Poche, 1997), 8619–8620, 8626–8627, 8630–8631, translation mine.

30. Christopher Baswell, "Men in the Roman d'Eneas: The Construction of Empire," in *Medieval Masculinities*, ed. Clare A. Lees (Minneapolis: University of Minnesota Press, 1994), 162; 151.

31. *Aeneid* 9.390–391.

32. *Roman d'Eneas*, 5232–36. See Raymond J. Cormier, *One Heart One Mind: The Rebirth of Virgil's Hero in Medieval French Romance* (University of Mississippi: Romance Monographs, 1973), 198–200, 217–219.

33. Louis Crompton, *Byron and Greek Love: Homophobia in 19th-century England* (Swaffham, England: Gay Men's Press, 1998), 13–14.

34. "To the Memory of Mr. Oldham," 7–10.

35. George Cockings, *War: An Heroic Poem* (London, 1762), III.253–266.

36. Crompton, 14–15.

37. Crompton, 16–18.

38. Byron, "The Episode of Nisus and Euryalus. A Paraphrase from the 'Æneid,' Lib. 9," 397–400, in *Lord Byron: The Complete Poetical Works*, ed. Jerome J. McGann (7 vols., Oxford: Clarendon Press, 1980–1993), I, 90.

39. *The Great War and Modern Memory*, 278.

40. Ferguson, *Empire*, 263–264.

41. Edmund Blunden, "1916 Seen from 1921," in *The Poems of Edmund Blunden* (New York: Harper and Brothers, n. d.), 163–164.

42. Shakespeare, Sonnet 66.

43. Pope, *An Essay on Criticism*, 356–357.

44. Ivor Gurney, "To His Love," in *Collected Poems of Ivor Gurney*. ed. P. J. Kavanagh (Oxford: Oxford University Press, 1982), 41.

45. See *Stars in a Dark Night: The Letters of Ivor Gurney to the Chapman Family*, ed. Anthony Boden (Stroud: Sutton, 2004), 134–137. My thanks to Mr. Boden for his helpful correspondence.

46. "Alba ligustra cadunt, vaccinia nigra leguntur." Virgil, *Eclogue* II, 18.
47. Herman Melville, "Shiloh," in *Collected Poems of Herman Melville*, ed. Howard P. Vincent (Chicago: Packard and Company, 1947), 41.
48. Melville, "The Victor of Antietam," in *Collected Poems*, 47.
49. Thomas Hardy, "The Man He Killed," in *The Complete Poetical Works of Thomas Hardy*, ed. Samuel Hynes (5 vols., Oxford: Clarendon Press, 1982–95), I, 344–345.
50. Kipling, "Fuzzy-Wuzzy," in *Selected Poetry*, 173–174.
51. Owen, "Strange Meeting," in *Complete Poems and Fragments*, 148–149.
52. William Wordsworth, "Ode: Intimations of Immortality," 188–189; 201–204, in *William Wordsworth: The Poems*, ed. John O. Hayden (2 vols., New Haven: Yale University Press, 1977), I, 529.

6: THE CAUSE OF LIBERTY

1. See Stanley Weintraub, "The Christmas Truce," in *The Great War*, ed. Robert Cowley (New York: Random House, 2003), 50–64.
2. Joseph Priestley, *Letters to the Rt. Hon. Edmund Burke* (Birmingham, 1791), 141.
3. See Julie Ellison, *Cato's Tears* (Chicago: University of Chicago Press, 1999).
4. Addison, *Cato* (London, 1713), II, i, p. 26.
5. Patrick Henry, Speech in the Virginia Convention, March, 1775, in William Wirt Henry, *Patrick Henry. Life, Correspondence and Speeches.* (New York: Burt Franklin, 1969), I, 266.
6. *Cato*, IV, i, p. 53.
7. This is the version that appears on Hale's monument in Coventry, Connecticut. For earlier and different versions, see the *Independent Chronicle* (Boston, 17 May 1781); Hannah Adams, *Summary History of New England* (1799), 359; and *The Diary of Frederick Mackenzie* (2 vols., Cambridge: Harvard University Press, 1930), I, 61–62. I owe these details to Professor Cedric Reverand II.
8. Francis Scott Key, "The Star Spangled Banner," in *Poems of the late Francis S. Key, Esq.* (New York, 1857), 31–32.
9. Woodrow Wilson, "War Message," 65th Congress, 1st Session. Senate Document No. 5, Serial no. 7264 (Washington, D.C., 1917), 3–8.
10. John Greenleaf Whittier, "Worship" (1848), in *The Poetical Works of John Greenleaf Whittier* (4 vols., Boston: Houghton Mifflin, 1894), II, 230.
11. "A Poem to his Majesty," in *Miscellaneous Works*, 41.
12. Addison gives a learned account, with excerpts from Horace, Ovid, Martial, Persius, and Claudian, in his *Dialogues upon the Usefulness of Ancient Medals* (London, 1726), 66–68.

13. James Thomson, *Liberty*, I, 25–34, in *Liberty, The Castle of Indolence, and Other Poems*, ed. James Sambrook (Oxford: Clarendon Press, 1986), 43.

14. James Thomson, "An Ode," from the masque *Alfred*, in *The Plays of James Thomson*, ed. Percy G. Adams (New York: Garland, 1979), 227.

15. *Liberty*, II, 244–251.

16. *Liberty*, I, 89–92.

17. Joel Barlow, *The Columbiad*, Preface, viii.

18. *Columbiad*, Preface, x.

19. *Columbiad*, Preface, x–xi.

20. *Columbiad*, IV, 138.

21. Julia Ward Howe, "Battle Hymn of the Republic," in *Sunset Ridge* (Cambridge: The Riverside Press, 1898), 1–2.

22. Revelation 19.11–15, KJV.

23. For a text and analysis of this rejected verse, now restored in many hymnals, see the helpful notes by Robert Willis Allen at http://johnbrownsbody.net/Battle_Hymn.htm.

24. Abram J. Ryan, "The Conquered Banner" (1868), in *Southern Poems*, ed. Charles William Kent (Boston; New York: Houghton Mifflin, 1913), 62–64.

25. James Ryder Randall, "Maryland, My Maryland," in *Southern Poems*, 59–60.

26. Samuel Byers, "When Sherman Marched Down to the Sea," text provided at http://www.civilwarzone.com/.

27. "Lo! Victress on the Peaks," in *Leaves of Grass*, 358.

28. Lynn Hunt, "Engraving the Republic," in *History Today*, 30 (1980): 11–17.

29. George Frederick Cameron, "Our Hero Dead," in *Lyrics on Freedom, Love and Death* (Boston: Lewis W. Shannon, Alexander Moore, 1887), 55–58.

30. Hervey Allen, "Soldier-Poet," in *Wampum and Old Gold* (New Haven: Yale University Press, 1921), 60.

31. Christopher Marlowe, *Doctor Faustus* (A-text), [5.1.92] in *Doctor Faustus and Other Plays*, ed. David Bevington and Eric Rasmussen (Oxford: Clarendon Press, 1995), 178.

32. Randall Jarrell, "The Death of the Ball Turret Gunner," in *Complete Poems* (New York: The Noonday Press, 1969), 144.

33. William Vaughn Moody, "Ode in Time of Hesitation," in *The Poems and Plays of William Vaughn Moody* (Boston: Houghton Mifflin, 1912), 14–25.

34. Paul Laurence Dunbar, "Robert Gould Shaw," in *The Collected Poetry of Paul Laurence Dunbar*, ed. Joanne M. Braxton (Charlottesville: University Press of Virginia, 1993), 221.

35. *Congressional Record*, 19 June 1902.

36. e. e. cummings, "next to of course god america i" in *Complete Poems, 1904–1962* (New York: Liveright, 1994), 267.

37. Denise Levertov, "Prologue: An Interim," in *Poems, 1968–1972* (New York: New Directions, 1987), 130–131.

38. Robert Lowell, "For the Union Dead," in *For the Union Dead* (New York: Farrar, Straus and Giroux, 1966), 70.

39. Letter quoted in full in Anna Mary Wells, *Dear Preceptor: The Life and Times of Thomas Wentworth Higginson* (Boston: Houghton Mifflin, 1963), 180.

40. Letter of Charles Russell Lowell, quoted by Helen Vendler in *The Given and the Made: Strategies of Poetic Redefinition* (Cambridge, MA: Harvard University Press, 1995), 13.

41. C. Day Lewis, "Where are the War Poets?" in *The Complete Poems of C. Day Lewis* (London: Sinclair-Stevenson, 1992), 335.

42. Philip Appleman, "Waiting for the Fire," in *Carrying the Darkness*, 5–6.

43. Oscar Fay Adams, "Sicut Patribus," in *Sicut Patribus* (Boston, 1906), 10.

44. Bruce Springsteen, "Born in the U. S. A.," lyrics printed on the album *Born in the U. S. A.* (Columbia Records, 1984).

45. George Will, *The Washington Post* (September 13, 1984).

Index